W9-BCA-471

Yasser Arafat—
An Apocalyptic
Character?

Yasser Arafat— An Apocalyptic Character?

An Urgent Call to the Nation of Israel and the Body of Christ

Marvin Byers

© Copyright 1996 — Marvin Byers
All rights reserved. This book is protected under the copyright laws of the United States of America. This book may not be copied or reprinted for commercial gain or profit. The use of short quotations or occasional page copying for personal or group study is permitted and encouraged. Permission will be granted upon request. Unless otherwise identified, Scripture quotations are from the New King James Version of the Bible. Scripture quotations marked (NIV) are taken from the New International Version. Scripture quotations marked (KJV) are taken from the King James Version. Scripture quotations marked (ASV), (RSV), and (NRSV) are taken from the American Standard Version, the Revised Standard Version, and the New Revised Standard Version, respectively. Emphasis is the author's own.

Hebron Press
Section 0374
P.O. Box 02-5289
Miami, FL   33102-5289

Previously published as *Yasser Arafat—A Biblical Character?*
First Edition: February, 1996
Second Edition: September, 1996
First Reprint: November, 1996

ISBN 0-9647871-5-6

For Worldwide Distribution
Printed in the U.S.A.

1-800-LAST DAY

To obtain copies of this, and other books by the same author, in English or Spanish, see the addresses listed at the end.

Yasser Arafat - Apocalyptic Character

Yasser Arafat (Cont.)

Acknowledgments

Since I know nothing as I ought to know it, and since I have a severe case of the spiritual blindness that came on Adam's race, I am always amazed at the Lord's kindness when He permits me to see and understand His Word in any area. I thank Him for allowing me to see what I share in this book.

I also express here my deep gratitude to my wife, Barbara, who spent many long hours doing much of the research that was needed to find the facts concerning Yasser Arafat. She was also willing to give up her husband for many weeks while I wrote this book. Because of where we were living at the time, she spent most of her days alone. Throughout our thirty years of marriage and ministry she has known many difficult situations, and this was one of them. In our entire life together, I have never heard her complain once about her circumstances—not even when we lived in the Philippine jungle. She never complained during this hard time either. Thanks, Barb.

Contents

Index of 78 Details About The Little Horn (Chapter 6)

Introduction

A few days after I had finished writing this book, Israel experienced one of its worst traumas since the founding of the state in 1948. Within a period of nine days, between February 25 and March 4, 1996, four Islamic suicide bombers killed or injured over 200 Israeli citizens. This book explains why the frequency and severity of such attacks upon the Jewish people will continue to grow in heart-rending ways in the near future. It also gives an abundance of documentation to demonstrate who is the source of these atrocities. This book reveals how many Western nations, including the US, are giving millions of dollars in aid to the "peacemakers" who are, in fact, the perpetrators of Islamic terrorism against Israel. This aid is pouring into the coffers of the father of modern terrorism, Yasser Arafat, because the West has been won by his fraudulent condemnation of terrorism and his bogus peacemaking efforts. The world will soon witness one of the greatest bloodbaths in the history of the Jews. Instead of hundreds of Jewish casualties, there will be untold thousands beginning in 1996 and 1997.

In February 1996, Yasser Arafat met with a group of Arab ambassadors in Stockholm and explained to them what he has planned for Israel. According to the Norwegian daily *Dagen* of February 16, the Nobel Peace Prize laureate himself predicted that "he expects Israel to collapse in the foreseeable future."[1] As he has done repeatedly since signing a peace accord with Israel, Arafat then spelled out exactly how he plans for the state of Israel to be destroyed. He declared that the "establishment of a Palestinian state is imminent." He continued by predicting that Jews would not want to live under Palestinian sovereignty, and "they will give up their dwellings and leave for the US." He added, "We Palestinians will take over everything, including all of Jerusalem. Peres and Beilin have already promised us half of Jerusalem...At least a million rich Jews will leave Israel...We will make life unbearable for Jews...Jews will not want to live among Arabs. I have no use for Jews. They are and remain Jews. We now need all the help we can get from you in our battle for a united Palestine under Arab rule." As he has consistently done from the day he signed a peace accord with Israel, the "peacemaker" called on his Arab brothers to join him in his "battle"— holy war until Israel has been annihilated!

The majority of true Christians today believe that Jesus is coming soon. Are there any signs in the earth that confirm this belief? The

Lord promised that before His return there would be "**wonders in the heavens** above and **signs in the earth** beneath" (Acts 2:19). There *have* been wonders in the heavens above and there will be more. One of several heavenly wonders of late was the collision of 21 pieces of a comet with Jupiter in July 1994. Astronomically speaking, this event was one of the most awesome celestial occurances in all of history. It was described as "the first time humans had ever observed the impact of one member of the solar system on another."[2] It was called a "celestial fusillade whose like had never before been seen by the eyes of earthlings."[3] Astronomers reported that "just a single fragment...triggered fireballs as powerful as a 6 million-megaton explosion (the largest H-bomb ever detonated weighed in at a piddling 58 megatons)."[4] The fact that we understood the scientific explanation of what was happening did not make this celestial event any less a sign in the heavens. What about the "signs in the earth" that Jesus promised would point to His soon return? Have there been any? I believe that this book presents many. In fact, there have been so many recent signs on the earth that they actually became one of the problems I encountered in writing this book. Lately, things have been happening at such an incredible pace that, on a number of occasions, I had to go back and change what I had written. Instead of writing, "This is what *will* happen," I had to change it to, "This is what has *already* happened."

Some have scoffed at Christians in past generations for declaring that certain world figures of their day, such as Napoleon, Stalin, and Hitler, were the long awaited antichrist. If we recognize two simple truths, maybe we will not participate with the scoffers. First, the Apostle John declares that there have been *many* antichrists (I Jn. 2:18). Second, one of the beauties of the Bible is that its message has been applicable to every generation. Therefore, in every generation there have been men on earth through whom Satan has manifested himself in ways that seemed to indicate that the antichrist had finally come. The mistake that many past Christians made was not the linking of certain men of their day with the characteristics of the antichrist found in the Bible. Rather, their mistake was to assume that the antichrist of *their* generation was the *last* antichrist who would manifest himself just before the return of Christ. Their antichrist was not the *last*, but he was definitely one of the many!

I do *not* believe that Yasser Arafat is the antichrist. He *has*, however, fulfilled in the most incredible ways almost 50 of the more than 80 details that Daniel gives concerning a man called a "little horn." According to

Daniel, that little horn will be used in the last days to deal with Israel to bring them back to their God. Could Arafat actually be that little horn or is he merely one more man through whom Satan is revealing his nature? In this book, we consider the answer to this question and discover that the answer has a lot to do with whether or not the Second Coming of Christ is near. A question that some have asked me is, "What if Yasser Arafat dies before fulfilling the remaining 30 details?" I deal with that question in this book and show that it does not affect this message. However, I would also like to ask every honest heart two questions. One, Have you observed that Yasser Arafat is at least an incredible foreshadow of Daniel's little horn if he is not indeed the little horn? And two, If Arafat has been fulfilling prophetic Scriptures at least in some measure—without us noticing—is it possible that God could fulfill other endtime prophecies without us noticing? This should be a sobering thought, because this is what happened to God's people in the First Coming of Christ. It is one reason most of them did not participate in the blessing of His coming. May God grant us sufficient understanding of the days we live in to not make the same mistake!

My hope is that the many signs of the Lord's soon appearing that are presented in this book will inspire an urgency in you to get ready for His coming, and will help you seek and find a deeper love relationship with the Lamb of Calvary. I also pray that you receive a clear understanding of what is happening to God's people in the Middle East as you read this book. Maybe it will affect your attitude toward the situation there so much that you will obey the psalmist's exhortation to "pray for the peace of Jerusalem" as you never have before (Psa. 122:6).

Marvin Byers

Chapter 1

The Peace That Brings Sudden Destruction

Revelation 11:2 declares that in the last days the city of Jerusalem will be **under the feet** of the Gentiles for a period of 42 months. According to the Bible, when something or someone is "under the feet" of another, it refers to being under the dominion or authority of that person. For example, the Bible tells us that the Lord placed His creation "in subjection under [man's] feet" (Heb. 2:8).[1] During the 42-month period just prior to the Lord's return, Jerusalem will once again be subjected to the rule of the Gentiles. At the end of that short period, Christ will establish His Kingdom over the nations of the earth.[2] Is the beginning of that 42-month period at hand?

Since the Six Day War in 1967, Jerusalem has been under the sovereignty of the Jewish state. When Israel took control of the city in that war, many centuries of Gentile rule came to an abrupt end. However, this will soon change. Jerusalem is destined to be ruled by the Gentiles once again. Sometime in 1994, the government of Israel began conducting secret high level talks with the Palestine Liberation Organization (the self-styled government of the so-called "Palestinian people")[3] concerning the future of Jerusalem.[4] It is widely believed, and often discussed by the news media, that the final arrangement will most likely establish a Palestinian government over East Jerusalem, which includes the biblical city of Jerusalem, often called "The Old City."[5] It has also been reported in the Israeli media that one option discussed in the talks is the possibility of the Vatican being more directly involved in Jerusalem.[6] As usual, the Israeli Labor government that was in power until the May 1996 elections denied such reports. However, their track record was to consistently deny politically damaging reports at first and then admit the truth later.[7] The United Nations is strongly in favor of placing Jerusalem under a Gentile government again. In December 1995, a UN resolution declared Israel's control over Jerusalem to be "illegal, and therefore null and void."[8] **The resolution was approved with a vote of 133 in favor, one against (Israel), and one abstention (US).**

One of the goals of the Israeli Labor government under Yitzhak Rabin and Shimon Peres was to leave the legacy of having brought peace to the Middle East and of having resolved the problem of Jerusalem, a problem that the Prophet Zechariah declared would trouble the nations just before Christ returns (Zech. 12-14). The final status talks concerning the future of Jerusalem began officially on May 5, 1996. However, even before that date, Professor Ruth Lapidot, an Israeli who is involved in the talks, suggested that the negotiations over Jerusalem should be conducted in secret. Her statement was published in an article that confirmed what had been previously only rumored in Israel—that Israeli officials were already secretly discussing the future of Jerusalem since 1994.[9] Apparently, by the time the final status talks began, the major decisions had already been made in secret by Israel's Labor government. However, since the Labor Party was replaced in the May 28, 1996 elections by the Likud, Israel's conservative party, we will have to wait and see how Jerusalem will ultimately be placed under the control of the Gentiles.

Under the provisions of Israel's peace accord with the PLO, the city of Ramallah was handed over to the PLO on December 27, 1995. Three days later, Yasser Arafat visited the city and addressed a huge crowd. He told them that Jerusalem would be next. Does he know something that the world doesn't know, or is he simply setting himself up to look like a fool before his Palestinian subjects? Mr. Arafat has a history of making fools of others while doing whatever is necessary not to be made a fool himself.

An important detail that should be understood is that the word "Palestinian" comes from the Hebrew word "Philistine." The Romans began calling the holy land "Palestine" around AD 135 in an attempt to eradicate Jewishness from the land. Even though the Palestinians are not *literal* descendants of the Philistines, they certainly seem to be *spiritual* descendants, and they are definitely Gentiles. Therefore, whether biblical Jerusalem is placed directly under the Palestinians, under the Pope, or under some other international governing body, one thing is clear: when it happens, Jerusalem will be "under the feet" of the Gentiles once again. The Bible reveals that this arrangement will last for only 42 months before Christ returns to reign and bring justice to this corrupt world!

Since Israel's miraculous victory over its enemies in 1967, it has been governing over a good portion of the land that the Lord promised to Abraham and his descendants, including both East and West Jerusalem. Many nations among the international community have opposed what they call Israel's "occupation of Arab territories" conquered in that war. Today, many are delighted that Israel's so-called "occupation" finally seems to be coming to an end. By the choice of the Labor government, Israel has been involved in handing over the control of 450 cities, towns, and villages within the limits of the biblical holy land to the Palestine Liberation Organization. What is known as the "West Bank" has been promised to the PLO, and is rapidly becoming an "autonomous area" under Yasser Arafat's Palestine Authority (PA). In 1995, the Israeli military began withdrawing from one area after another as the Palestinian "police" (or more correctly, terrorists, as we will see) moved in to take control. Why would Israel ever decide to do such a thing? It has all been done in the name of peace. The Israeli left-wing Labor government decided that if they could placate their perennial enemies by giving them land, the Jewish state would be allowed to live in peace.

Among the many places that have been given back is Bethlehem, which is King David's birth place as well as the birth place of the King of the Jews and Christians. Then there is Hebron. For practicing Jews, this is the second most important city in Israel. The father of the nation, Abraham, and his son, Isaac, once lived there. The tombs in which they were buried are still there today. It was the place from which Moses' 12 spies took the grapes of Eshcol, and the place that Caleb (one of the believing spies) desired for his inheritance. King David first reigned in Hebron and moved from there to Jerusalem. Hebron is one of the last places that will be given to the PLO. It seems certain that, like David, they will continue on from Hebron and enter Jerusalem. Jericho was the first city given to the PLO. Israel, Arafat, and many throughout the world understand the significance of Jericho. Under Joshua, it was the first city conquered in the conquest of the entire holy land. Arafat's conquest of Jericho through peace has been considered to be a prophetic message foretelling the conquest of the rest of the holy land as well.[10] Also, Shechem (now called Nablus), the place of Jacob's well, has been handed over in the name of peace. (See Map 6 in Appendix A.)

We know from the Book of Revelation, and from information that leaked out of the peace negotiations of the former Israeli Labor government, that ultimately the Gentiles will even rule over Jerusalem. Fortunately for the Jewish people, the Gentile rule will be very short. This is fortunate because it will also be very violent. Thankfully, it will be interrupted by the glorious appearing of the great King over all the earth, the Lord Jesus Christ. He has declared that Jerusalem, along with all of Canaan, is *His* land, and that Jerusalem will be *His* capital city, not the capital city of an unbelieving Gentile government!

Israel is already beginning to experience the awesome consequences of their so-called "peace process." Many citizens are discovering exactly what the real cost of this peace will be to the nation. An article entitled "Peace on Wheels" was published in *The Jerusalem Post* of December 11, 1995, stating that "Prime Minister Shimon Peres has said that virtually all Israelis are willing to make sacrifices for peace." The article then proceeds to explain that few expected the price to be so high. As one city, town, and village after another have become autonomous under the PLO, many Arab delinquents who were previously held in check by the Israeli military are now fanning out among the nearby Jewish neighborhoods and pretty much taking any goods they want, often in broad daylight and "before the very eyes of their owners," according to the *Post* article. This is part of what the Lord said He would do to deal with His people. He promised that He would send "a plunderer at *noonday*" (Jer. 15:8).

Presently, in a nation of only 5 million citizens (numbering less than one third of the population of metropolitan Los Angeles), 35,000 new cars are stolen by Palestinians yearly. This represents one third of all new cars bought in Israel. The thieves don't have to concern themselves about being prosecuted. They need only concern themselves about crossing back over the "Green Line" with their newly acquired possessions. The Green Line is an imaginary line that runs between the territory conquered in the 1967 war and Israel's previous borders. The new autonomous areas under the PLO are said to be "outside the Green Line."

Once the thieves cross back over the Green Line, which is sometimes only a few yards away from where they have stolen the belongings of their victims, they are safe from any prosecution. Israel's government has decided not to authorize the Israeli police or the military to pursue any Palestinian criminal beyond the Green Line even though the peace agreement they signed gives them this right. As a result, many Israelis admit that now when they are robbed, they do not even bother calling the police because they will do nothing to help them. The plunderers actually "bring carts and donkeys across the fields to carry their loot back!"[11] Some Israeli farmers have lost hope of making a living because their implements are carried away as they watch helplessly.[12]

The burglars need not fear being prosecuted under the new Palestinian Authority (PA) either—because in many cases, they are actually stealing a car to fulfill an order that was placed by one of the newly-appointed PA officials.[13] Life for criminals under the PA is a Utopia. Even when convicted of the most serious crimes, criminals spend only a few days in prison. Israel's complaints to the PLO concerning convicted criminals being released in a matter of days are answered with a denial of the facts.[14] If the prosecution of murderers is a total farce, how could anyone expect justice to be meted out to the common armed robbers who are working for the new government? The *Post* article ("Peace on Wheels") explains that the PA officials actually order from the burglars the make, color, and model of the new car they want. Under the new Palestinian regime, an almost-new Volvo can be bought for as little as five hundred dollars.[15] Most likely, as long as the Israelis have any belongings left, the PLO won't have to worry about inflation or the cost of living in their new autonomous areas!

Jeremiah wrote a prophetic message for the people of Israel who would be living in these last days. Oh, that Israel would consider what he wrote over 2500 years ago, for it predicts what the outcome of their peace process will be! Twice Jeremiah explains that his message is for Israel living in the last days (Jer. 23:20; 30:24). A careful reading of the Book of Jeremiah shows that although he had a message for God's people of his day, the primary fulfillment of his message awaits the last days. For example, he declares that a descendant of David (Christ) will rule the earth, and that in His days, Judah and Israel will dwell safely (Jer. 23:5-6). This has not yet happened, but it will! Jeremiah goes on to prophesy that "the days are coming... that they shall no longer say, 'As the Lord lives who brought up the children of Israel from the land of Egypt,' but, 'As the Lord lives who brought up and led the descendants of the house of Israel from the north country and **from all the countries** where I had driven them.' And they shall dwell in their own land" (Jer. 23:7-8). When God has finished dealing with Israel and the world, not one Jew will remain among the nations (Ezek. 39:28). He has not yet accomplished this amazing work of gathering Israel, but He will! Then, in this context, Jeremiah clearly states that we will understand his message in the last days (Jer. 23:20).

Another aspect of Jeremiah's last-day message is also being fulfilled before our eyes at this very moment and it is extremely tragic. Throughout his prophetic message, Jeremiah refers to those who proclaim, "Peace, peace." He laments that they give to God's people a false hope of peace, when in fact great sorrow and spiritual travail awaits them (Jer. 6:14; 8:11,15; 14:13,19). Over and over, Jeremiah makes it clear that God's people cannot have peace until they repent of their sinful ways and turn to Him. He forewarns, "We have heard a voice of trembling, of fear, and **not of peace**" (Jer. 30:5). He further explains what is going to come upon God's people—instead of peace they will experience extreme suffering likened to **the travail of a woman with child** (Jer. 30:6). According to Jeremiah's vision, there has never been a day of affliction like the day that is coming upon Israel; not even the Holocaust in Europe was as dreadful (Jer. 30:7). He calls this time, "the time of Jacob's troubles" (Jer. 30:7b), but then gives a glorious hope: "But he [Jacob or Israel] will be saved out of it" (Jer. 30:7c). Once again, Jeremiah explains that we will understand this message in the latter days (Jer. 30:24).

If the Jewish residents of areas adjacent to the newly surrendered autonomous areas are already losing everything they own, who can imagine the time of trouble that Jacob will face when almost all the major population areas of Israel are at most a few miles from the autonomous areas of the PLO? This will be the case once Israel finishes withdrawing from all 450 population centers of the Arab controlled West Bank. A quick glance at Israel's new map confirms this. (See Map 6 in Appendix A.) In spite of all the material loss that Israel now suffers, and will yet suffer in the near future, many of us in Israel know that this cannot begin to describe the anguish, travail, and injustice that the nation will soon face when it experiences a dramatic increase in the loss of life. Oh, that God's chastenings of Israel through material losses in these last days could somehow turn the nation back to Him, but the prophetic message does not give much hope of that happening! Tragically, very soon, the maiming and loss of life through terrorism that this small nation has frequently mourned in the last few years will seem as nothing compared to what is coming. It is always a shock to the nation when fanatical Arab suicide bombers board a bus and blow themselves up along with the passengers.[16] Israel is a tough nation that can go to war and cope with the loss of life on the battlefield; but the killing of women and children produces an indescribable impact on a nation whose memory of the Holocaust is still so vivid. In later Chapters, we will discover that the Bible warns of deep sorrows to come for which nothing in the past was sufficient to prepare the hearts of God's people for their final travail.

There has never been a time in the history of modern Israel when the leaders have promised the nation peace as they are doing today. Jeremiah surely saw our day when Israel's leaders would be saying, "Peace, peace." Since the first step in the Israeli-PLO peace process—the signing of the Declaration of Principles with the PLO in Washington on September 13, 1993—the vast majority of the daily headlines in the newspapers of Israel has been speaking about the peace and security that has come, or is yet to come to Israel. During a one-and-a-half year period after the initial peace agreement (from September 1993 to July 1995), there were over 650 articles in *The Jerusalem Post*[17] in which the word "peace" was actually part of the title of the article. This equates to more than one each day. In addition, there were hundreds of other articles concerning peace that did not directly mention the word "peace" in the title. On most days, at least one article speaking of peace was on the front page, and this continues to be the case at this writing. The message of peace is on the nation's lips today as never before in their history.

Israeli politicians have assured the people that this will be a peace that will bring them security as a nation. They felt comforted because Yasser Arafat, the leader of the PLO, signed a Declaration of Principles in Washington, DC, and later signed a peace accord in Cairo, promising to change certain phrases in the PLO Charter that call for the total elimination of the State of Israel.[18] In the past, Mr. Arafat's lifelong goal to annihilate Israel was disconcerting to the Israeli leadership in their headlong rush toward peace. Therefore, they considered a change in the Charter to be important. It apparently did not occur to them that a change in the Charter was not necessarily equivalent to a change in the PLO's goals, especially since that organization does not have a reputation for telling the truth even if they put it in writing! However, during the two years after the peace accord was signed, it appeared that the written goals of the PLO no longer troubled Israel's leaders. They continued to give the PLO the land even though Arafat made no attempt whatsoever to change the Charter. In April 1996, he was finally forced to convene a meeting of the Palestine National Council (PNC) or face losing $500 million in US aid.[19] Prime Minister Shimon Peres raved that what the PNC did was one of the most important events in the last 100 years. The world raved also, only to find out that the only thing the

PNC voted on was permission to establish a commission that will, at some unspecified future date, present a draft of a possible new Charter. There was no discussion of annulling the old Charter. The day might come when the PLO functions with two Charters instead of one if they never annul the old one. Either way, whether or not the PNC actually annuls the old Charter will not affect the goals of Israel's enemies. Their avowed goal is the end of the State of Israel.

The great hazard of being blind is that one cannot see the risks posed by even one's next step. So it is with the incredible blindness that has been covering the eyes of Israel's recent leaders. They seem to have been incapable of seeing the horrendous danger just ahead. In spite of many sad disillusionments, the Jewish people have the tendency of seeing their enemies in the best possible light. Sometimes this is foolhardy. For this reason, some Jews were willing to pay their own train fares to be carried to their death in the Holocaust. They believed what the soldiers told them—that the train was carrying them to freedom. They also believed that their captors were being kind enough to allow them to take showers as they were herded into the gas chambers. How trusting! The virtue of thinking well of others must be mixed with an equal portion of discernment, otherwise there is little hope of avoiding the snares of the Wicked One and his followers. Israel's trust of their enemies today and the resulting "peace" they have made with them will ultimately place them in a worse situation than even the diabolical German Holocaust, concerning which their cry has been, "Never again!"

Israel made peace first with a distant enemy, Egypt, in 1979. In 1993, they made peace with an enemy that lives in their midst—the PLO. In October 1994, they made peace with Jordan. Then, at the beginning of 1996, it seemed evident to most that some sort of "peace" with Syria was at hand, in spite of the fact that the Syrian-backed and -controlled terrorist organization, Hizbullah, almost daily has been raining death and destruction on Israel with their bullets and missiles from their base in Syrian-controlled southern Lebanon. On December 31, 1995, the headlines of *The Jerusalem Post* were, "US urges Syria to restrain Hizbullah." At least the US knows who controls the Hizbullah terrorists!

The Western news media has failed to tell the real story of Syrian President Hafez Assad, with whom Israel wants to make "peace," partly to satisfy the Bill Clinton White House. Assad is one of the most brutal murderers that has ever lived on earth. One of the many sacrifices he has made to his god of political power and position was that of the entire town of Hama in northern Syria. That town no longer exists.

To quiet that city's opposition to his government, he simply sent in his troops in February 1982 and killed over 20,000 inhabitants—men, women, and children.[20] He then turned the city into a new hill in Syria by bulldozing the entire town and covering it over. Although this is a well-known and well-documented fact, it was not even mentioned in the US news until *The Washington Post* ran a piece about it almost two months after it happened![21] Can Israel trust Assad to treat them any better, especially when he hates Jews and claims that "Palestine" really belongs to Syria, not to the Palestinians or to Israel?[22]

The Apostle Paul confirms Jeremiah's message, showing what is just ahead for Israel during the time of unprecedented peacemaking in the nation. In the context of end-time events—the Rapture of the Church and the coming of Christ—Paul picks up Jeremiah's message and explains what Israel will soon experience (I Thess. 4:14-5:5). Just as Jeremiah warned Israel about its travail in the last days, Paul warns, "For when they say, 'Peace and safety!' then sudden destruction comes upon them, as labor pains upon a pregnant woman. And they shall not escape" (I Thess. 5:3). According to Jeremiah and Micah, it is precisely the people of Israel in the last days who will experience travail like a woman with child (Jer. 4:31; 6:24; 13:21; Mic. 4:9-10). Therefore, in the context of the Lord's coming, we understand who will be saying, "Peace and safety." Paul is referring to the people of Israel also.

Like Jeremiah, Paul makes it clear that sudden destruction will come upon Israel at the very time they are saying "Peace and safety." The word "safety" in the Greek can also be translated as "security from enemies."[23] Along with peace, Israel seeks this "security," which is another word that constantly appears these days in the Israeli press. As a people, Israel longs for secure borders, and for the assurance that the Arab nations will no longer pursue their goal to annihilate the entire Jewish nation. Of course, only Israel's Messiah can give them peace, as well as the borders *He* has established for His people.

If any man on earth has personified the modern nation of Israel it was the late Yitzhak Rabin, Israel's recently-assassinated Prime Minister. He began to fight against Israel's enemies as a commando even before Israel's homeland was given back to them. Later, he fought in the War of Independence in 1948. He was the commander of Israel's armies in the glory of the Six Day War in 1967. He was continually involved in the nation in its rise from ashes to glory. Unfortunately, he was closely associated with the nation of Israel in another way—he was a man who rejected God and the covenant that God made with Abraham.

Yitzhak Rabin's last message to his country was probably his most significant and it was surely prophetic. On November 4, 1995, he concluded his address to a "Peace Now" rally of 100,000 people in Tel Aviv. His last *words* to Israel declared that it is time for peace and safety. However, the *message* to Israel was acted out prophetically as he stepped down from the podium and was immediately assassinated. What a warning from the life of the man who personified Israel—as he spoke of "peace and safety" sudden destruction came to him in a very literal way! The glorious aspect to Rabin's final prophetic message is that just as he was greatly loved by many in Israel, likewise, Israel is greatly loved by her God, and God will have the last word!

Not only Israel, but much of the world is talking peace these days; yet, with regard to peace, the eyes of the world are principally on the Middle East, because there can be no lasting **world** peace until there is peace there. One reason for this is that one fourth of the world's population is Moslem, and an avowed goal of a great number of the world's Moslems is armed conflict until they succeed in destroying the State of Israel. For this reason, as well as others, much of the world is doing what they can to promote peace in the Middle East.

Something that the leaders of most Western nations do not seem to understand is that the struggle in the Middle East has little to do with territory; of which the Moslem nations have plenty. (See Map 1 in Appendix A.) For almost 1.5 billion Moslems,[24] what really is at stake is their religious belief. According to their holy book, the Koran, Israel cannot be blessed unless they turn to Allah, the god of Islam.[25] The dilemma for Islam and its adherents is that Israel has already received great blessing and the nation has *not* turned to Allah. Nevertheless, this nation has actually been resurrected after experiencing 2,000 years of God's judgment that caused them to be scattered among the nations of the world. They have also been blessed as a nation in amazing ways and have become stronger than all the surrounding Moslem nations put together, proven by Israel's victory in every war! Israel has literally become a military superpower! Israel's prosperity and blessing is daily proof that 1.5 billion Moslems believe in a false religion and a false book. Therefore, they *cannot* make peace until they either cast Israel into the sea or reject the claims and demands of Islam. Furthermore, they cannot make real peace with any non-Islamic nation, because Islam calls for armed struggle until the world is completely converted to Islam.[26] Therefore, peace will never come to the Middle East or anywhere else until the Prince of Peace has come and conquered the nations of the world and men's hearts.

In spite of these facts, Israel has never talked about peace and safety as it does today. Historically, Israel has been anything but a dovish nation. In fact, since their War of Independence in 1948, Israel has often been accused by much of the world community of having far too little interest in making peace. Part of what the world often views as Israel's "problem" is that many Jews still believe that the Bible is Israel's title deed to all the holy land. Every war in Israel seemed to demonstrate that God was giving the land back to Israel through conquest. Israel was forced into every war it fought; yet, after every war, Israel possessed additional areas of the land that God had promised them! God also promised that in the last days He would bring His people back to the land He has given them as an everlasting inheritance (Hos. 3:4-5; Jer. 24:1-24; Deut. 30:1-9). In various Scriptures, the Lord makes a comparison between how He brought them out of Egypt into Canaan 3,500 years ago, and how He would bring them out of the nations into Canaan in the last days (Jer. 23:7). They had to fight for the land then, and they have had to fight for it again in these last days!

Sadly, after so many armed conflicts by which they possessed ever greater portions of their inheritance, today Israel is actually giving up huge parts of the land to their enemies to obtain a peace of their own making—a peace that ignores the Prince of Peace. The irony of this peacemaking effort is that it will end in war and sudden destruction, and Paul says that on this occasion "they shall not escape!" In the coming war with their enemies, the people of Israel will not only end up losing land; they will also lose many lives. (See Isaiah 1:7-9 and Zechariah 14:2.) As Jeremiah does, the Prophet Daniel also speaks of the time of Jacob's trouble, but he uses different terms. He says that the people of Israel will experience a time of distress like never before, but they will be delivered out of it (Dan. 12:1). This time their deliverance from trouble will come only from the Lord and not from their own armies, because their armies will be broken. Daniel explains this, saying, "When the power of the holy people has been finally broken, all these things will be completed" (Dan. 12:7 NIV)—including the deliverance Daniel had just promised Israel in Daniel 12:1. Moses also forewarned Israel, saying, "Evil will befall you in the latter days; because ye will do evil in the sight of the Lord" (Deut. 31:29).

Very often in life, as with electricity, there is a positive and a negative side to our actions and motives. Paul was happy that the gospel was being preached—the positive side—even though it was being done by people with wrong motives—the negative side (Phil. 1:15-18). Israel is giving away *God's* land, in order to make peace with their enemies. They do so in order to find peace without turning to their God. That's the negative side of this peace process. However, they are doing much the same that Abraham, their father, did about 4,000 years ago. In order to make peace with Lot, Abraham meekly gave Lot what appeared to be the best part of the Promised Land. Israel, today, is giving away some of the very best parts of the holy land to their enemies in order to make peace. Their desire for peace instead of conflict is definitely noble. That's the positive side of this peace process.

PLO, beware! The worst thing that the Palestinians could possibly do is to accept land that belongs to God and to install their government there. Two things happened after Abraham made peace by giving up land, and those two things will happen again. First, God told Abraham to lift up his eyes and look to the north, south, east, and west, because He was giving *all* the land to him! I believe that in these last days God's response to Israel's meekness will be much the same, regardless of world opinion or the attitude and reaction of the nations. God will give Israel *all* their land! Second, the worst thing that could have happened to Lot was to take for himself land that God had promised Abraham, because he ended up in the place of God's judgment—Sodom. As the PLO takes the land from Israel they are literally placing themselves under the judgment of God according to Joel 3. Through Joel, God promises to judge all those who have participated in dividing His land and oppressing His people.

Joel 3 is a warning to the United States of America also, which is one of the principal promoters of a peace that has been forged by dividing the Lord's land. God declares in Joel that He will fight against *all* nations for that folly, and this includes the US! Anyone who believes that they are called to arbitrate a peace treaty that involves dividing God's land is just as blind as Israel has been for agreeing to it. Yes, Israel's cry of "peace, peace" will end in the worst travail and suffering of her history, but the end will not bring the total destruction and final defeat of Israel as her enemies are hoping. The end of this final conflict will be the destruction of every nation that has had a part in dividing the holy land or that allies itself with other nations to make war with Israel (Joel 3:2). The Messiah will defeat all of Israel's enemies, and then He alone will have the right and authority to rule over all the nations of the earth, and He will do so from Jerusalem, the city of the great King! (See Zechariah 14.)

Chapter 2

Daniel's Vision of Four Beasts

The Prophet Daniel had a vision of four great beasts coming up out of the sea in Daniel 7:2-3. The first was a lion, the second a bear, the third a leopard, and the fourth beast, which was different from the first three, had ten horns. The interpretation of what these beasts symbolize was also given to Daniel. He was told, "The four great beasts are four **kingdoms** that will rise from the earth" (Dan. 7:17,23 NIV). Some students of the Bible have assumed that these four beasts reveal the same basic truths as Nebuchadnezzar's dream in Daniel 2. Nebuchadnezzar dreamed of an image or statue with four parts, each made of a different material, and Daniel interpreted the dream by matching these four parts to a series of four kingdoms. History confirmed the accuracy of Daniel's interpretation. He explained to Nebuchadnezzar that the head of gold was symbolic of his own kingdom, Babylon. The breasts and arms of silver represented the kingdom of the Medes and Persians that arose in place of Babylon. The belly and thighs of brass pointed to the kingdom of Greece, and finally the kingdom of Rome was to come last, represented by the legs of iron and the feet made of a mixture of iron and clay. Historically, this interpretation was fulfilled with such precision that unbelievers foolishly assume that the Book of Daniel was not really written by the Prophet Daniel who lived in the sixth century before Christ. They do not understand that our God knows and controls the future!

Since Daniel's vision of four beasts in chapter 7 was likewise figurative of four kingdoms, it is understandable why some have assumed that his vision is another revelation of the same four kingdoms that Nebuchadnezzar saw in his dream. There is a major difference between the two revelations, however. Nebuchadnezzar's dream revealed four great kingdoms that would arise before the **First Coming** of Christ.[1] In Daniel's vision we find proof that he was seeing four great kingdoms that would arise before the **Second Coming** of Christ. One proof is that all four beasts are present on earth at the time of the Second Coming in Daniel 7:9-12. Daniel saw that the fourth beast with ten horns was destroyed and cast into the fire. This is precisely what happens at the Second Coming of Christ to a beast with ten horns found in the Book of Revelation. (See Revelation 13:1 and 19:20.) So Daniel's vision is definitely a revelation of events in the last days that culminate with the Second Coming. Daniel saw in his vision that when the fourth beast is destroyed at the Lord's coming, the other three beasts will have their lives prolonged for a time (Dan. 7:12). The only way their lives could be prolonged at His coming is if they are alive on earth at that time. The life of something that is already dead cannot be "prolonged;" it could be resurrected, but not prolonged.

The Book of Revelation links all four of Daniel's beasts with the last days in an even clearer way. In Revelation 13:1-5, we are shown Daniel's beast with ten horns again, but more details are provided there concerning its characteristics. We are told that it will have power in the earth for 42 months, or for the last three-and-a-half years before Christ's physical return. As seen in Revelation 13, this beast is a wicked, antichrist, governmental system that will exist on the earth in the end. Notice, however, that this beast is a composite of three other beasts—a lion, a bear, and a leopard. These are the same three beasts that Daniel saw arising in the earth before the fourth beast arose. In other words, even though the fourth beast is different from the first three (Dan. 7:7), those first three will be incorporated into this fourth beast and will participate in that kingdom in some way. Therefore, all four beasts are alive and present in the end.

Note also that Daniel sees "another horn, a little one, coming up among" the ten horns on the fourth beast (Dan. 7:8). The focus of this study is to determine what this little horn does, where he does it, and to whom he does it. Also, if possible, we want to discover if he is someone who is alive and well-known in the earth today. In other words, is there anyone on earth who is presently fulfilling this prophetic message? In order to begin our investigation of the little horn, we first need to have a basic understanding of the ten horns from among which the little horn grows up. We will consider what these horns are, as well as what they *cannot* be. Sometimes, just knowing which interpretations of prophecy are impossible clarifies things tremendously because then there is less probability that we will be looking for a fulfillment in the wrong place. One of my great concerns is that many people in the Body of Christ are looking in the wrong direction to see the fulfillment of the Bible's prophetic message.

The enemy is a master of deception, especially with regard to the fulfillment of prophecy. One of his tactics is to do everything he can to misdirect our attention when a biblical prophecy is being fulfilled. He wants us to be gazing toward the south if the action is going on in the north; and he wants to draw our eyes toward the west if the really important events are occurring in the east. To a great degree, his tactic has worked. Therefore, as a first step toward understanding what Daniel's fourth beast and its little horn will be, let's stop looking for the fulfillment in the wrong place!

The Ten Horns Cannot Come From Europe

For many years we have all heard that the Roman Empire will rise again, and that the ten horns found on the beast of Daniel 7:7 and Revelation 13:1 are ten nations from the European Common Market. One obvious problem with this interpretation of prophecy is that, at this writing, the Common Market already has 15 member nations, and is talking about opening the door to even more nations—those of Eastern Europe. So what happened to the ten horns? Wouldn't it be tragic if, while we are gazing at Europe, the whole prophetic message were being fulfilled somewhere else in the world?

There are a number of biblical reasons for rejecting Europe as the place from where these horns arise in the last days. The main reason has to do with another vision that Daniel received in chapter 8. It gives a vital key for being able to determine from where the horns will arise. It also gives additional details about the little horn—our main focus in this study. There, Daniel received a vision of a ram with two horns and of a male goat with a "notable horn" (Dan. 8:1-8). The male goat destroyed the ram and grew very great. When he became strong his notable horn was broken and in its place came up four horns toward the four winds. Once again the interpretation is given to us in the same chapter so that we are not left to our own devices and ideas. Gabriel explains to Daniel that the ram with two horns symbolizes the kingdom of the Medes and Persians (Dan. 8:20). The male goat symbolizes the kingdom of Greece, and its notable horn represents the first king of the Grecian Empire (Dan. 8:21). That king was seen conquering the Medes and Persians, symbolized by the ram with two horns (Dan. 8:3-7). After the king of Greece becomes very strong, he is broken, and his united kingdom is divided into four weaker kingdoms (Dan. 8:22).

Fortunately, we have access to indisputable historical facts related to these events. We know that the kingdom of the Medes and Persians was, in fact, conquered by the Greek Emperor, Alexander the Great, who was indeed the first king of the Grecian Empire. We also know that when he was 33 years of age, at the height of his power, Alexander died in 323 BC,[2] and his kingdom was divided into four smaller kingdoms.[3] The Antigonids ruled over Greece and Macedonia.[4] The Seleucids ruled over Syria, called "the king of the north" in Daniel 11 since it was north of the holy land. The Ptolemies ruled over Egypt, called "the king of the south" in Daniel 11.[5] Persia, to the east of the holy land, was the fourth kingdom and was controlled first by the Parthians and later by the Sassanids.[6]

These historical facts give us the key to determining the origin of the ten horns from among which another "little horn" comes up—an eleventh horn. (See Daniel 7:7-8,20,24.) Daniel explains in very clear terms the geographical origin of these eleven horns. Before we look at his explanation, it is important to note one other historical fact: Alexander began his conquest in Macedonia and Greece, and moved from the west to the east as Daniel 8:5 foretold he would do. He conquered everything in his path until reaching Punjab, India, in the east. He also moved toward the south and entered Egypt in northern Africa. It should be carefully noted here that, with the exception of modern-day Greece, Alexander **never conquered Europe, nor was Europe ever part of his kingdom**.

Equipped with these historical details, we are able to see clearly that according to Daniel, neither the ten horns nor the little horn arise out of Europe. **In Daniel 8:9, we are told that the little horn arises out of one of the four kingdoms into which Alexander's kingdom was divided.** (For those who are interested, most encyclopedias have a map depicting Alexander's conquests and the boundaries of his kingdom.) Therefore, the little horn must arise from some location that lies between Greece and India—that is, within the boundaries of Alexander's kingdom. This fact serves to identify the geographical origin of the ten horns as well. Daniel 7:8 reveals that the little horn comes up **among** the ten horns that are on the beast. Therefore, if the little horn arises from someplace between Greece and India, then the ten horns must be found in that same region. If the ten horns are from Europe and the little horn is from Alexander's kingdom, it couldn't be said that the little horn comes up **among** them!

Another common belief is that the little horn is the antichrist himself who will arise during the last few years before Christ's physical return. What if the little horn is not the same man as the antichrist, and what if he arises long before the antichrist comes on the scene? Could he possibly be a well-known person already? Please read on.

Chapter 3

Why the Little Horn Cannot Be the Antichrist

It has been frequently taught that the little horn found in the Book of Daniel is the antichrist who will rule over the whole earth in the last days. In no way do I consider myself to be an expert on end-time truth. In fact, God's word assures us, "If anyone thinks that he knows anything, he knows nothing yet as he ought to know" (I Cor. 8:2). For many years, I, too, have believed that the little horn and the antichrist would be the same person. I do not ridicule those who believe this. There are understandable reasons why many have believed this and continue to do so. One reason is that Daniel prophesies, "... by him [the little horn] the daily sacrifices were taken away" (Dan. 8:11). Most English versions of the Bible translate the original Hebrew[1] into these, or similar, words. We will come back to this passage later. Students of the Bible often link this thought with other Scriptures that are interpreted to mean that the antichrist will be found seated in a rebuilt Jewish temple. To better understand the rest of this study, let's look at some weighty biblical evidence that should at least cause us to consider the possibility that the little horn will not be the antichrist himself. The evidence indicates that the little horn will be a much lesser power than what most of us expect the antichrist himself will be.

Regarding Daniel's revelation of the end, there is one thing we can be certain of—that it agrees with what is revealed in the Book of Revelation concerning the last days. The two visions are never contradictory; instead, some of the details provided by the two are actually complementary, serving to amplify and clarify one another. In the context of the last days, Daniel sees a beast with "ten horns" (Dan. 7:7). In the interpretation of his vision, Daniel is told that the beast is a kingdom that shall arise and "devour the whole earth," and that "the ten horns out of this kingdom are ten kings" (Dan. 7:23-24). In the Book of Revelation, the Apostle John likewise sees a beast with "ten horns" (Rev. 13:1). This beast also receives power over the whole earth (Rev. 13:7). In the interpretation of his vision, the angel tells John, "The ten horns which you saw are ten kings who have received no kingdom as yet, but they receive authority for one hour as kings with the beast" (Rev. 17:12). In both Daniel's vision and John's vision, the beast is destroyed by the Lord at His coming and then cast into the fire. (See Daniel 7:9-11 and Revelation 19:20.) There is little doubt that the two visions are talking about the same evil kingdom in the last days, even though John gives us details about this beast that Daniel does not give. For example, John says that the beast not only has ten horns, but that it also has "seven heads" (Rev. 13:1).

The purpose of our study is to examine the little horn. Therefore, we will not attempt to examine all the details that the Book of Revelation gives us about this beast since understanding them is not essential for us to identify the little horn. However, we do need to understand the basic relationship between the little horn and the beast.

The divine "interpreter" of Daniel's vision explains that the fourth **beast** "shall be the fourth **kingdom** upon earth..." (Dan. 7:23). Take note here: It is a **kingdom** as Revelation 13 likewise reveals it to be. The angel explains to John that the beast is also a king (Rev. 17:10-11). In other words, he is a man. The beast is also linked to a man in Revelation 13:18 where we are told, "Let him who has understanding calculate the number of the beast, for it is the number of a man: His number is 666." It is not incongruent or illogical symbolism to use a beast to represent both a king and his kingdom. Rather, this is done to reveal a truth that is quite obvious—a kingdom is always an outgrowth and extension of the king to whom it belongs. This is a fearful revelation for the last days because it is telling us that anyone who chooses to participate in the antichrist kingdom will take on the characteristics of the king of that kingdom—the antichrist himself. The king and the kingdom will ultimately be one and the same, with all his subjects manifesting the same satanic nature!

Concerning the ten horns or ten kings, the angel tells John, "These are of one mind, and they will give their power and authority to the beast" (Rev. 17:12-13). Just as the beast is symbolic of a king, these ten horns represent ten kings also. However, all ten give their authority and allegiance to the beast. Daniel sheds light on the relationship that exists between these ten kings and the beast who is also a king. He calls Nebuchadnezzar, the king of Babylon, a "king of kings" (Dan. 2:37). According to Revelation 17-18, Babylon will rise again in the last days, and, once again, there will be a "king of kings" over that empire. All other kings will pay him homage. That king is often referred to as "the antichrist" or the beast of Revelation.

All the various parts of this wicked, antichrist system that the Bible likens to a beast, including the seven heads and ten horns, are actually **a part** of what the beast is. As with any animal, each **part** reveals certain unique characteristics which belong to that animal. However, just as the horns of a cow are not the whole cow, likewise, the ten horns on this beast are not the whole beast! The ten horns *belong* to the beast; they are *controlled* by the beast, and become an outgrowth and manifestation of what he is. They are ten kings who submit to the mind and will of the beast, and for that reason, they take on his nature. (See Revelation 17:12-13.) In light of this, it is clear why **the little horn that comes up among the other ten horns is not the whole beast.** In Revelation, the beast in its entirety is seen to be the antichrist and his kingdom. Since the little horn is not the whole beast, he is not the antichrist. Rather, he is merely one of the many manifestations of the spirit and nature of the antichrist and his system in the earth.[2]

Since both the little horn of Daniel and the beast of Revelation have a mouth that speaks great things, some teachers use this fact as proof to show that both symbols refer to the same man. However, be careful to note that the mouth of the beast is the mouth of a lion; it is this mouth that speaks great things, not the mouth of a little horn. The lion is one of the other three beasts that Daniel saw arising in the earth before Christ's Second Coming. The fourth beast will incorporate the first three beasts into its system, as we mentioned in Chapter 2. (Compare Daniel 7:2-7 and Revelation 13:1-5.) It would be a faulty analogy to liken one horn on the beast to the lion that is incorporated into the beast.

Let's compare now what the Bible tells us about the little horn and what it tells us about the antichrist to see that they cannot possibly be the same man. We will limit ourselves to what the Bible actually says instead of engaging in speculation. Of course, later, we will be taking a close look at the details given by Daniel about the little horn and these things will become clearer.

What We Know About the Little Horn

1. He subdues three other nations (Dan. 7:8,24), and is given authority over God's people for a "time and times and the dividing of time" (Dan. 7:25). This period is defined by both Daniel and John to refer to about three-and-a-half years. (See Daniel 12:7,11 and Revelation 12:6,14).

2. His three-and-a-half years of authority end when the Lord comes in the clouds and establishes His Kingdom on earth (Dan. 7:8-10,13-14,25-26). Therefore, we know that this period of three-and-a-half years comes just before Christ's physical return.

3. Daniel 11:41—The modern nation of Jordan, made up of ancient Moab, Ammon and Edom, escapes from the control of the little horn.

4. Daniel 11:25-28,43—The little horn decides to attack Egypt. One motive for doing so seems to be that he wants to gain control of Egypt's finances.

5. Daniel 11:30—"ships from Cyprus" (from the Mediterranean Sea) come against him.

6. Daniel 11:40-44—We are given important details here about the little horn:
   a. This happens at the time of the end, so his three-and-a-half years of authority are almost over.
   b. At this time, he is attacked by the king of the north and the king of the south.
   c. Finally, because of the resistance of countries in the east and north, he is angered and destroys many.

What We Know About the Antichrist

1. The antichrist or "beast" has authority over *all* nations of the earth for three-and-a-half years (Dan. 7:23; Rev. 13:5-7).

2. His authority ends with the physical return of Christ, because the beast is destroyed and cast into the lake of fire at Christ's coming (Rev. 19:11-20 and Dan. 7:11).

3. Therefore, we *do* know that the beast and the little horn are at least functioning during the same period—the last three-and-a-half years. (But the question remains, Are they the same political leader?)

4. The antichrist leads *all* the nations of the world into battle against the Lord at His coming:
   a. Rev. 19:19a—"I saw the beast, the kings of the earth, and their armies, gathered together to make war against the Lord."
   b. Zech. 14:2-4—All nations are actually fighting against Jerusalem at the time the Lord returns to save Israel from destruction.
5. Therefore, at the end of the beast's reign he is found fighting against the Lord along with all the nations.

How Then Can the Little Horn Be the Antichrist?

1. At the end of the last three-and-a-half years, the little horn is attacked by a number of other nations, and the country of Jordan is not under his control. According to the Bible, this is *not* the way the beast or antichrist will conclude his reign. He will have authority over *all* nations (including Jordan), and the armies of *all* the nations will fight with him against Israel and against the Lord Himself. At the end, other nations are not fighting against the beast as we see happening to the little horn.
2. Daniel 11:25-30, 40-44—The little horn attacks Egypt and carries away "great riches" from Egypt. After he attacks Egypt the second time, other nations come against him (including "ships from Cyprus" or from the Mediterranean, the king of the north, the king of the south, and at least one country from the east). These actions and events are not consistent with what we know about the beast (or antichrist) in Revelation. Consider:
   a. Daniel 11:25 shows that Egypt's army will be bigger than the army of the little horn. This could not be the antichrist because he will have authority over all the nations of the earth, so how could Egypt have a bigger army than he does?
   b. Daniel 11:28—The little horn returns from his conquest of Egypt with "great riches." The antichrist could not possibly consider Egypt's possessions to be "great riches," even if he carried away every penny the nation has. Remember, he has authority over all nations, and no one can buy or sell without his mark (Rev. 13:17). Under his control are extremely wealthy nations like the US, all of Europe, Japan, and so on. It is inconceivable that the little money a worldwide antichrist could take from Egypt would be termed "great riches." This would be similar to a rich man robbing a true beggar and afterwards declaring that

he had taken "great riches" from the beggar. Egypt is so poor today that it would sink financially if billions of dollars in US aid were not poured into the country annually.

c. Why would a worldwide antichrist suddenly decide to attack an insignificant military power like Egypt?

d. Daniel tells us that when the little horn attacks Egypt other nations will then attack him. If the antichrist were to attack Egypt, what nations would come against him if he already has them all under his authority? Remember, the antichrist has control over all the nations during the entire period of three-and-a-half years (Rev. 13:5,7).

Conclusion

As we can see, and will yet see with greater clarity, the little horn is simply too little and too poor to be the worldwide antichrist! The little horn will end up being attacked by other nations around him rather than leading the armies of all the nations of the world in a war against Israel and the Lord. Throughout his visions, Daniel uses the horns of animals to be symbolic of kings. The bigger the horn, the more powerful the king who is represented by it. (See Daniel 8:3-9.) Once we understand this, it is hard to imagine that Daniel would call Alexander the Great a "big horn" as he does in Daniel 8:8 (which is what the Hebrew literally means), and then, in the very next verse, call the antichrist, who will be the most powerful world ruler in history, a "little horn." Alexander ruled over the territory between Greece and India. The antichrist will rule over the whole earth. The terminology that Daniel himself uses gives us a strong indication that the "little horn" is not nearly as big as we have imagined him to be. The Spirit of God did not make a mistake in naming him!

If the little horn is not the antichrist in the end, then who is he and what will he do? The next Chapter and the rest of the book answers these questions. The prophecies of Daniel reveal that this little horn is involved in the events of the Middle East, *not* in the control of the entire earth.

Chapter 4

Daniel Never Heard of a "Gentile Church"

Before we can understand Daniel's *message* for the last days, we must first understand Daniel's *heart and faith*. For many Christians, a continual problem that arises when reading the Old Testament is how to determine if the passage they are reading is for the Church or for natural Israel. I have actually heard it said by a respected teacher of God's Word that if the passage is judgmental and negative, it is for Israel; on the other hand, if it promises blessings and is positive, it is for the Church. This is certainly convenient! It would be difficult for Jews to accept *that* "gospel!" If you think that this teacher's idea is strange, you should take a look at one of my study Bibles.[1] Apparently the editors promote the same concept. The introductory comments they added as headings in Isaiah 40-66 are a shocking revelation of what many seem to believe in the Body of Christ today. Their comments follow precisely the concept that the aforementioned teacher promotes. Over and over, the passages that deal with a promise of blessing are introduced with something like "The Lord comforts the Church." The passages that relate to judgment are presented as "The Jews reproved." In fact, one section is introduced as "The Gentiles called. The Jews rejected." We would do well to note that throughout history, a just God chastened Israel for their sin and blessed them for their obedience, and He surely does the same today with *all* His people.

The concept that God is dealing with Israel in one way and the "Gentile Church" in another is a serious contradiction of Scripture. In God's eyes there is no such thing as a "Gentile Church!" In Ephesians 2:11-22, the Apostle Paul makes it very clear that Christ's work on the cross made two peoples into one people and into one Church or "holy temple." Paul declares that in Christ, Gentile believers have become true "citizens" of Israel (Eph. 2:12,19). Some in the Church teach that because Israel rejected their Messiah, God rejected Israel, and that because of this, the "Gentile Church" took Israel's place in the purposes of God. This is a serious heretical doctrine. It has birthed many other strange doctrinal errors in the Body of Christ, especially concerning the last days and Christ's Second Coming. This doctrine is often referred to as "Replacement Theology." This idea was conceived about 200 years after the cross and then, later, birthed at the same time the Catholic church was birthed—during the Council of Nicaea in AD 325.[2] Although by that time the Church had been in spiritual decline for years, that Council represented a sharp turn in the road that led the Church into the Dark Ages where, except for a very small remnant, it totally lost its spiritual life.

The Apostle Paul dedicates three chapters of Romans (chapters 9-11) to an explanation of God's truth concerning Israel "according to the flesh" (Rom. 9:3-4). In the midst of this discourse, Paul writes, "I ask then: Did God reject his people?" (Rom. 11:1a NIV) His emphatic answer is, "By no means! I am an Israelite myself, a descendant of Abraham, from the tribe of Benjamin. God did not reject his people, whom he foreknew" (Rom. 11:1b-2a NIV). How can we take this to mean that God rejected Israel and chose the Gentiles instead? He could not have defined in any clearer terms what he meant by "his people." Paul definitely was not talking about the Gentiles!

In Romans 11, Paul continues defending his declaration that God never rejected His people Israel. Found here are some very humbling thoughts. Paul reveals that God Himself gave Israel spiritual blindness (Rom. 11:7-10). The Lord's purpose in this was to bring salvation to the Gentiles so that His visible blessing on *them* would provoke Israel to jealousy (Rom. 11:11). Imagine this. One of God's purposes in saving the whole world was simply to reach Israel! And yet some Gentiles have been so presumptuous as to assume that God has rejected the very people He is trying to provoke to jealousy. No wonder Paul continues in Romans by warning the Gentile believers, "Do not be arrogant, but be afraid. For if God did not spare the natural branches, he will not spare you either" (Rom. 11:20b-21 NIV). How tragic that many believing Gentiles down through the ages have not understood this. If they had, they might have walked with greater humility, and might have looked upon Abraham's children with an attitude of compassion and thankfulness for what came to the Gentile world through their race.

Instead, many adopted the slogan (or at least the spirit) of the Crusaders in Europe—"Kill a Jew and save your soul!"[3] The words of others were, "The only good Jew is a dead Jew."[4] Others called the Jews "Christ killers."[5] They must not have noticed that Jesus declared that the "Gentiles" were the ones who "put Him to death!" (Lk. 18:32-33) After all, it *was* the Roman Gentiles who actually crucified the Lord! Obviously, the Lord allowed the Jews and the Gentiles to work together in crucifying Him, and both are equally guilty, since the sins of both placed the Lord on the cross.

The attitude of the Crusaders still permeates much of true Christianity today. I have discovered this attitude even in the true, born-again, blood-bought "Gentile Church" of today—even in places of national leadership in the US. On one occasion, when the subject of the Jews came up, one well-known charismatic leader in the US told me, "Regarding Israel, the only thing that I want is for someone to drop an atomic bomb on the whole nation to clear out the Jews so that I can go inherit my land!" The spirit behind this is not the Spirit of Christ that was revealed in Paul. Concerning natural Israel, he cried, "I have great sorrow and continual grief in my heart. For I could wish that I myself were accursed from Christ for my brethren, my countrymen according to the flesh, who are Israelites" (Rom. 9:2-4a). While the leader I know wished for their death so that he could reign, Paul wished that he could die in their place so that they would be blessed! Do you feel toward the Jews what the Spirit of God felt and manifested through Paul?

Some may ask, Why then does Paul say that in Christ there is "neither Jew nor Gentile"? (Gal. 3:28) In the Greek text, this is not what Paul says, as the New Revised Standard Version correctly shows. This version properly translates Paul's words as, "there is no longer Jew **or** Greek [Gentile]." There is a vast difference between "neither one nor the other" and "no longer one **or** the other." In Christ, two options no longer exist. We are not all either a Jew or a Gentile. The Body of Christ does not consist of a mixed congregation where some are Jews and others are Gentiles. In Christ, there is only one option for all—we are all *true* Jews as defined by Romans 2:28-29. This interpretation of Galatians 3:28 is confirmed as Paul goes on to say that "there is no longer slave or free." As the next two chapters in Galatians confirm, these two options do not exist in the Church either, because Paul assures us that we are all free men. (See Galatians 4:1,6-7,26,31; 5:1.)

How then do the Church and Israel flow together? And how do Middle East events in Israel relate to the worldwide Body of Christ? It is not possible to understand this until we accept the Bible's declaration that both peoples have been made one. All Christians are part of God's plan for His people Israel because they are part of Israel. The only reason that Israel's present government does not declare that all true Christians are also Israeli is that they have not yet understood that Yeshua (Jesus) is their King and Messiah as well as the Gentile's King and Messiah, and that He has made us both to be one people in Him. Lest someone deduce that I believe that all natural-born Jews automatically form part of the Body of Christ, let me clarify what I am saying.

Unfortunately, most of the "Jews" in Israel today are not true Jews biblically speaking. Only those who have been born again, or born according to the promise of God, are true Israelites as Romans 9:6-8 explains. However, the Bible makes it clear that within present-day Israel, there is a remnant of people who will survive the horrendous days ahead, and will turn to their Messiah. When Paul declares that "all Israel shall be saved" (Rom. 11:26), he is speaking only about the "remnant" that he introduced in Romans 9:27—"Though the number of the children of Israel be as the sand of the sea, **a remnant shall be saved.**" According to Romans 11:5, *part* of this Jewish remnant is already saved. Only the remaining members of that remnant will turn to the Lord Jesus Christ in the last days. Even though most of the Jews whom God sees in that remnant are still "lost sheep of the house of Israel," they are nonetheless sheep and not rebellious goats. God, who lives in the future, sees them as our brothers and sisters in Christ, even though we cannot yet call them that. The leader I know who wants a bomb to fall on Israel to clear out the land for him may well see all the failures, sins, and iniquity that are manifested in natural Israel today. What he *cannot* see are the precious jewels that God is forming there under intense pressure in order one day to present them to His Son, the Messiah. God has not rejected Israel, and He *will* bring that remnant through to salvation!

Just as the remnant of Israel is called to inherit the earth, all the ex-Gentiles who are now in Christ—and therefore citizens of Israel—are called to inherit it along with them. Remember: Both peoples form the Church. Do you long to be a part of the Kingdom that Christ will soon establish in Jerusalem? The land must be taken back from the enemies of Israel in both the spiritual and natural realms before that can happen. The struggle in which natural Israel is involved is a struggle in the natural realm for the promised land. The question is, while they are involved in the natural struggle, are you involved in the spiritual struggle for the land? Are you willing to do your part? Are you willing to join your heart to theirs and get involved in the struggle for the land by praying for the peace of Jerusalem as Psalm 122:6 admonishes us to do, and by interceding for your future brothers and sisters in Christ?

Israel will never know peace until the nation has succeeded in removing its enemies from the land. The Lord explained this fact to Israel regarding the first conquest of Canaan, and it is still valid today. The Lord instructed Israel, "But if ye will not drive out the inhabitants of the land from before you; then it shall come to pass, that those which ye let remain of them shall be pricks in your eyes, and thorns in your sides, and shall vex you in the land wherein ye dwell" (Num. 33:55). Far from driving its enemies out, Israel is making peace with them today. The Book of Judges shows what Israel can expect when it fails to defeat its enemies—continual attacks, plundering, and death. Israel is ignoring God's command when He said, "You shall make no covenant with the inhabitants of this land... But you have not obeyed My voice. Why have you done this?" (Judg. 2:2) The Lord's word for that day is just as valid today. He forewarned, "Therefore I also said, 'I will not drive them out before you; but they shall be thorns in your side' " (Judg. 2:3). Can you imagine what it must have been like in those days for mothers in Israel who knew that their children were never safe from attack because wicked enemies were still roaming the land? If it is difficult for you to imagine this, the current events in Israel provide a graphic and tragic example as Israel's enemies slaughter them these days in one terrorist attack after another just as they did in the days of the Judges.

Are you praying for God to intervene for Israel and give them a heart to return to Him so that He can save them from the hand of their enemies and give them their land? As you pray for God to bring peace to Jerusalem in this way, you can be part of God's answer. Sadly, some Christians are still part of the problem because they believe that Israel has been replaced by the Gentiles, and that Israel no longer has any right to the land God promised to Abraham and his children. If Israel's failures disqualify them from being under God's covenant, then I should assume that my failures will bring the same judgment on my life. But if I pray that God's mercy would come on them, maybe He will show me mercy and allow me to inherit the land also!

Daniel Reveals What Will Happen to *Israel* in the Last Days

And what does all this have to do with Daniel's endtime message and the little horn? It is impossible to understand the message of Daniel if we do not understand to whom and for whom his message was written. The Prophet Daniel began to intercede for his people, asking the Lord to rescue them from their captivity in Babylon and to restore the nation. (See Daniel 9:1-4,16-19.) As he prayed, he reminded the Lord that He had brought **His people** out of Egypt (Dan. 9:15). Daniel also recognized that because of their sin, **God's people** had been judged. He also reminded the Lord that **His people** are called by His name. Then Daniel explained, "Now while I was speaking, praying, and confessing my sin and the sin of **my people Israel**... the man Gabriel... reached me about the time of the evening offering" (Dan. 9:20-21). Gabriel then explained to Daniel, "Seventy weeks are determined for **your people**" (Dan. 9:24). These passages leave no room for doubt regarding who "Daniel's people" are. They are the people that God brought out of Egypt. They are the people in Daniel's day who were under judgment in Babylon for their sin. They are the people who are called by God's name; they are also Daniel's people, called "Israel" in this passage.[6]

Later, in chapter 10, an angel (or the Lord) appears to Daniel and declares, "Now I have come to make you understand what will happen to **your people** in the latter days, for the vision refers to many days yet to come" (Dan. 10:14). Note that the angel's message to Daniel is related to **his people**—Israel—**not** to the Gentile world or even to a so-called "Gentile Church."

A considerable number of biblical prophecies cannot be understood without understanding who Israel and the true Jews are. As we attempt to understand prophetic passages in the Bible, great confusion results when we apply part of a passage to natural Israel and other parts of the same passage to a "Gentile Church." This has been done with Daniel's prophecies almost universally in the Body of Christ in the most shocking ways. This is done in spite of the fact that the angel told Daniel he was being shown what would happen to **his people**, Israel, in the last days. Daniel had never heard of a "Gentile Church" or of Replacement Theology. No one could have convinced Daniel that his God would someday break His everlasting covenant with Israel and replace the nation with Gentiles! Daniel knew the promise that God gave through Jeremiah. The Lord said, "If you can break My covenant with the day and My covenant with the night, so that there will not be day and night in their season, then My covenant may also be broken..." (Jer. 33:20b-21a). In the context of this declaration, the Lord leaves no room for doubt that He is speaking about the covenant He made with natural Israel—the people who were destroyed and went into captivity—people whom He promises to bring back to the land of Canaan, causing them to dwell safely. (See Jeremiah 33:4-16,24-26.)

Daniel also knew Deuteronomy 4:27-31 and 30:1-9, which states that before Israel had ever entered Canaan the first time, the Lord forewarned them that they would be scattered throughout all the nations of the earth because of their sin. This warning was not speaking of the short Babylonian captivity because He promises that after their captivity they will be gathered back to Israel **in the last days**. He assures them, "When you are in distress, and all these things come upon you **in the latter days**, when you turn to the Lord your God and obey His voice (for the Lord your God is a merciful God), **He will not forsake you nor destroy you, nor forget the covenant** of your fathers which He swore to them" (Deut. 4:27-31). He also promises, "The Lord your God will bring you back from captivity, and have compassion on you, and gather you again from all the nations where the Lord your God has scattered you" (Deut. 30:3). What a merciful God! He promised He would never forsake Israel, and that in the latter days He would visit them again! If Daniel believed that God's promises are trustworthy as we believe today, then he surely understood that the restoration of the scattered nation of Israel was a key part of the endtime scenario. He knew with certainty that his people Israel would continue to be God's people. The twist that has been given to his prophecies—that he was receiving a revelation about a "Gentile Church"—was the furthest thing from his mind!

In our study of Daniel's little horn, we will not switch back and forth between Jews and Gentiles when considering Daniel's prophecies. We will strictly adhere to the interpretations given in the Book of Daniel itself, applying them only to "Daniel's people," as the angel did. As we do so, we will discover that many of the events foretold in Daniel have already been fulfilled, and that many others are in the process of being fulfilled at this very time. Lord, open our eyes and our understanding!

The little horn in Daniel is seen to be a tool in the hand of God to deal with His people in the Middle East to turn them back to Himself. This horn grows up among the ten horns on the beast of Daniel 7 and is an eleventh horn. (See Daniel 7:8,20,24.) Interestingly, we find no reference to an eleventh horn in the Book of Revelation. The reason seems quite clear. Unlike the Book of Daniel, Revelation was not written to natural Israel. It was a message directed to the entire Body of Christ, as seen in Revelation 2-3. It is understandable, then, why there is no mention in Revelation of this tool, the little horn, that is used to deal specifically with Israel.[7] Although the Book of Revelation is a repeat of how God dealt with Israel in the beginning, in Revelation God is not dealing with natural Israel alone. Rather, He is dealing with the worldwide Body of Christ, composed of both Jews and Gentiles.

For Daniel "The Whole Earth" Was a Limited Area

Before we look at Daniel's prophetic message concerning the little horn, we need one other key to help us unlock his secrets. When Daniel spoke of "the whole earth," he did not have in mind the entire planet earth as we might mistakenly assume. He repeatedly refers to one specific area on this planet as "the whole earth." One example of Daniel's usage of this term is found in his vision of the male goat in Daniel 8. The divine "interpreter" explains that this is the king of Greece who would defeat the Medes and the Persians. We know that Alexander fulfilled this prophecy. Concerning this king, Daniel observes that "a male goat came from the west, across the surface of the **whole earth**" (Dan. 8:5b). Alexander conquered only from Greece to India and parts of northern Africa. Therefore, when Daniel declares that the male goat crossed the surface of "the whole earth," we understand that Daniel's concept of "the whole earth" was this limited area. In other words, it is the whole *biblical* earth or the whole *prophetic* earth—from Greece to India, the land Alexander conquered. From this "earth" the little horn springs up. It was all the earth known to men like Daniel and his fellow Israelites. Remember that as recently as 500 years ago, "the whole earth" still only included the area from Europe to India. Fortunately, Christopher Columbus had a wider perspective!

Daniel's usage of this concept appears several times in the Book of Daniel. When Daniel interpreted Nebuchadnezzar's dream, he told him, "Wherever the children of men dwell... [God] has given them into your hand, and has made you ruler over them all" (Dan. 2:38). To our way of thinking, if someone were to use the phrase "wherever the children of men dwell," we would take this to mean the whole planet; but for Daniel, it meant only the bounds of the Babylonian Empire. Later on in the Book of Daniel, Nebuchadnezzar writes a letter to all his subjects throughout his domain. He begins the letter, "Nebuchadnezzar the king, to all peoples, nations, and languages that dwell in **all the earth**: Peace be multiplied to you" (Dan. 4:1). His concept of "all the earth" certainly did not include the entire planet, unless he thought that he was also talking to the Aztecs in Mexico! Again, it was all the earth that was directly involved with God's people, their land, and the fulfillment of the prophetic message of Daniel.

How Does All This Affect Us As Believers?

"Keep your heart with all diligence, for out of it spring the issues of life" (Prov. 4:23). One morning, some years ago, I was awakened by the following words, "The most important thing in life is the attitude of heart, and the most important attitude of heart is unfeigned love of the brethren." The beatitudes that the Lord enumerated in His sermon on the mount are actually attitudes of heart that will bring great blessing on our lives (Matt. 5:3-11). As the Epistle to the Hebrews reveals, faith and unbelief are also attitudes of heart, and they are vital factors in determining our eternal destiny. The writer of Hebrews warns that Israel went "astray in their heart" (Heb. 3:10b), and exhorts us, "Beware, brethren, lest there be in any of you an **evil heart of unbelief** in departing from the living God" (Heb. 3:12). It is staggering to consider that our attitude of heart in the area of faith or unbelief will actually determine where we spend eternity!

What about our attitude of heart toward Israel? Do we have God's attitude of heart regarding the relationship between Gentiles and Jews that the cross of Christ established? Throughout the Word of God, the attitude of heart that the nations maintained toward Israel was also a determining factor in their destiny. Since God never changes, it surely must be a factor still today for both nations and individuals. As we mentioned already, God has declared that the covenant He made with Abraham will never be broken and continues with the people who were scattered among the nations. A Gentile Church was not scattered among the nations because of its sin. This covenant continues to be for Abraham's physical descendants. If God's covenant with Abraham is still in effect, then those who bless Israel will be blessed and those who curse God's people will be cursed, even if they only curse them in their heart as Esau did to Jacob. The Prophet Nahum speaks judgment against Esau (Edom) because of wrong thoughts, words, and actions regarding Israel. If we long for more blessing on our lives, let's begin to bless Israel in our hearts, as well as with our words and actions!

For many centuries the Church has set about to "Gentilize" and generalize the Bible and its message. It has forgotten that the Bible was written *by* the Jews, *about* the Jews, and *for* the Jews, and that biblical history and prophecy center in the holy land, the only land that God calls His own. It has forgotten Paul's message telling Gentile Believers that they have not only been "grafted in among" the ever-present Jewish remnant that believe in Christ, but that they are also citizens of the nation of Israel. (See Romans 11:1-5,17 and Ephesians 2:11-13,19.) The Gentile Body of Christ today needs to recognize that it is one with believing Jews and that the struggle for the place of God's throne, the holy land, is one we should all be involved in through our prayer and support in every way that the Lord leads us. The enemy is powerful and our options are clear—either defeat him or be defeated.

The enemy, Satan, manifests his character and his goals with regard to Israel through many hostile nations today. The most ardent enemies of Israel are also the most vocal—the Islamic nations. Unfortunately, many in the world today, even many Christians, have been swayed by Islam's rhetoric that is frequently broadcast and printed. So that we do not one day find ourselves siding with Israel's enemies in our attitude of heart, it is important that we not only understand who Israel is but also who Israel's enemy is—Islam. The tiny nation of Israel has been used in a measure to restrain Islam in its march toward world domination, but it is time for the Church to get involved in this battle in a spiritual way as never before lest it be swallowed up by the forces behind Islam. Let's take a look at this enemy of God's people and God's ways.

Chapter 5

Islam and the Deadly Horns

Horns are dangerous and deadly on a wild beast, and Daniel's beast has eleven of them. Daniel shows that the little horn on the beast originates from Alexander the Great's former kingdom, and that he grows up among the other ten horns or nations. (See Daniel 8:8-9 and 7:8.) Since he grows up among them, the ten nations that those horns represent must be from the same geographical location as the little horn—Alexander's kingdom. Therefore, all ten nations must be Islamic nations because, with the exception of Greece and tiny Israel, Islam controls every square inch of Alexander's former kingdom and much more. There are no nations on the earth today that are more dangerous, deadly, and anxious to rip apart every other person and nation on earth. Islam's openly declared goal is to destroy every person on earth who is unwilling to convert to Islam. The theology of Islam pervades every area of a Moslem's life. As Moshe Sharon, professor of Islamic history at the Hebrew University in Jerusalem correctly observes, "Western opinion tends to view the Arab world and the Middle East as being made up of basically 'secular' modern societies, in which Moslem activists are just 'fanatics' representing minority groups with no real political power or popular base. Even Ayatollah Khomeini's reappearance in Iran and the establishment of his Islamic state and the sweeping movement of return to Islam all over the Islamic world did nothing to change this perception."[1]

The truth is, many of the nations that occupy the territory of Alexander's former kingdom are not only comprised of an Islamic majority, but they are actually religious states. Islam is not only their official religion, but the laws of Islam are the laws of the nation. Even in non-religious Moslem nations, most of the population—including the president or king—participate in the Islamic daily prayers, bowing toward Mecca. Islam pervades the entire area and is the principal influence.

The ten horns on the beast of the last days are an outgrowth and manifestation of what the beast is. They reveal his nature and desires. The effect of those horns is the first thing a person experiences when he encounters the beast! If a wild bull were to be turned loose near where we are, we would have no fear of his eyes or of his tail. We would fear his horns, because with them he would reveal his mind, his nature, and his purpose. In both the Hebrew and the Greek, horns are symbolic of strength.[2] The strength of a wild beast to bring death and destruction is directed through its horns—they are the tools he uses to this end. The angel explains to John that these ten horns (kings) "have **one mind**, and shall give their power and **strength** unto the beast. These shall make war with the Lamb, and the Lamb shall overcome them" (Rev. 17:13-14). They totally yield themselves to the beast, becoming one with him and having one mind or "purpose"[3] among themselves and with him. In fact, the angel explains to Daniel that the beast with ten horns is a kingdom from which the ten horns arise (Dan. 7:23-24). This statement also reveals the unity and oneness between the beast and the horns. In fact, if the beast is a kingdom from which ten horns or kings arise, and at the same time these ten horns arise from Alexander's kingdom, then the beast must be intimately linked with Alexander's former kingdom. Since Alexander's former kingdom is under Islam today, we conclude that the beast must be intimately linked with Islam itself.

These horns will actually make war against the Lord Himself, but there will be a glorious end to the battle because the Lord will overcome them and establish His Kingdom on the earth! The angel also reveals that these horns are, in fact, the beast's way of bringing death and desolation, proclaiming, "And the ten horns which you saw on the beast, these will hate the harlot, make her desolate and naked, eat her flesh and burn her with fire" (Rev. 17:16).[4] Nothing could describe the nature of this beast better than what is said here about these horns— they are depicted as being so vile that they **eat flesh!**

Let's compare Daniel's description of the nature and mind of the ten-horned beast, point by point, with the nature and mind of Islam. Islam is surely the clearest revelation in the earth today of Satan's violent, destructive, and abominable nature. Please note that I am not dealing here primarily with Arabs. There are many wonderful Arab people in the world, and God will surely visit them in these last days. I am speaking about Islam, the principal influence over the Arab world today. For all those who submit to it, it definitely becomes an influence that affects their character, way of thinking, and actions.

Daniel writes, "*After this I saw in the night visions, and behold, a fourth beast, dreadful and terrible, exceedingly strong. It had huge iron teeth; it was devouring, breaking in pieces, and trampling the residue with its feet. It was different from all the beasts that were before it, and it had ten horns*" (Dan. 7:7).

1. The Beast is Dreadful and Terrible

This is a **wild** beast, not a family pet! Islam was founded in Medina by Mohammed around AD 622. In other words, it came from the land and people of Ishmael.[5] The Lord Himself described the spirit that would characterize Ishmael, saying, "And he will be a wild man; his hand will be against every man, and every man's hand against him" (Gen. 16:12a). (Note that the Bible's usage of the word "hand" usually refers to a person's works, plans, ideas, will, and ways.[6]) Although all Arabs are not from Ishmael, if they submit to the spirit manifested in the religion that Ishmael's people birthed, they come under Ishmael's spirit. The Islamic world has definitely identified itself with Ishmael, declaring that it was Ishmael, not Isaac, who was offered on the altar by Abraham. They not only admit, but proudly declare, that their religion is based on Abraham and Ishmael, not Abraham and Isaac. God said that Ishmael would be wild and that his hand would be against the world and the world's hand against him. The wild and warlike spirit of Ishmael has been imbibed and embraced by all the followers of Islam—the religion that promulgates Ishmael's theology and spirit.

Are we being bigoted or narrow-minded to think that the Moslem world is against every man and every man is against the Moslem world? How can this concept be bigoted when it is what Islam itself and the Moslem world teach? Islam declares that there are really only two "houses" or groups of people on earth today—all Moslems belong to Dar al-Islam (The House of Islam), and the rest of the world belongs to Dar al-Harb (The House of War).[7] Islam teaches that "jihad [holy war] is Allah's will, dictated to the prophet from heaven. Moslems must either beat unbelievers into submission, or kill them."[8] Unless you plan on becoming a disciple of Mohammed, you had better understand that your "hand" (your ideas and ways) definitely needs to be against Ishmael's "hand" very soon if it is not already!

Be certain that Ishmael's plan, in accordance to the demands of Islam, is to kill every human being on earth who is unwilling to convert to Islam. Of course, no one in the United States need worry, because these attitudes are only found in the fanatical Moslem world... or are they? Please recall that 1995 was the year of a "million-man march" on Washington, DC. Who organized and orchestrated this march? In case you hadn't noticed, it was Black Muslim leader Louis Farrakhan, a major figure in the Nation of Islam in the US. A large percentage of the marchers were black men who have placed their lives under the spirit of Ishmael by converting to Islam. Maybe you should check to see just how near Ishmael's "hand" (ways) is to you. These days, the nearest minaret-topped mosque is not very far away in most places in the US, England, and other Western nations! There are over 1,000 in the US alone, where approximately five million Muslims meet.[9]

While some Christians are talking about reaching the world for Christ by the year 2000, Islam is winning the worldwide war for souls. Islam is the fastest-growing religion in the world today, and its mosques are springing up everywhere throughout the US and the world. As Christians, we desperately need a visitation from on high! Does it really matter that millions of Black Americans have now embraced the teachings of the Koran and Islam that require whole-hearted disciples to kill and maim until everyone submits to Islam? Apparently, they have not been convinced that the Church of Jesus Christ has the answer for them. Does it matter that some of our best-known athletes are leading the way in the worldwide revival of Islam, showing the youth of the world their key to success, and even changing their names to Moslem names? Is it only a fad? Is Islam in America different, less serious, or less dangerous?

Dr. Connor Cruise O'Brien, a veteran Irish diplomat and one-time personal representative of the UN Secretary General, warned, "Islam is indivisible. It's a tragic error to regard Islamic fundamentalism as something distinct and separate from Islam itself."[10] He went on to explain that "for the past two centuries, Islam has been dominated by the 'House of War' (dar al-harb) which advocates permanent war to subjugate unbelievers... [the Moslems'] remedy is jihad, which is a religious duty imposed by Mohammed on all Moslems." Dr. O'Brien concludes: "It is dangerous to talk about fundamentalist Islam. It implies that there is some other kind of Islam which is well disposed to those who reject the Koran. There isn't another kind." As in every religion, there are Moslems who only give lip service to what they believe.

However, all Moslems who *truly* believe in Mohammed's message are duty bound to subjugate the world by force. Interestingly, Mohammed's name in Greek, the language of the New Testament, has a number value of 666.[11]

In January 1996, *Reader's Digest* published an article entitled "Islam's Real Agenda." As an inhabitant of the Middle East, I only wish that the article were fact and not fiction. The author, Sai'd Al-Ashmawy, assures us, "My Islam is a religion of tolerance and brotherhood." In his case, that may very well be true, but unfortunately, *his* religion is accepted by only a very small percentage of the almost 1.5 billion Moslems on earth. Al-Ashmawy then equates the God of Israel with Allah, making them one and the same, as many Christians have mistakenly believed. The truth is, Allah is the name of one of many Arabian genies that lived in a stone house in Mecca that the Koran says was built by Abraham.[12] Mohammed destroyed the others and chose Allah to be the god of Islam. In other words, Allah was a demonic idol. There was another glaring oversight in Mr. Al-Ashmawy's description of Islam—the Hadith. The Moslems have more than one religious book that dictates their religious beliefs and their way of life, just as Jews do also. The Jews live by the Old Testament as well as by the Talmud—ancient Rabbinical writings that interpret the Old Testament Scriptures for them. Moslems live by the Koran as well as by the Hadith—statements attributed to the prophet Mohammed.[13]

Maybe Mr. Al-Ashmawy has decided to invent his own modernized branch of Islam that rejects the Hadith. He has every right to do so, but if he gets too vocal about it, he may be risking what Salman Rushdie faces—an Islamic sentence of death. Rushdie's written statements concerning the Koran and the brand of Islam that most Moslems endorse has brought the wrath of the Islamic world upon him. Mr. Al-Ashmawy should also be honest with his readers and admit that Islam is also led by the Hadith. Just one of many passages from the Hadith should further clarify the great "tolerance and brotherhood of Islam." All the "faithful" are admonished, "You will fight against the Jews and you will kill them until even a stone would say, 'Come here, Muslim, there is a Jew (hiding himself behind me) [sic]; kill him.' "[14] If you are one who has believed that the god of Islam is also the God of the Jews, the chosen people, consider what the Hadith teaches Moslems about the nature of their god when it proclaims, "Let Allah destroy the Jews."[15] Sadly, *Reader's Digest* unwittingly became a tool through which the Islamic world was permitted to propagate a serious lie, claiming that Islam is motivated by a benign and loving spirit!

If *any* Moslem, either in the US or in Arab countries, is not actively involved in waging war (jihad) until all the world becomes part of the Nation of Islam, they do not *really* believe and are not faithful disciples! This call to violence is what Israel and the entire world face today. This is the reason that peace in the Middle East is impossible as long as Israel exists. The root problem there is not primarily territorial, but rather spiritual. God's people have managed to survive miraculously in the midst of a sea of Islamic hatred, and as long as Islam exists, it will never allow this affront to its god to go unchallenged. The issue in the last days will not be a struggle between Europe and the "Gentile Church," or Europe and Israel, or even the United States and Russia.[16] The issue is primarily between Ishmael and Isaac, and secondarily between Ishmael and the rest of the world. The bombing of the World Trade Center in New York was precisely what the Moslem world has in mind—not only for Israel but for all other human beings who belong to the "House of War" because they are non-Moslems! The plans to plant other bombs in New York were subsequently frustrated, but that minor success of the FBI will not stop the war—more bombs and terrorism will definitely come or Islam is not Islam!

If Islam is a religion of tolerance, as Mr. Al-Ashmawy purports, or is less fanatical in the US, why did Louis Farrakhan, the leader of the Black Muslims' million-man march on Washington, meet with Colonel Muammar Gaddafi of Libya *after* that march? The purpose of his meeting with Gaddafi was to "organize 10 million Moslems and Arabs in the United States to make them influential there."[17] Gaddafi pledged one billion dollars in aid to Farrakhan and his organization to help him reach that goal.[18] The only kind of "influence" that Muammar Gaddafi has ever known how to exercise is terrorism and violence! If the Islam of Farrakhan is peaceable and only seeks to be an influence for good in the US, why did he meet with one of the most violent, lunatic-fringe elements of the Islamic world to get advice on how to exercise that influence? What sound, sage-like advice could Gaddafi have to offer anyone? Lest I be accused of smearing the character of Mr. Farrakhan, I will allow him to speak for himself here. In February 1996, he warned, "You can quote me: God will destroy America by the hands of Muslims."[19] More bombs and destruction are surely on the way—and with a billion dollars to spend some will almost certainly be nuclear!

The conflict of the ages that began in Genesis will end in Revelation—between Ishmael and Isaac. Unfortunately, Mr. Al-Ashmawy does not understand that this is a *spiritual* battle that will know no end until Christ and *His* disciples have won the war! How blind we have been to assume that our problems will arise from Europe in the last days. The declaration of war has already been signed with the blood of thousands of so-called Islamic "martyrs" who have died fighting the "infidels." Every time another Moslem dies, whether it's in a suicide bomb attack or in a successful Israeli retaliation, the "faithful" are whipped into a greater frenzy for the blood of Israel and the Western world.

On January 6, 1996, a funeral was conducted in Gaza, the first autonomous area placed under the PLO. The funeral was for 30-year old Yihye Ayyash. He was known as "The Engineer" in both Israel and the Palestinian world because he was a chemical engineer who produced the bombs that were used in car bombs and by at least five suicide bombers on Israeli buses. Israel tried to deal with him through legal channels. Prime Minister Rabin personally asked Yasser Arafat to extradite Ayyash to face Israeli courts. Arafat refused.[20]

Although the Israeli intelligence circles knew that Ayyash was living openly in Gaza, the Palestine Authority in Gaza conducted a "thorough search," and concluded that he was nowhere to be found.[21] While Arafat was claiming he had no idea where Ayyash was, his own security chief, Jibril Rajoub, was in constant contact with the explosives expert.[22] According to Israeli intelligence, Arafat and Rajoub were planning to authorize Ayyash to launch more suicide bombings in Israel as soon as Israel handed Hebron over to the PLO.[23] Arafat and the Hamas terrorist organization had decided together that it would be better to curb further terrorism inside Israel until Arafat had first gotten everything he wanted from Israel.[24] Of course, the Western news media gives the idea that Arafat cannot control Hamas. Their reporting makes people think something like: "Poor Mr. Arafat; if only he could convince Hamas that making peace is a good idea—but they are uncontrollable extremists. We all hope that they don't harm his wonderful plans of peace for Israel!" As *The Jerusalem Post* explained, "In front of Western audiences, Arafat plays the 'good guy' who negotiates with Israel, while allowing Hamas to play the 'bad guy' who attacks Israel."[25] If you have been one of those who have believed that the Hamas terrorists are out of control, and you have doubts about this, I thoroughly document the intimate working relationship that exists between the PLO and Hamas in points 14 and 31 in Chapter 6.

No one is quite sure why Ayyash's cellular phone would suddenly explode while he was using it, since cellular phones are not normally prone to do that. However, the inhabitants of Gaza assumed that their hero had been killed by the Israelis who wanted to avoid future bus bombs. The explosives expert met his end at the hands of other explosive experts who were even more proficient than he was and who gave him a friendly, personal call from Tel Aviv—the Israelis! Once the Israelis were sure he was actually talking on his cellular phone, they sent the fatal signal to the explosive device that had been planted in the phone. "He that killeth with the sword must be killed with the sword" (Rev. 13:10b). It was a little embarrassing for Mr. Arafat that Israeli intelligence was able to find Ayyash while his own "investigators" could not—right in Arafat's own territory! Arafat then blamed Israel for the death of a hero and martyr.[26] The funeral struck fear into the hearts of many Israelis, because it was attended by a vengeful mob of 250,000 Palestinian citizens, the largest Arab demonstration in Israel's history.[27] The Palestinians promised revenge.[28] That revenge was carried out between January 25 and February 4, 1996, in the form of four suicide bomb attacks in which over 200 Israelis were killed or wounded.

More "martyrs" for Islam are inevitable because the line of volunteers to become the next suicide bomber is growing. At the end of 1994, just one of the many terrorist groups in the Middle East reported they had 50 more who were willing to be suicide bombers.[29] That was then. Recently, Israeli intelligence reported to the Knesset (the Israeli Parliament) that Hamas alone has hundreds of Palestinians who are waiting in line to die as suicide bombers.[30] This does not count volunteers in other Islamic terrorist groups. Is it stretching things to conclude that, just as the Lord foretold, Ishmael is a wild man? Can we begin to see any relationship between Islam and the beast whose horns rip people apart with utter hatred and malice?

For some years, the nations of the world, through the UN, have been constantly backing the Arab-Moslem nations. Unknowingly, they do so to their own serious detriment because God is weighing the actions and attitudes of the nations in His balance. My documentation for demonstrating that the UN supports the Arab world against Israel is indisputable—except for Saddam Hussein's Kuwait fiasco, the UN, since its founding, has never once imposed sanctions on an Arab country for wrongdoing but has continually imposed sanctions on Israel. A tiny nation of five million people, one thousandth of the world's population, has the honor of being the subject of about one third of the UN

Security Council's resolutions.[31] The Security Council has issued "31 expressions of concern, seven warnings, and 49 condemnations against Israel."[32] In November 1975, the UN even passed a resolution that equated Zionism with racism.[33] In 1994 alone, the UN General Assembly passed 21 anti-Israel resolutions.[34] On February 18, 1995, the UN Human Rights Commission condemned Israel for "rights violations in [Arab] territories" and insisted Israel end its "illegal occupation and settlement of the Golan."[35]

How is it possible that the world of Islam could have actually gained such control over the UN? There are certainly a number of factors involved. First, Satan surely controls both the UN and Islam, and, as we will discuss in a moment, Islam promotes Satan's goals and reveals his character more than any other kingdom on earth today. It is therefore quite understandable that the UN and Islam would flow together quite nicely, especially with regard to anti-Semitism and God's plans for His people and His land. Second, Islam controls much of the world's oil reserves that many of the other member nations in the UN desperately need. They can't afford to anger the Islamic nations too much! Third, nations that Islam considers to be "enemies" face a greater threat of terrorists acts directed against their people. Fourth, the sheer strength of 55 Islamic nations that have a vote in the UN give them tremendous clout.

A recent example of the UN's bias against Israel, as well as the bias of the world's news media, could be observed in April 1996 during Israel's offensive against Hizbullah guerrilla targets in Lebanon. During that offensive, dubbed "Grapes of Wrath," Israeli mortars landed in a refugee camp in Lebanon and killed over 100 civilians. The world was outraged against Israel's brutality. The anger grew as the cameras that filmed one news clip after another were focused on the cadavers of the dead and the wounded bodies of little children and adults. It is interesting to contrast what the world saw when over 200 Israeli men, women, and children were killed or wounded during the four suicide bomb attacks in a period of nine days in early 1996. The cameras were usually focused on either the rescue workers who were running around at the scene of the attack, or else on the twisted metal of the bombed-out buses. How many cadavers of little children and adults did the world see? Maybe there were some shown, but I do not recall having seen any during the several hours that I watched the news on TV after each of those bombings. In the case of the news coverage of the Lebanon tragedy, the dead or wounded were constantly in the cameras. Was that because Israel was involved?

There was something far more sinister in the reporting on the tragedy in Lebanon. Not once was the blame for the death of the refugees placed where it belonged. In a few cases, some reports mentioned that Hizbullah had launched missiles into Israel right next to the refugee camp. The inference was that the guerrillas carried at least some of the guilt since they were once again hiding behind civilians, though this was only mentioned in passing just one time on the many news reports that I saw personally. There were two things that I never once heard mentioned. First, that Hizbullah has been attacking Israel almost daily for several years, killing or maiming civilians and destroying Israeli property. Israel's offensive was not an ill-conceived, uncalled-for reaction. Second, and by far the most important point, never once was the blame placed on the UN where it belongs.

Many will recall that during the news coverage of the carnage in Lebanon, UN soldiers were seen among the rescue workers. Where did they come from? They were stationed in that very place. In fact, the refugee camp was within a UN-controlled base in Lebanon. The question that begs asking is, Why did the UN military authorities stationed at that camp allow Hizbullah guerrillas to haul in their missiles and launch them against Israel from within a UN base? They allowed this knowing very well that a full eight days before these launches Israel had automated their response to the Hizbullah rockets. Israeli radar simply picked up every launch and then fed the exact location of the launch into the computerized aiming devices of the big guns. Within minutes mortars would fall on the launch site to destroy Hizbullah's capability of launching another missile from the same site. The UN officials knew this. They also knew that after the launch of not one but *two* missiles from just outside the refugee camp, Israeli mortars would be landing in that zone within minutes. Did they do anything to move the refugees who were under their responsibility? No! Who, then, carries the greatest responsibility for this disaster in Lebanon? Israel or the UN? Though it is hard to believe, the UN actually passed a Resolution condemning Israel and saying that they killed the civilians in the refugee camp on purpose.[36] Israel surely had some idea of how it happened and responded by saying that it was not only an accident but that the UN was guilty of harboring Hizbullah guerrillas in the UN camps.[37] Fortunately, divine justice rather than human justice will ultimately decide who was most guilty.

Another example of the world's bias against Israel and the news media's collaboration to favor the Arab world is what happened when Iraq killed 5,000 innocent civilians among the Kurds with poisonous gas. The *Boston Globe* considered that event worthy of four articles—only one of which appeared on the front page, along with merely two photographs, and one editorial during the month after the massacre. During the same period, the *Boston Globe's* routine coverage of the Israeli-Palestinian conflict included 60 stories, 13 of these were on the front page, in addition to 15 photographs and six editorials! Other newspapers, such as the *New York Times* and the *Los Angeles Times* reported in much the same way.[38] The motivation for this is at least three-fold: 1) a satanic conspiracy, 2) petrodollars, and 3) fear. The outcome in each case is certain: 1) Satan's collaborators will partake of Satan's end unless they repent, 2) appeasing the enemy because he has money is both ungodly and disastrous and will surely bring God's judgment, and 3) appeasing him out of fear, with the hope that he won't plant quite as many bombs in one's country, is an example of Isaiah's "covenant with death" that will not stand (Isa. 28:15-18). Humanity's only hope is to make a covenant with the God of righteousness! The Western world will likely discover too late that Israel's enemy is also their enemy as well as the enemy of every other non-Islamic nation on earth. The Moslem world *will* not and *cannot* be placated or appeased as long as they are faithful disciples of Mohammed who calls them onward to bloodshed!

The Western world still mocks Saddam Hussein's declaration that "the mother of all wars" had just begun at the outset of the Gulf War. How do we know that he wasn't right? The war isn't over yet! Although the US considers it to be finished, an Islamic militant like Saddam Hussein only lays down the sword when he is dead. The newest evidence indicates that he was directly involved in the World Trade Center bombing. Laurie Mylroie, a former Harvard teacher and Middle East expert, recently published a book filled with evidence linking Hussein to the bombing. Regarding Mylroie's book, an Associated Press article states, "James Fox, the former chief of the FBI's New York bureau, who oversaw the agency's probe into the World Trade Center bombing for 10 months, said: 'Her analyses are pretty impressive to me' "[39] Possibly, Saddam has decided that it would be to Iraq's benefit to fight the war on American soil instead of inside Iraq. It remains to be seen whether or not the Gulf War was the beginning of "the mother of all wars." The beast and its horns are dreadful and terrible!

2. The Beast is Exceedingly Strong

The "whole earth" that Daniel refers to—Alexander's kingdom— has been under the dominion of seven empires since the beginning of time.[40] According to *National Geographic*, they are the following empires: 1) Egyptian, 2) Assyrian, 3) Babylonian, 4) Medo-Persian, 5) Grecian, 6) Roman, and 7) Islamic.[41] The last empire, the so-called "Nation of Islam," which is comprised of the Moslem nations, is exceedingly strong. Compared with the empires that have controlled the prophetic world of Daniel, it is stronger than any other in history in every way— demographically, geographically, financially, and militarily.

With 1.5 billion followers,[42] it is by far the strongest empire in history, **demographically**. **Geographically**, this empire not only controls all of Alexander's kingdom, but it has extended far beyond those limits and controls much of Africa, Pakistan, many countries of the ex-Soviet Union, and others. Some will recall that if Charles Martel of France had not detained the march of Islam in AD 732, Europe, and consequently, the rest of the world would almost certainly have fallen into the hands of the Moslems.[43] In terms of **financial strength**, Islam is easily the strongest empire in history because of its oil wealth. Finally, the combined **military strength** of the Nation of Islam can best be described by Daniel—"exceedingly strong." The US and many other Western powers, as well as China, have armed the Moslems to the teeth with many of the most advanced arms on earth. Military analysts claim that even Iraq today is stronger militarily than it was before the Gulf War. Large portions of the enormous oil revenues of the Moslem countries are continually being poured into arms. Between 1973 and 1993, the nations of the Middle East have spent a staggering one trillion dollars on arms, as they beat their plowshares into swords![44] Of course, this is strictly for "defensive purposes" so that the aggressive Israelis don't take over the region! The truth is, after so many embarrassments in past wars with Israel, the Islamic nations are preparing for a war that they believe cannot possibly be lost regardless of what mistakes they might make. This is their plan, but heaven's Man of War has a different outcome in mind, and He is just waiting for the enemy to make its move!

3. The Beast Has Great Iron Teeth

Since the beast is not a literal animal, then neither are his teeth— they, too, are symbolic of something. Of course, the Bible itself must give us the answer, rather than our own mind or imagination. Speaking of the wicked, Psalm 64:3 states, "Who sharpen their tongue like a sword, and bend their bows to shoot their arrows—bitter words." As seen here and elsewhere, the Bible likens arrows to words. However, in Psalm 57:4 we are told that the **teeth** of the wicked are **arrows**, and their tongue a sharp sword. This passage relates **teeth** to arrows (or **words)** and relates words, or the tongue, to a sharp sword. Most Christians know that a sword also speaks of words. God's sword is His Word and the sword of the wicked are *their* words, as the psalmist tells us. Proverbs 30:14 ties this all together, clarifying how the Bible uses teeth as a symbol of people's words. It states, "There is a generation, whose **teeth** are as **swords** [symbol of words], and their jaw teeth as knives, to devour the poor from off the earth, and the needy from among men." The Bible's symbolism makes plain sense if we consider that normal speech depends on the coordinated use of the tongue, teeth, lips, palate, and jaw (which are all likened to our words in different places of the Bible).

According to Peter, the words of a Christian should be an expression of the word of God. He admonishes us, "If anyone speaks, he should do it as one speaking the very words of God" (I Pet. 4:11a NIV). The word of God should just naturally come pouring out of the mouth of a true Believer. So what are the "teeth" or "words" of the beast? What does the beast speak? He speaks the words of Satan. If Islam is the manifestation of the beast in the earth, we should expect that its "words" are an expression of Satan's nature and message. The Koran is the expression of that "word." Interestingly, a man who was born into the world of Islam, Salman Rushdie, wrote a book entitled *Satanic Verses*, which exposes some of the original passages of the Koran that were messages Mohammed received from Satan. We can well understand why he is still in hiding to avoid being killed by the Islamic world— he revealed the truth!

The word of Islam (the Koran and the Hadith[45]) is not like our Word (the Bible). Their spiritual teeth are not like our spiritual teeth. The Bible calls for us to win the world by showing the world love; the Koran and Hadith call for winning it through bloodshed and the sword of Islam. The Bible exhorts us to reveal meekness to those who differ with us. Islam demands that they be killed. The Bible inspires humility; the writings of Islam inspire pride and self-esteem. The Bible encourages us to confess our faults; Islam encourages its followers to do anything they have to do to hide their faults and save face.

Three **words of testimony** from its own leaders are sufficient to show us what kind of "teeth" this satanic religion manifests through its words. The late Ayatollah Khomeini of Iran often said, "The purest joy in Islam is to kill and be killed."[46] Also, a Syrian minister of education said, "The hate which we indoctrinate into the minds of our children from their birth is sacred."[47] Haj Amin al Husseini, the Grand Mufti of Jerusalem during the Second World War, and second cousin of Yasser Arafat[48] proclaimed, "Allah has bestowed upon us the rare privilege of finishing what Hitler only began. Let the jihad begin. Murder the Jews. Murder them all."[49] The West has no idea what spirit it is that is invading their land, or with what spirit they are cooperating by mediating peace with Israel's enemies and collaborating in dividing God's land!

4. The Beast is Devouring

The Aramaic word used here for "devouring" is the same as the corresponding Hebrew word.[50] Daniel uses it seven times. Two of those seven times he uses it as "to accuse." (See Daniel 3:8 and 6:24.) In Daniel 3:8, this word is translated in English versions of the Bible as "accused" (KJV, NKJV), "denounced" (NIV, NRSV), "brought accusation" (ASV), and "maliciously accused" (RSV). For at least two reasons, it seems that this "devouring" is related to "malicious accusations" with words. First, this description of the beast "devouring" follows immediately after the revelation of its teeth, which we have seen to be its words. Second, over and over the Bible presents the concept that we can devour one another with the words of our mouths. Jeremiah also learned the power of words. God spoke to him, "I will make **my words** in thy mouth fire, and this people wood, and it shall **devour** them" (Jer. 5:14). Paul warns all of us, "If you keep on biting and devouring each other, watch out or you will be destroyed by each other" (Gal. 5:15). I never heard of Paul addressing the problem of cannibalism in any of the churches!

We are already familiar with the meaning of Proverbs 30:14: "There is a generation, whose teeth are as swords, and their jaw teeth as knives, to **devour** the poor from off the earth." We can be sure that Daniel was also using the word "devour" metaphorically. Note that just two verses before Daniel's description of this fourth beast he describes the second beast, a bear, that is commanded to "**devour** much flesh" and it is seen with the flesh "in its **mouth** between its **teeth**" (Dan. 7:5). How easy it is for us, as human beings, to become identified with this beast and not only use our mouth to eat but also to speak words that devour others through backbiting!

Today, the Islamic enemy seeks to devour Israel "from off the earth" by its devouring words, slanderous accusations, and abominable lies that it tells and that the news media happily feeds to the world. It is abundantly clear that Satan, "the ruler of the kingdom of the air" (Eph. 2:2 NIV), is in control of the "kingdom of the air" that the media has built. By far, most of what is printed in the media or broadcast on radio and TV about Israel is at least biased against the nation, if not outright lies. For those who have any doubt about the unfairness of the news media in their reporting on Israel, *The Media's War Against Israel*[51] carefully and thoroughly documents the facts. The Introduction to this 426 page book was written by US Congressman Jack Kemp.

On January 3, 1992, *The Jerusalem Post* printed an exposé of a recent report that appeared in the US press.[52] The US article was written by syndicated American columnist Mary McGrory. The *Post* exposé begins, "In a recent column she included a description of a few 'outrages of the [Israeli] occupation [of the West Bank].' " The *Post* proceeded to quote McGrory's list of supposed outrages: "There are guidelines directing when an Israeli soldier may shoot a child under 12; there are 17,000 Palestinian political prisoners in Israeli jails, and there is detention without trial for six months for Palestinians who look cross-eyed at Israeli military authorities."

The *Post* article continues, "Reading McGrory one cannot but surmise that Palestinians have supernatural powers. They can torture and murder 550 Arabs, kill 97 Jews, cause 4,000 injuries, burn hundreds of cars and buses, fling stones and petrol-bombs on moving vehicles (punishable by 40 years in jail in Maryland, 10 in New Jersey), and ambush civilian cars... and they can do all that by crossing their eyes!"

In her syndicated column, McGrory told of a press conference in Madrid with Hanan Ashrawi who was, at that time, the PLO's press secretary.[53] McGrory wrote that during the press conference a newsman representing a Christian publication asked, "How [Ashrawi] could expect Israel to give up Judea and Samaria after they have served as launching pads for attacks against Israel at least twice." The following is how the McGrory column presented Ashrawi's answer (without even mentioning the content of the question that had been asked): "Asked about Judea and Samaria, the biblical names of the occupied territory, Ashrawi replied: 'I am a Palestinian Christian and I know what Christianity is. I am a descendant of the first Christians in the world, and Jesus Christ was born in my country, in my land. Bethlehem is a Palestinian town. So I will not accept this one-upmanship on Christianity.' " The *Post* concludes, "Not only McGrory, but the correspondents of the British press wildly applauded Ashrawi's answer. In a veritable swoon, McGrory thus described Ashrawi's triumphant riposte: 'It was pretty much game, set and match.' " Tragically, the 200 news correspondents from different countries who were there got up and cheered instead of being "offended about this mockery of the truth."[54] Nor did it seem to matter to anyone that her answer completely ignored the question.

This type of distortion of the facts is not new to the Palestinians, and unfortunately, the collaboration of the Western news media in propagating their lies is not new either. Could McGrory have actually believed that Jesus was a Palestinian? Has she never heard of King David, and that his home town was a totally Jewish town called "Bethlehem"? Does she really believe that Americans are so stupid that "Jesus the Palestinian" will get by them unnoticed? It is highly doubtful. What she most likely believes is what the communists have discovered and employed for years—that if you tell a lie long enough and often enough, people will finally believe it. If the West continually hears that the Jewish people just sauntered into the holy land and began to take possession of ancient Palestinian cities and towns, they will probably start believing that version. This is just one example of the corruption and the twisting of truth that has constantly bombarded the world through the news media. These deliberate attacks do not only affect Israel. They will ultimately affect the attitude of a nation toward Israel, and then the attitude of any nation toward Israel will affect *God's* attitude toward that nation!

In *The Media's War Against Israel*, authors Stephan Karetzky and Peter E. Goldman expose the hypocrisy that pervades much of the news media in its reporting on Israel. Concerning *Time Magazine*, they write, "For the last seven years [beginning in 1970], and with accelerating tempo after 1977, *Time* has engaged in vigorous adversary journalism against Israel... Israel has been able to do no right."[55] Speaking also of the *New York Times*, the most influential newspaper in America, they write, "One of the major elements of the *Times* news reports... was the presentation of Arabs as helpless, innocent victims... people being brutalized by calculating, cruel, anti-democratic, voracious Israelis. The Arabs, one is led to believe, used force only when compelled to by the Israelis."[56] Could anything be more twisted? With very little research, just about anyone could fill a book with *documented* examples where

Arab governments and their terrorist groups have carefully planned and executed terrorist attacks against Israelis where hundreds of Jews have been killed. The only reason for the vast majority of these attacks was pure, unadulterated Islamic hatred of Israel. Although there have been individual Israelis who have taken the law into their own hands and attacked Arabs, I would challenge anyone to find just *one* such attack planned and perpetrated by the government of Israel against innocent Arabs!

The news media never seems to hesitate in promulgating twisted "facts." From time to time, the West hears of Israeli military raids into southern Lebanon—into the refugee camps of "innocent civilians." Sometimes it sounds like Israel has no greater justification for sending their planes in than to give their new pilots a target for practice. What the West does *not* hear is that the Islamic terrorists attack northern Israel from those "refugee camps" in Lebanon almost daily with Russian-made katyusha rockets, bombs, and gunfire. Usually, when Israel decides to do something to protect itself after many serious provocations with loss of life and property, the news of Israeli raids hits the press, often presented to make Israel's reaction seem totally uncalled-for.

From the time it became apparent that Israel was actually going to survive as a nation against impossible odds between 1948 and 1973, the only *right* the world gave the Jews was to suffer patiently at the hands of terrorists. Apparently, the world no longer believes that the nation has the right to defend itself. Israelis live under constant threat of attack—and attacks constantly occur. Terrorists are continually destroying Israeli life and property. When Israel is finally provoked into action, the news correspondents are there to validate and broadcast the terrorists' accusations of Israel's "armed aggression" and "unprovoked assaults." With such cooperative allies like the media working with Israel's enemies, those enemies have perfected the art of "devouring" Israel with their mouths!

I wonder how those same news correspondents would label a US response to continual World-Trade-Center-type attacks from coast to coast? I believe that we will soon find out, both in the US and in other countries of the world where the press has helped Israel's enemies devour Israel with their words. Will the hypocritical news media consider the nation's response "uncalled-for" when *their* homes are being destroyed and *their* families killed or maimed? The Just Judge is weighing our hearts and actions. Thankfully, He will soon bring justice to a corrupted world. Let's pray for the peace of Jerusalem!

The continual onslaught of devouring words that Israel's enemies proclaim are printed and broadcast daily by the media. These messages will ultimately affect the news correspondents' own nations. Great Britain is a graphic example. Before Israel became a nation, some British officials, who were anti-Zionists, actually encouraged the Arabs to engage in violent acts and words against Britain's "Jewish National Home" policy as outlined in the Balfour Declaration.[57] The British governor of Jerusalem, Richard Waters-Taylor, even encouraged Haj Amin, the Grand Mufti in Jerusalem, "to show the world that the Arabs of Palestine would not tolerate Jewish domination in Palestine."[58] As the Arabs reacted and spoke with increasing violence, their devouring words and actions were duly reported in the British press. Soon, so many political leaders in Britain were against the immigration of Jews to Palestine and a Jewish homeland that the official position of the British government became antagonistic to the Zionists.

In time, Britain became one of the greatest opponents on earth to the creation of the State of Israel. Colonel Richard Meinertzhagen, the British chief of intelligence in the Middle East who played a key role in driving the Turks out of "Palestine" in 1917, was pro-Jewish. When he realized what Britain was beginning to do, he lamented, "We are backing the wrong horse and, my God, we shall suffer for it if and when another war is sprung on us."[59] Did they suffer? The tremendous damage that Hitler's air force did by dropping tons of bombs on London and other English cities was minor compared to the damage the British Empire suffered after World War II had ended. After a journey through history of almost 1,000 years, and after becoming one of the greatest empires on earth, Britain not only lost its empire but also lost the blessing of God both at home and abroad in one area after another—spiritually, morally, financially, politically, and socially. They had been afraid of losing the favor of the Arabs who occupied the oil-rich lands that Britain so much wanted to continue controlling. What happened? They not only lost the favor of the Arabs, but they soon lost every square inch of their holdings in the Middle East.

Today, the spiritual condition of England is one of the most lamentable in the world, and their finances are in shambles. I once heard a European call Britain a "third-world country." The nation has gone from the heights of respect to the depths of shame. Even their illustrious "crown" is being defamed, exposed, and mocked continually today! What went wrong? The same thing that went wrong in an ever-growing number of nations throughout history—nations that decided to oppose both God's people and His plan for the Jews. The influence of the news media is known to be enormous. Apparently, the Western media has set its course and will continue to influence their nations to oppose Israel unjustly. Sooner or later, this always incurs divine displeasure and judgment on a nation.

5. The Beast Is Breaking In Pieces

If slander and lies do not get the world's attention, Islamic terrorists are more than willing to "break into pieces" anything, everything, and everyone—from killing 270 on Pan Am flight 103, to killing or injuring over 1,000 at the World Trade Center, to throwing a helpless, elderly Jew, Leon Klinghoffer, into the Mediterranean Sea, while he was still in his wheelchair.[60] Some look on and say, "Those poor Palestinians! They certainly must be frustrated over what Israel is doing to them if they feel compelled to go to such extreme measures!" Much of the Western press promotes the notion that if Israel just didn't exist in the Middle East, peace would come to the region. From absolutely indisputable historical facts, it can be demonstrated that even if Israel ceased to exist today, the Islamic world would continue killing themselves and others—*today!* Violence is as much a part of Islam as baseball is a part of the US, and, tragically, Islam does not seem to consider violence to be any weightier than most Americans consider baseball!

Consider a few of the historical facts: At this writing, the Secretary General of the United Nations is Boutros Boutros-Ghali, an Egyptian Moslem. He has written that the Arab nations of the Middle East were involved in more than 30 conflicts between themselves during a period of 30 years.[61] Some of those conflicts were actually all-out war.[62] The intra-Arab wars and violence continue to this day but receive very little press coverage. For example, the world considered 1985 to be an "uneventful" year in the Middle East.[63] However, in a one-month period during that year, there were 18 major acts of violence involving Arabs.[64] Apparently, nothing registers on the world's violence scale unless Israel is a factor. One of the reasons the Arabs have not been able to annihilate Israel is that, fortunately for Israel, they spend much of their time and effort trying to annihilate one another.[65] The Arab nations experienced "30 successful revolutions and at least 50 unsuccessful ones during the twenty-five year period from the establishment of the State of Israel in 1948 until 1973. During the same period, 22 heads of state and prime ministers were murdered."[66] A partial list of the continued acts of Arab violence against their own leaders, up to

1992, is available in *A Place Among the Nations.*[67] The murder of Anwar Sadat of Egypt in 1981 was one, along with 48 related political murders in less than five years in which influential people who supported Sadat's peace with Israel were removed.[68] Another act of Arab violence was committed against King Feisal of Saudi Arabia, who was assassinated in 1975.[69]

The nature of Islam is to "break in pieces." Is there any people or nation on earth that is blowing things up throughout the world like Islam is doing today? The vast majority of the world's worst terrorists are from Islam. For most people, recent world history provides sufficient proof that this is so. Bombs and bomb threats are so universally linked with Islam in people's minds today that when the Federal Building in Oklahoma City was bombed, almost everyone immediately looked toward the Moslem world. When it turned out that, on at least this occasion, the Moslems were apparently not involved, it was amazing to read and hear the repentant attitude of many people in the US for having been so unjust and bigoted in always blaming the Islamic world for terrorism. Suddenly it looked like we were all unjustly turning the innocent Moslems into the scapegoat! I don't think anyone needs to feel condemned for having jumped to the wrong conclusion. Rather, we do well to recognize *why* we jumped to that conclusion. Islamic terrorism has a fairly consistent track record and has proudly taken credit for more destruction and death than any other group of people on earth. The spirit of Islam has continually revealed its propensity to "break in pieces," whether by the bombing of the Israeli embassy in Argentina in 1992, or the bombing of the Jewish community center there in 1994, or the bombing of the World Trade Center in 1993, or the frequent bombings of public buses in Israel.

6. The Beast Tramples the Residue With Its Feet

Islam is by no means content with merely killing its victims. It loves to glorify its god by gloating in its victories, and by demonstrating its contempt and disrespect for human life. This is the thought that is depicted by Daniel's next description of the nature of the beast— "trampling the residue," or what remains, after "breaking in pieces" its victims. The thought of the word "trample" is "to humble."[70] Islam takes pleasure in "humbling" the "residue" or the remains of its victims (their corpses). If the Islamic terrorists on the seized ship, the *Achille Lauro*, had simply wanted to make their point by killing an elderly American Jew, they could have simply shot the wheelchair-bound Leon

Klinghoffer in the head and left him there. That was not enough. After shooting him in the head at point-blank range in front of his wife, they picked up his wheelchair and threw him into the sea. It would have given too much honor to the body of Leon if his poor wife had been permitted to bury him with dignity and weep over him. The leader of the terrorist group responsible for this act, Abul Abbas, revealed the wretched heart of Islam in a subsequent interview with Yoram Hazony. Concerning why they cast the corpse into the sea, his hard-hearted, brutal response was, "Perhaps he enjoyed the swim."[71]

Few events could show the utter contempt that Islam has for its victims like those surrounding the assassination of King Feisal II of Iraq in 1958. He was murdered along with all but one of the members of the royal family. What the Moslem populace did with the body of the heir apparent gives an idea of just how Islam tramples the remains of their victims. It also shows just how peace-loving the Moslems really could be if only Israel weren't around. One witness said, "With ropes the regent's body was attached by the neck and the armpits to the back of a lorry [truck] which dragged it through the streets to the shouts of 'Allah is great!' Men armed with knives and choppers dismembered the body, and the young men ran off waving the limbs with joyful shouts. When the procession reached the ministry of defense, the body was no more than a mutilated trunk, but it was hoisted to a balcony where a young man with a knife climbed a lamp-post and repeatedly stabbed the corpse in the back. He then began cutting off the flesh, working from the buttocks upwards. From the street, a long white stick was brought which was inserted into the corpse and forcibly pushed inside. What was left of the regent's body that evening was soaked with petrol and set on fire, the remains being thrown in the Tigris."[72] This is Islam; these are the "horns;" and this is a sobering manifestation of the nature of the beast.

Lest anyone be tempted to conclude that these were nothing more than isolated events, I would be quick to add that the "isolated events" go on and on. In another example, Palestinian terrorists in Jordan killed a Jordanian soldier. They then "beheaded him and played soccer with his head in the area where he used to live."[73] On November 28, 1971, Wasfi al-Tal, the Prime Minister of Jordan, was gunned down in the Cairo Sheraton by Mansur Suleiman Khalifah. "As he lay dying, al-Tal moaned, 'I've been murdered... murderers! They believe only in fire and destruction.' His wife, Sa'diyya, came running to him. 'Are you satisfied now, Arabs,' she sobbed and shouted, 'you sons of dogs.' A

Jordanian officer knelt and kissed the dying man's forehead. And one of the assassins also knelt down and licked the blood that was flowing on the marble floor."[74] The beast tramples the residue with its feet!

7. The Beast Is Different
From All the Beasts That Were Before It

It seems that the difference between this beast or kingdom and previous kingdoms on earth is described by Daniel himself in the next phrase—"it had ten horns." Again, the horns are a manifestation in the earth of the nature and character of the beast. One obvious difference between this kingdom and past kingdoms is that the "horns" or principal strength of this beast derives from the religious system, Islam, and is not a political or military system as were all past kingdoms. In light of all that we have seen, we should ask ourselves an obvious question, Is there any other people or human system—political, religious, or social—on the face of the earth that would be more prone to "make war with the Lamb" in the last days, instead of repenting of their own ways?

So Who Are the Ten Horns?

I do not want to commit myself regarding the ten precise Islamic countries that God considers to be the ten horns. However, I will offer a *plausible* list. My main reason for being cautious here is two-fold. First, some of the countries that exist today may not be recognized by God as one of the horns of destruction. Maybe the Lord does not consider every little Islamic nation as a justifiable entity. Some were possibly created on land that He still considers to be part of the nation from which it was originally taken. Second, unless *God* shows us who the countries are, we should not speculate. I am not certain of which ones are on *His* list. For example, Saddam Hussein claims that Kuwait belongs to Iraq. It is true that it used to, but Texas once belonged to Mexico. The question is, Does God still consider Kuwait (or Texas) to be part of its parent nation?

Having said that, here is my plausible list. My main criteria for including an Islamic nation in the list is that they must be "horns" that are at least near Israel and who are directly involved in efforts to see Israel destroyed. A second criteria is their place in history with regard to their conquest or involvement in the holy land. The ten nations *could* be the following: 1) Turkey, 2) Lebanon, 3) Syria, 4) Iraq, 5) Iran, 6) Saudi Arabia, 7) Jordan, 8) Egypt, 9) Libya, and 10) Sudan (Cush).

The Ten Horns Receive a
Kingdom for Only One Hour

"And the ten horns which thou sawest are ten kings, which have received no kingdom as yet; but receive power as kings one hour with the beast" (Rev. 17:12). This detail that the angel gives could be one of the strongest confirmations of all that the Islamic world is, indeed, the source of the ten horns—ten kings or ten kingdoms (nations). Note first, that frequently when the Bible speaks of a "king," such as the "king of Egypt," it is not speaking of a particular individual, but rather, of a political position. There were many different Pharaohs who ruled over the kingdom of Egypt, but the Bible makes no distinction between them when it refers to "the king of Egypt."[75] Also, the Bible's usage of the word "king" refers to a head of state, not necessarily to someone who sits on a literal throne and wears a crown. This becomes obvious if we consider that there is no contiguous region on earth today within which exist ten nations that are ruled by literal, classic-type kings. In fact, even if we take into account the entire earth today, there are very few *true* kingdoms still in existence. We are in the age of "democracy," and the international community frowns on autocratic kings who are seated on thrones, even though a few have managed to survive.

What does the angel mean when he explains that the ten kings will only reign "one hour"? Most of us would probably assume that even though he is referring to a very short time, he is *not* speaking about an "hour" of only sixty minutes. If ten kings were to reign for only one literal hour in the end, their "reign" would be so inconsequential to God's overall plan that it is unlikely they would be mentioned in Scripture. However, if the Lord is speaking about another type of "hour," He may very well be giving us another key to understanding from where these kings arise.

If we refer to Peter's explanation of the Lord's prophetic "day," we discover that the Lord's "days" are days of 1,000 years (II Pet. 3:8). Could the "hour" the angel refers to be speaking about an hour of God's prophetic day? If a "day" is 1,000 years, then "one hour" of that day would represent 41 years and 8 months.[76] It is doubtful that the angel was speaking in precise terms when he said that the ten kings would reign for "one hour." If this time period refers to a very precise period of years, then all ten kingdoms would have to be birthed at exactly the same time. That has never happened at any time in history and is probably not what the angel means. Knowing that the ten horns receive a kingdom for "one hour" can help us determine the geographical location of these kingdoms. Are there any kings or kingdoms on the earth that are approximately 40 years old? European nations certainly do not qualify since most of them have existed for many centuries.

Great Britain controlled much of the Arab world for the first half of this century. At the beginning of this century there were very few independent nations in the Middle East. The boundaries of many modern Arab states were established, and the new nations were granted independence, in relatively recent times. Egypt has been generally recognized as the real leader among the Arab nations (although other Arab nations, particularly Syria, have vied for that recognition for years). Biblically speaking, Egypt has also played a central role in Israel's history. *Official* independence came to Egypt in October 1951, when the Wafdist government terminated the Anglo-Egyptian treaty and ordered British troops off Egyptian soil.[77] In spite of the date of independence that Egypt actually celebrates (February 28, 1922), it could hardly be said that Egypt was independent as long as British troops were still in charge. They relinquished their control in October 1951. With the exception of Ethiopia and Oman, all of the present Islamic nations received their independence shortly before or shortly after Egypt became truly independent.[78] If the Lord is returning soon, these nations definitely qualify to be considered kingdoms of a very short duration. In fact, most of these "kingdoms" are close to being 40 to 50 years old—approximately one "hour" of God's thousand-year day!

Daniel tells us that the little horn comes up *after* the other ten horns. (See Daniel 7:8,24.). If the ten horns are leaders over ten nations in the Middle East, then we should expect that *after* those nations are established another horn or leader comes up among them and establishes one more nation near the time of Christ's Second Coming. As we will see, Daniel even reveals where that new nation will be located— right within the Holy Land itself! As a result of the Oslo, Norway agreements that Israel made with Yasser Arafat in 1993, a Declaration of Principles was signed on September 13 of that year on the White House lawn which ultimately led to the signing of a peace accord in Cairo on May 4, 1994. This was one giant step toward giving Yasser Arafat and the PLO permission to establish a Palestinian nation within the nation of Israel. We will see the significance of what Israel did in that agreement as we look now at Daniel's little horn.

Chapter 6

The First Indications of the Identity of the Little Horn

I was walking up the stairs that lead to our house. It was two days before the signing of the now famous Declaration of Principles between Israel and the PLO on the White House lawn on September 13, 1993. I had been closely following world events for the past thirty years, and especially God's work of restoring the nation of Israel. It seemed to me that what was about to occur was an extremely important piece of God's end-time puzzle and a further fulfillment of Scripture. However, I did not understand exactly how the piece fit into the puzzle. Nor did I understand just *how* important that coming event would actually be for Israel and the world.

As I walked up the stairs, I heard a little voice that I would soon discover had come from the Lord. The little voice said to me, "Count the days between the date of the signing ceremony and the first day of the new millennium—January 1, 2,000." I quickly got a calendar and did just that. To my amazement, I discovered that there would be precisely 2,300 days between the day Israel would be "making peace for the first time in history with Ishmael," (as President Clinton declared) and the first day of the new millennium.[1] I remembered, from Daniel 8:14, that Daniel's "little horn" will be involved with Israel for 2,300 days during the last days. As happens with most prophetic Scriptures, this will have at least two fulfillments.[2] It was partially fulfilled by Antiochus Epiphanes, the king of Syria, between about 170 BC and 163 BC.[3] The context of Daniel, however, makes it clear that it will also have a fulfillment in the last days, as we will see.

In spite of this amazing "coincidence," I still saw no connection between what was about to happen at the White House and Daniel's "little horn." The principal impact that my "discovery" had on me was simply to confirm once again that we are living in the last days. It also made me even more aware that what was about to happen in Washington was extremely significant from the standpoint of end-time prophecy. Two things related to the signing ceremony astounded me even more than my discovery. The first was the monumental importance that the world itself placed on the Israeli-PLO agreement. On the front page of the *Detroit Free Press*, these words appeared: "There are very few moments in history that are comparable to this moment."[4] It was hailed as a major turning point on the road that is leading the world to universal peace. It was also announced that this ceremony had been considered to be of such transcendental importance on earth that it **produced the greatest gathering of the world's dignitaries on the White House lawn in the history of the US.**[5]

The other thing that astounded me was the reaction of the Body of Christ to this awesome, historical and monumental event. After all, the Church has preached for years that the day would come when Israel would make a covenant with a wicked leader seven years before the Lord's return.[6] It has been preached and believed for decades that this event would signal the beginning of the end. One would have thought that even Yasser Arafat knew something about this. After signing the agreement, he declared, "This is the beginning of the end!"[7] Regarding the many signs that would indicate the end is near, Jesus said, "When these things begin to come to pass, then look up, and lift up your heads; for your redemption draweth nigh" (Lk. 21:28). To my way of thinking, this was a time for us to begin looking up in a new way, and to seek the Lord with new fervor. Therefore, I was awestruck by the amazing response of most Christians in the Body of Christ to this event—none! For many in the Church, it was just another day!

Why would the Body of Christ ignore all this as though it were a non-event? Will it require an even *greater* fanfare and gathering of world leaders whose message is "Peace, peace," to awaken the Church from her deep sleep to understand in what day she is living? I slowly began to perceive why so many Christians either ignored or discounted the importance of Israel's covenant of peace with the enemy. The fundamental reason is that for many, this peace agreement cannot be of any real importance because it does not line up with some of the details they believe about the last days. For many, their personal belief about the sequence of events in the end precludes placing any importance on Israel and Mr. Arafat's internationally acclaimed peace accord. What if none of us (including myself) have all the details straight? Do we risk anything by clinging to what we have been taught and to our own preconceived ideas about the last days if those ideas turn out to be incorrect? Each of us should answer this question only after considering the facts.

Ignorance of the facts may well be another reason few Christians have placed much significance on the Israeli-PLO peace process. Few Christians realize what the consequences of Israel's "peace" will be. Fewer still are aware of what is happening *to* Israel and *in* Israel at this very moment. It is an awesome and apocalyptic road that the nation has chosen in their quest for "peace and safety." Few people in the Western hemisphere have even begun to grasp the seriousness of what Israel has done. Few have grasped it because few have a clear understanding of two important issues. First, there is a sad lack of understanding regarding the importance of Israel in God's endtime plan— even among Christians. Once we understand that God has never thrown in the towel on His plans for His land or His people, we begin to perceive that everything is coming back around and will center once again in the Middle East. Second, few people realize just who Yasser Arafat and the PLO really are. This is true for both the Christians as well as their political leaders. It behooves us to find out! Mixed with an ignorance of the facts is the popular but serious misconception that the little horn of Daniel is the antichrist. We have already seen several reasons why he is not the antichrist. He is only one small part of the endtime beast, a part that deals only with Israel. In the coming pages, it will become clear that the little horn deals with Israel and not the world as we see what Daniel reveals and what he does *not* reveal about this little horn.

In March 1995, another "little thought" passed through my mind, and once again, I realized afterward that it had come from a loving Lord. The little thought was simply that Yasser Arafat is the fulfillment of Daniel's little horn. This thought was not based on any foregone conclusions, personal study, or evidence that I was aware of, and I did not continue meditating on it. Two months later my wife Barbara and I returned to Israel, where we have a home and have been spending about six months each year. While there, I remembered that "little thought" and decided I would re-read Daniel's description of the little horn and jot down each detail given concerning him. Just as many Bible readers would probably conclude, I assumed that Daniel most likely didn't give more than five or ten details about this person. I didn't expect my study to be very long. To my surprise, the list of details kept growing until it reached more than 80! I knew immediately that the Lord had a reason for so many details—He wants us to be able to recognize this person when he appears on the world scene.

What I previously knew about the history of Yasser Arafat showed me the incredible way in which he had already so perfectly fulfilled many of Daniel's details concerning what the little horn would do and what he would be like. I then began to search for all the books and information that I could get my hands on about this man. Based on the facts, I can now declare that Yasser Arafat has already fulfilled, with stunning precision, at least 47 of the approximately 80 details found in Daniel. When someone is describing a third party to us, for the purpose of determining if their acquaintance is the same John Doe we know, most of us do not need 47 confirming details to reach our conclusion. Neither should we need that many to identify confidently the little horn, but the Lord has given us enough to preclude the possibility of misidentifying him when he comes.

Why, then, did the Lord continue describing the little horn in Daniel with about 30 additional details? I believe they were given so that, after properly identifying him, we will also be able to see what the little horn plans to do and how he will accomplish his wicked plan. According to Isaiah, God's ability to foretell the future brings glory to Him and shows that He is the only true God. (See Isaiah 41:21-23; 44:6-8; 46:9-10; 48:5.) The many added details about the little horn also permit Israel and the Body of Christ to be forewarned so that we know what we face in the end and understand the significance of world events in our day. If we correctly discern that the prophetic message is being fulfilled, and we understand in what way it is being fulfilled, it will almost certainly affect our relationship with the Lord. Suddenly, our personal goals and ambitions in this world will seem less important, and we will be quicker to make the Lord's plans our plans. The Lord's life will less likely be merely a spiritual additive in our lives.

Knowing that their city would soon be destroyed surely caused the early church in Jerusalem to have a different perspective on life. (See Luke 19:41-44.) No wonder many of them were so willing to sell all their property and give the money to the Lord as they did in Acts 5. They must have reasoned, "Why should we hold on to things that will soon be lost when we can invest them in the Kingdom of God and save them forever?" Would you handle your own finances in a different way if you knew that you were going to lose everything you own within a few short years? Would an assurance of the Lord's soon coming change your commitment in the realm of giving, since instead of losing everything, you could give it to Him and keep it forever?

In my search for the facts and documentation concerning Arafat's life, the Lord made me aware of His providential guidance on a number of occasions. It became clear that He was leading me to the information required to discover who this man is. On one of those occasions, my wife and I went to a large secular bookstore in downtown Jerusalem. We were amazed and disheartened to find it closed for inventory. We decided to walk about 10 blocks to another large bookstore rather than to look for another parking space in downtown Jerusalem—an exercise that turns into perpetual motion at times! During the walk, we were delayed once again when we just happened to meet some friends on the street.

After what seemed like forever, we finally arrived, and I headed straight for the area in that large bookstore that would most likely have what I needed. I asked a salesperson concerning the availability of two specific books. She informed me that they were no longer available. Next to me, kneeling down to examine books on one of the lower shelves, was a man. When he heard the salesperson's response, he stood up and said, "I have one of those books, and you can use it if you like. I also know where to get the other from a used book shop. I'll take you there right now if you have the time." As we talked further, it turned out that one of his interests in life was to read and study everything he could find on the Israeli-Arab conflict. He not only ended up selling me his own book, but also did me the favor of searching out a number of other key references.

My wife and I were amazed at God's ability to guide people so deaf and blind as we are! To accomplish that on this occasion, the Lord had to: 1) close a store, 2) arrange for our friends to meet us on the street to slow us down, and 3) move someone we didn't even know to go to that specific bookstore at that exact moment. He did all this just so we would arrive at the exact bookshelf in that particular store at the precise moment to be able to get expert help finding key information on Yasser Arafat's life! We knew that the Lord wanted us to understand the facts, and we believe that He also wants His people to understand the facts. I believe that for this reason I was led to write this book.

There was one other thing I needed to do in preparation for sharing this message with others: investigate the precise meaning of the entire Hebrew text that deals with the little horn in chapters 7, 8, and 11 of Daniel. Most of us know that the only totally reliable version of the Bible is the original Hebrew, Aramaic, or Greek. We must be cautious about being dogmatic regarding the accuracy of the particular translation we may use.

To determine what the Hebrew actually says in these chapters, I went to some friends who are Jewish Believers in Yeshua (Jesus). They have the qualifications I was looking for. First, they have been Believers for a long time and have loved and studied the Bible for years; and second, their mother tongue is Hebrew. We compared my English Bible with their Hebrew Bible, verse by verse. Therefore, what I will be sharing about the little horn is based on what the Hebrew actually says. However, almost everything I mention that the reader finds to be different from his particular version of the Bible, can be verified and confirmed by using the *Strong's Hebrew Dictionary*.

Some may wish to remind me that Daniel 2:4b-7:28 was originally written in Aramaic and not Hebrew.[8] For those who are not aware of the relationship between Hebrew and Aramaic, it helps to understand that Aramaic is simply an older form of Hebrew. A comparison of the Aramaic words in Daniel 7 with the corresponding Hebrew words shows that there is often little or no difference between the two. This comparison can also be done using the *Strong's Hebrew Dictionary*.

"Thank you, my friend, for your generous gift.
I'm preparing one for you, too!"

Chapter 7

Is Yasser Arafat the Little Horn of Daniel?

Could the little man who wears the little horn on his head, and who is the greatest enemy the modern nation of Israel has ever had, be the little horn about whom Daniel gives almost 80 details? The political cartoon on the preceding page was not drawn by a Christian who was trying to demonstrate that Arafat does, in fact, wear a little horn on his head. It was drawn by a Jewish artist for the *Jewish Press* in New York.[1] Besides showing Arafat's little horn, this cartoon also demonstrates Arafat's perverse goals.

Another graphic cartoon, which I was unable to include here, appeared in *The Jerusalem Post* on January 12, 1996. It not only revealed Arafat's little horn, but it also revealed that he is a little man in both his physical and political statures. In that cartoon, he is standing between King Hussein of Jordan and Prime Minister Peres of Israel, who were strengthening their peace ties at that time. He is shown to be so short that his head only reaches their shoulders, and they are shaking hands over his head as he looks up with a worried expression on his face. This cartoon reveals how Arafat seeks to hinder the new peace that King Hussein has made with Israel, but he is seen to be only a little man and a little obstacle.

The Bible teaches us that the natural realm reveals spiritual truth.[2] Could the little horn on Arafat's head be symbolic of who this man really is? Two things about Arafat are certain: 1) he is recognized more for his headgear with the little horn formation on top than for any other visible characteristic, and 2) he has definitely been declared to be Israel's greatest enemy by a man who knows as well or better than anyone else—Ariel Sharon, one of Israel's best-known Defense Ministers.[3]

Who is this man, known as Yasser Arafat? His name at birth was Rahman Abdul Rauf Arafat al-Qudwa al Husseini.[4] "Arafat" is the name of the sacred mountain near Mecca where Mohammed experienced a spiritual transformation in his life.[5] Having briefly examined Islam for what it is, we now understand the *source* of that spiritual experience. Arafat's family called him Rahman, but his boyhood teacher and first verifiable homosexual partner, Majid Halaby, gave him the name Yasser.[6] So his last name calls to mind the very spiritual source of Islam and his first calls to mind Sodomy!

Concerning Arafat, Danny Rubinstein, an Israeli columnist for the Hebrew daily *Ha'aretz*, who has met with Arafat on a number of occasions, writes, "He is one of this century's best-known personalities."[7] At least five biographies have been written about him and he is the central theme in literally hundreds of books.[8] Rubinstein declares, "Knesset member Uri Avneri, once said that nobody has been hated in Israel as much as Arafat."[9] Journalist Thomas Friedman wrote that Arafat is "without doubt one of the most unusual characters and unlikely statesmen ever to grace the world stage."[10] Along with others, Rubinstein observes, "Arafat has enjoyed a mysterious sort of power"[11] and also, "his leadership has almost miraculously survived."[12] He asks, "How is it that someone who looks so strange and is so lacking in seriousness can at the same time be considered a statesman... of the first order?"[13] Other Rubinstein observations concerning Arafat are: "Perhaps the most recognizable political leader in the world;[14] most [of the world] is perplexed over this strange phenomenon;[15] [he is a] recipient... of the highest international honor."[16]

The Jerusalem Post gives one of the most amazing facts of all about Arafat, stating that his name is a worldwide "household name."[17] We know this is true today, but we should ask ourselves, How can it be that even the world recognizes something mysterious, strange, and miraculous in this man, yet the Church hardly takes notice of him and almost totally ignores his significance. If this is the Church's reaction to *this* messenger of Satan, sadly, it might be an indication of how well the Church would discern the antichrist himself. He would probably have to come with horns, a tail, and dressed in a red body suit before the Church would begin to recognize him! I include myself in this Church—we are *all* blind unless the Lord opens our eyes.

Let's look at the facts. By considering what Yasser Arafat *is* and what he has *done*, and by comparing this with Daniel's description of the little horn, I have personally become convinced that he is the long-awaited little horn of Daniel. I encourage the reader to *first* consider all the facts, and then decide for himself. One observation that will emerge from this study is that if Yasser Arafat is *not* the little horn, then the coming of the Lord is not yet at the door. We will see from the context of Daniel that the works of the little horn will require a considerable number of years to accomplish. Those years end with a specific three-and-a-half-year period that leads up to the Second Coming of Christ. If Arafat is not that horn, then someone else must yet appear on the Middle East scene and *begin* to fulfill this rather extensive prophetic message. However, if Arafat *is* the little horn, then the coming of the Lord is much nearer than most people believe, and much nearer than many Christians are willing to accept. Sadly, some have unfulfilled carnal dreams that they desire more than the coming of the Savior!

Whether Christ is coming soon or not, may you allow this study to instill in your heart a new urgency to seek the Lord as never before. One motivation for doing so will be a new burden for Israel, God's people. Possibly another motivation in your heart for doing so will be a deeper desire to allow the Lord to change you as you see the degradation and wretchedness that we, as human beings, are capable of giving ourselves to if we choose our own way instead of God's way.

As we look at Daniel's description of the little horn, we need to keep in mind two points that we have already discussed: 1) according to the angel, Daniel's vision reveals what will happen to **Israel in the last days**, not what will happen throughout the whole world, and 2) the little horn is not the antichrist. The little horn is only one of the horns found on the beast in the last days. He is therefore, only one of the many manifestations of Satan and the antichrist system in the earth. This horn, however, is used by God for a specific purpose—to deal with Israel in the Middle East.

We will consider each detail Daniel gives about this little horn, quoting the specific passage from Daniel for each. The biblical quotes for each individual passage are not all taken from the same English version of the Bible. In each case, I used the version that most exactly translates what the Hebrew itself says. Unless otherwise indicated, the quotes are taken from the New King James Version. I used four methods for determining the true meaning of each Hebrew or Aramaic word and phrase. First, I determined if Daniel himself used the specific word in other passages and how he used it. Second, I determined how the word is used throughout the Old Testament and how the translators themselves most often translated it. Third, I placed considerable weight on the definitions found in the *Strong's Dictionary of Hebrew*. Fourth, I took into account the translation I was given of each passage by my friends whose mother tongue is Hebrew.

For each detail that Daniel gives about the little horn that has already been fulfilled by Yasser Arafat, I include documentation that demonstrates the fulfillment. The details that remain unfulfilled at this writing provide us with a description of what the little horn will *yet* do in the Middle East. Although I have commented on each of the details, I have attempted to avoid speculation concerning how these things will be fulfilled unless the speculation is based on known facts. In those cases I have presented plausible scenarios. I have placed an asterisk (*) before each detail that has already been either partially or totally fulfilled.

* 1. He Is a *Little* Horn

"I considered the horns, and, behold, there came up among them another little horn" (Dan. 7:8a).

Why is this horn called "little"? Yasser Arafat can indeed be called "little" for several reasons. First, he is **physically** little. He's only five feet four inches tall.[18] I have a photograph that shows him standing on a stool behind the podium during his discourse at the White House signing ceremony in September 1993. Second, he is **politically** little. Later, we will see just how little real political power he actually possessed when Israel decided to make peace with him. Even Arafat knows that he was rescued from political oblivion by Israel's decision to make peace with him.[19] Third, he is **territorially** little. Even after he has obtained part or all of the West Bank, and he has established his rule or "kingdom" over it, the new Palestinian state will be the smallest Arab country on earth. Fourth, he is **financially** little. Although Arafat himself is wealthy, when he has finished establishing his new government over the Palestinians, it will be the poorest of all the Moslem nations. Last, he is **morally** little. It could be argued, as we will see, that he is the most morally bankrupt of all the Islamic leaders on earth.

* 2. He Comes Up *Among* the Ten Horns

"I was considering the horns, and there was another horn, a little one, coming up among them" (Dan. 7:8a).

As already discussed, the little horn is a king who arises in the midst of the ten horns who represent ten Islamic kings or nations. The thought that this little horn comes up *among* the other horns conveys the idea that, naturally speaking, they are all in geographic proximity of one another, and spiritually speaking, they all proceed out of the same head. Therefore, they are all controlled by the same head—the satanic, antichrist system which manifests itself through all eleven horns. It can definitely be said that Yasser Arafat has come up among these other heads of state or horns for at least four reasons: 1) **geographically,** he has physically grown up among them in the Middle East; (See Map 1 in Appendix A.) 2) **politically,** he has been associated with every one of them at different times over the last 30 years, even being a friend of some; 3) **economically,** the other horns have actually nurtured and supported him and his goals with financial help; and 4) **spiritually,** Arafat is one of them. He is a Moslem, not a Christian nor a Jew. Contrary to what some believe, Arafat was *not* born into a Christian family. His parents were Moslems before he was born.

* 3. He Comes Up *After* the Ten Horns

"The ten horns are ten kings who shall arise from this kingdom.
And another shall rise after them..." (Dan. 7:24a).

During the interpretation of his vision, Daniel is told that the ten horns arise first, and **afterward,** this little horn arises. He does not receive a kingdom at the same time they do. Today, all the other Islamic nations around Israel are already independent. Yasser Arafat has not yet succeeded in establishing an independent Palestinian state within the holy land. For over 50 years, he has totally dedicated his life to terrorism to reach that goal. Some Israelis suspect that Arafat, in flagrant violation of the Oslo agreements, will soon make a unilateral declaration of Palestinian independence.[20] In the autonomous areas, he is already beginning to issue passports, stamps, and independent Palestinian currency.[21] It has been correctly stated in the Israeli press that regarding the emergence of a Palestinian state, it is no longer a question of *if* but *when.*[22] Years after the other horns have received their kingdoms, this little horn will finally receive his.

4. He Plucks Three Horns Up By the Roots

"...there was another horn, a little one, coming up among them, before
whom three of the first horns were plucked out by the roots" (Dan. 7:8b).

This is one of the details about the little horn found in Daniel that has not yet been fulfilled, but we will see that circumstances indicate that the fulfillment is near. In his interpretation of Daniel's vision, the angel explains that the little horn "shall subdue three kings" (Dan. 7:24). It is important to note that the Aramaic word used here actually means "to humble." It does not *necessarily* mean that they are killed, but they are at least placed under the authority of the little horn. A logical question would be, How could Arafat take over *any* Arab country when he does not even have an independent Palestinian state of his own? According to Daniel, the little horn's army is going to increase dramatically before the end. Daniel even indicates over which three Arab nations he will gain control. We will wait and allow Daniel to tell us more about his army and the other three horns.

* 5. He Has Eyes Like the Eyes of a Man

"And there, in this horn, were eyes like the eyes of a man" (Dan. 7:8c).

As Daniel observed this little horn, he was sufficiently impressed by his eyes to mention this specific detail as something outstanding. Arafat's eyes are definitely one of his characteristics that create an impact in people's minds. Those who have personally known Arafat have been greatly impressed by his eyes just as Daniel was. They have mentioned them often and in powerful terms. Many things have been said about his eyes, including these comments: "He would just look right through you with his eyes."[23] "His eyes were hypnotic and they could stop you cold."[24] "When he looked at one, [he] seemed to peer into one's deepest interior recesses."[25] "He had picked up many mannerisms... bulging his eyes when he talked."[26] "He had two ways of looking at you with his large eyes—very softly, like a man looking at a woman... or blankly, as though his eyes were going right through you."[27] "He did not speak with his voice so much as with his body—his hands, his eyes."[28] It has also been said of his eyes that they "bore holes into you."[29]

Besides all these observations, for many years, Arafat's eyes were also known for a strange habit he had—of wearing sunglasses constantly whether inside or outside, and whether with friends or political leaders. He almost never took them off.[30]

What does Daniel mean when he describes his eyes to be like "the eyes of a man"? The Bible talks much of both the eyes of the Lord and also the eyes of man. If we see with the eyes of man instead of the eyes of the Lord, we have a problem with our spiritual vision. A man with only human vision sets his eyes on earthly goals and on an earthly inheritance. He will struggle and fight to reach that goal. Yasser Arafat definitely does not see things as God sees them.

A lack of divine vision is a problem that another man in the Bible also had. That man used natural vision to choose the best part of **the holy land** and was willing to fight for it. His name was Lot. Since there was strife between Abraham and Lot, Abraham asked Lot to choose what he wanted. Lot then "lifted up **his eyes**" and chose what he considered to be the best part of Canaan (Gen. 13:10). Afterward, the Lord told Abraham, "Lift up *your* eyes" (Gen. 13:14). As Abraham received vision from the Lord's perspective, he looked in every direction and the Lord told him that everything he could see would be his and his descendants forever!

Certainly Mr. Arafat is like Lot and has shown that he has the eyes of the natural man, not seeing as the Lord sees. He does not see the end. He sees through the eyes of the natural, carnal man. Therefore, his vision and goals are totally ungodly—he wants the land of Canaan, and like Lot, will end up losing everything! In fact, just as Abraham made peace with Lot by giving him land, so Israel today is making peace with Arafat by giving him land. The result of Abraham's decision was that Lot ended up in Sodom, under judgment, and he lost everything. The result of Israel's decision will be that Arafat will end up under God's judgment and will lose everything also—and very soon!

* 6. He Has a Mouth Speaking Great Things

"...and, behold, in this horn were eyes like the eyes of man, and a mouth speaking great things" (Dan. 7:8d KJV).

"Then I would know the truth of... the ten horns that were in his head, and of the other which came up... even of that horn that had eyes, and a mouth that spake very great things" (Dan. 7:19-20 KJV).

In Daniel's second description of this little horn, he doesn't only say that the horn speaks "great things," but that he speaks "*very* great things." Arafat is well-known for being an effective rabble-rouser and agitator. Since signing the 1993 peace accord, he is also now referred to as an international statesman. Daniel could be referring to these things, but I believe there is something much deeper here that is an awesome characteristic of Yasser Arafat.

As a young man, I used to hear some of Arafat's outlandish statements and laugh. I loved Israel and was excited over what God was doing for His people. Along with many others, I thought Arafat bordered on being a lunatic when he talked about taking Israel's land from them—land that God had obviously given to them forever. The last time I laughed at the "great things" Arafat spoke was after he signed the Israeli-PLO peace accord in Cairo on May 4, 1994. He immediately began to proclaim, "Jericho and Gaza first, and then on to Jerusalem."[31] He openly declared that Jerusalem would soon be the capital of a Palestinian state. Most of the world who heard it probably mocked his claims. After all, Israel had conquered East Jerusalem in the Six Day War in 1967, and then in 1980 the Knesset had issued a declaration stating that Jerusalem would be the "undivided eternal capital of Israel."[32] Who was Arafat kidding? Obviously, he was just letting off steam! Surely, he was just promising great things to the Palestinians, knowing he could never deliver!

By now, the whole world should begin to understand that this man not only *speaks* great things, but he actually reaches his goals. As the angel declares to Daniel, this little horn shall "prosper and thrive" (Dan. 8:24), or "succeed in whatever he does" (Dan. 8:24 NIV). As I mentioned in Chapter 1, from all indications, East Jerusalem will soon be in the hands of Yasser Arafat and the PLO.

* 7. His Vision Is Greater Than His Fellows

*"...that horn... whose appearance was
greater than his fellows" (Dan. 7:20b).*

Do you remember the ten Islamic nations I mentioned in Chapter 4 as plausible candidates for being the ten horns of the beast? How many heads of state of those ten countries could you identify in a photo? Few people would recognize more than four or five at the most. On the other hand, there are few people on earth who would not immediately recognize a photo of Yasser Arafat. His appearance is definitely "greater" in the sense of being better known. This is because his **appearance** in newspaper photos throughout the world is with far **greater** frequency than the other horns. There is another reason Arafat's appearance is so well-known. If he were in a contest with the other Islamic heads of state to decide who had the most striking appearance, Arafat would win, hands down—for striking fear into the hearts of all who see him!

In addition to these thoughts, there seems to be something much deeper in Daniel's description of the appearance of the little horn.

Virtually all translators of the Bible have felt that Daniel was referring to the "appearance" of the little horn in this verse, and that may well be one possible meaning here. However, it should be noted that the Aramaic word translated as "appearance" in this one verse is used by Daniel in 11 other verses in his book. In every other case, the same translators rendered this word as "vision" or "visions" or as the act of "seeing." The root of this word is used 31 times in the Old Testament. In the King James Version, it is translated as "see" 17 times and as "saw" six times, and "beheld" six times. On the other two occasions, it is translated as "had" and "wont" (meaning "usually"). Never once is it translated as anything close to "appearance." It is consistently related to vision or the act of seeing. Why should we assume that Daniel used this word to refer to vision or the act of seeing with the eyes 11 times and only once to refer to physical appearance? If we assume that Daniel's use of this Aramaic word was consistent, then we could also translate Daniel's description of the little horn in Daniel 7:20b as "whose vision was greater than his companions."

Unquestionably, throughout Yasser Arafat's life his "vision" or goals in both the natural world as well as in the spiritual realms of Islam have been far greater and far more well defined than the "vision" of any of his companions. I will give just three of many possible examples to illustrate this point. The first reveals that his *spiritual* "vision" has been far greater than his companions since early childhood, and the other two examples reveal that his *natural* "vision" or earthly goals related to the extermination of the Jews and the taking back of the holy land has been much greater also.

At the age of seven, Yasser began his religious training with his great uncle, Yusuf al-Akbar, who gave Islamic instruction to all the youth of the neighborhood.[33] At first, there were times when his uncle considered Yasser to be "as dull and stupid as a camel."[34] However, to Yusuf's great amazement, when he would begin quoting a passage from the Koran to the class, Yasser would frequently finish the quote from memory. Yasser's uncle was discovering something about him that would be vocalized many years later by Shimon Peres, who said, "Yasser Arafat is amazing both in his wisdom and stupidity."[35] Yusuf did not realize that young Yasser had nothing more than an amazing memory, and could recall the passages he had heard his father read to the family from the Koran. Unfortunately, Yusuf arrived at the outrageous conclusion that Yasser was a supernatural boy on whose mind the Koran had been imprinted from before birth. He was sure that it was due to the direct genealogical descent from Mohammed which the al-Husseinis claimed.[36] Once Uncle Yusuf had "discovered" who little Yasser was, he instructed all the family to be careful about how they treated such a holy and wise child.[37] They duly obeyed, at least for a time. Yasser had no reason to disbelieve his uncle, and for some years afterward, while his companions impatiently received the minimum religious instruction possible, Yasser's only interest was his great call to Islam and his vision of attaining the divine goal for his life. When the other children all ran out of the class to play, Yasser would stay behind and receive more instruction until after dark every day.[38] According to his sister, Halma, and brother, Nasir, Yasser would go into trances that would last for hours, and Halma confessed that she grew up being afraid of him.[39] Spiritually speaking, Yasser definitely had a "greater vision than his companions," as Daniel revealed, and it sounds like it came from the same source that Mohammed's visions came from!

Yasser also possessed a "greater vision than his companions" with respect to his earthly ambitions. This became evident at the age of 19 when he was already involved in terrorist acts. On one occasion, he was with a group of about 20 young terrorists who were on a secret raid to destroy a property. When they arrived at their target, they were ambushed by the owners of the property who had been forewarned by someone from within the terrorist organization to which Yasser and the others belonged. No outsider could have possibly known about the plans. One of the young men in the group was Rork Hamid. Several in the group had doubts about his full commitment to their terrorist activities. When all 20 fled and regrouped in a shed, Yasser looked at Rork and expressed what the others were thinking—that Rork must have been the informer. Yasser took immediate and deliberate action— he calmly walked over to Rork with his pistol drawn and shot him in the head. One of the members of the group later said, "We were astounded. Yasser turned to us with a weird smile on his face and said something like, 'Let that be a warning to any and all of you who would betray the holy Ikhwan' " (the Moslem Brotherhood of Egypt).[40] Arafat then ordered them to hang Rork's body in the town square; which orders they promptly obeyed! They discovered later that Rork had not been the informer. It had actually been none other than Haj Amin al Husseini himself, the leader of the organization and Arafat's second cousin. He had decided to sacrifice that whole group of young men to incite greater anger against the enemy.[41] Yasser never so much as said he was sorry for killing Rork. To the contrary, he inferred that Rork had not died in vain because his death helped to increase the clarity of vision in the others.[42]

Arafat's "greater vision" for the total annihilation of every Jew was also revealed while he attended the University of Cairo in Egypt. He was 22 years old and was a member of the Palestine Students' Federation, dedicated to the destruction of the Jews in Palestine. At that time he was dating young Jinan al-Oraby, with plans to marry her.[43] According to her own story, he came to her house one day while two of her girlfriends were visiting her—Rachel and Miriam. Her friends lived in the same neighborhood in Cairo and came from a Jewish family. When Yasser discovered that the girls were Jewish he suddenly seemed very interested in the girls and in their family. Among other personal questions, he asked them about where their father worked and where the family lived. Jinan had no idea about Yasser's feelings toward Jews. She would soon find out. Two days later, Rachel and Miriam's father was murdered. Jinan made no connection between Yasser and the murder until a few days later when he was visiting her again, and they were alone in the house. She told him about the girls' father and began to weep again for them. Yasser went into a rage and began to strike her, shouting at her never to weep for a Jew. When she explained that they were her friends, he totally lost control and tore her clothes completely off her in a rage. Finally, he admitted to her that he was the one responsible for the murder. I am sure that few if any of the students in the Palestine Students' Federation had a vision for the destruction of Jews as great as this young man's vision!

* 8. He Makes War With the "Saints"

"I was watching; and the same horn was making war against the saints" (Dan. 7:21a).

Here is where a major misconception has entered the interpretation of Daniel's vision. Since most English versions of the Bible have translated the Aramaic word in this passage as "saints," Gentile Christians immediately associate this passage with people that belong to the famous "Gentile Church." The New Revised Standard Version is one of the few versions that translates this properly as, "this horn made war with the holy ones." Is there a significant difference between "holy ones" and "saints"? The difference is great only if we misunderstand what Daniel means. Our misconception arises because "saints" is one of the principal New Testament words used to refer to the Body of

Christ. Therefore, it is difficult for a Christian to read "saints" in Daniel without getting the wrong idea. To help us understand Daniel, let's do a very brief word study.

The Aramaic word that many English versions translate as "saints" in Daniel is "qaddiysh" (*Strong's Hebrew Dictionary*, #6922). The corresponding word in Hebrew is "qadowsh" (*Strong's Hebrew Dictionary*, #6918). These words come from the root verb "qadash" (*Strong's Hebrew Dictionary*, #6942), meaning "to sanctify," which simply means "to set apart" or "to separate" for a specific purpose.[44] This word does not necessarily refer to a person's moral or spiritual character. For example, when Daniel uses the corresponding Hebrew word in connection with his people, Israel, and calls them "the holy people" (Dan. 8:24), he is not referring to their upright walk, something that few had in Daniel's day. Rather, he is referring to their position before God. They have been chosen by Him for His purposes. In Isaiah 13:3, even the Babylonians are called God's "holy ones" (the same word); because, as He explains, they were set apart by Him for a purpose—to bring judgment to the earth. Israel is called the "chosen people" not because they are righteous, but because God decided to choose them for His purposes. (See Deuteronomy 9:4-6.)

The Hebrew word "qadowsh" appears 106 times in the Old Testament and is translated as "holy" **95 times** in the King James Version. The corresponding Aramaic word "qaddiysh" appears 12 times (all 12 times are in Daniel). This word is translated as "holy" **seven times** in Daniel and as "saints" five times. However, note a very important point here: All five of the instances in Daniel where this word is translated as "saints" are in the context of this one vision in Daniel 7. Why did the translators choose "holy" in the vast majority of the places where this word and its corresponding Hebrew word occur in the Old Testament (102 times out of 118 occurrences of the two words), and then translate it as "saints" throughout this one vision of Daniel? Possibly, they were attempting to see Christians here also. My Hebrew-speaking friends confirmed to me that the correct translation here is "holy ones," and that no Hebrew-speaking person would ever think of Christians when reading this! This refers to the same people that Daniel calls "the holy people" in his book, using the corresponding Hebrew word (Dan. 8:24; 12:7). According to the angel that interpreted the vision, it is speaking about Daniel's people—Israel—in the last days. So what does this mean? Take heart, Christians around the world, the little horn will not make war with you! He has already been making war with the chosen people for almost 50 years!

Arafat Has Been Making War With Israel for Many Years

Israelis recognize that their greatest enemy since the founding of the State of Israel in 1948, has been Yasser Arafat![45] He has attacked Israel for a longer period of time, more often, and killed more Jews than any other single person alive on the face of the earth today! He is "the worst murderer of the Jews since 1945."[46] He began his attacks on Jews as a teenager, working with his hate-filled father and others to destroy the Jews.[47] Later, he organized a group of terrorists known as Fatah, which was incorporated into the PLO when Arafat gained control over that organization. From its inception, the PLO's Charter declared that its very purpose for existing is the destruction of the State of Israel. Consider just a few of the Articles in that Charter.[48] Article 9: "Armed struggle is the *only way* to liberate Palestine and is therefore a strategy and not tactics" (emphasis mine). Article 15: "The liberation of Palestine... is a national duty... to purge the Zionist [Jewish] presence from Palestine." (No wonder Arafat tortures those who do not want to participate with him in terrorism—he considers it a "national duty" to destroy Jews!) Article 19: "The partitioning of Palestine in 1947 and the establishment of Israel is fundamentally null and void..." Article 21: "The Palestinian Arab people... rejects every solution that is a substitute for complete liberation of Palestine." (Note: The peace process is a farce, then, since it is a solution short of this goal.) Article 22: "Israel is a constant threat to peace in the Middle East and the entire world." Of course, the Oslo accord demands that these statements be removed from the Charter, something that was delayed indefinitely by the April 1996 meeting of the Palestine National Council. Even if the Articles calling for the elimination of the State of Israel are ever removed from the PLO's Charter, nothing the PLO has done to date indicates that these goals will be removed from the hearts of the PLO's members!

Ironically, the last Article quoted above probably contains more truth than anything else the PLO has ever said. Israel *is*, in fact, a constant threat to world peace. Not because Israel wants to fight, but because the spirit of Satan manifested through Islam, the PLO, the UN, the news media, and other God-hating institutions will never let Israel rest in peace until either Satan's system is destroyed or Israel is destroyed! In Moses' day, God hardened Pharaoh's heart and the heart of Jannes and Jambres, Pharaoh's sorcerers in Egypt so that He could destroy them and bring Israel into blessing. (See Exodus 10:1; 7:11 and II Timothy 3:8-9.) It seems that something very similar is happening today with Arafat and his PLO. In these last days, God will once again destroy the sorcerers. Who are the sorcerers who are opposing His people? In Hebrew, the acronym "PLO" is also a Hebrew word that means "sorcerers!" We can be sure that the Palestinians did not realize the name they were giving themselves when they formed the PLO. Isaiah 2:6 tells us that the Palestinians (Philistines) are soothsayers or sorcerers. How sovereign our God is! He can even cause the names that the wicked choose to reveal who they are in His eyes.

After Israel had departed from Egypt and entered Canaan, God hardened the hearts of the enemies of Israel in Canaan also, causing them to fight against God's people. He is doing the same thing again today. He will ultimately harden the hearts of *all* nations, and they will end up fighting against God's tiny people. (See Joel 3 and Zechariah 12:9.) The Lord will fight on the side of Israel, and the nations will lose the war to the glory of Jehovah's name. (See Revelation 19:15.) The result will be that Israel will end up regaining possession not only of the West Bank and Judea, but it will possess the whole world! God promised Abraham that his descendants would inherit the whole earth. (See Romans 4:13.) It doesn't matter if Mr. Arafat and the PLO or the whole Islamic world join forces with the nations of the world to throw Israel finally into the sea. Ultimately, they will lose and Israel will win, although the cost to Israel is going to be enormous, because...

* 9. He *Prevails* Against the "Saints"

"...the same horn was making war against the saints, and prevailing against them" (Dan. 7:21b).

Just about anyone with a gun can "make war" to one degree or another, but not everyone can "prevail." The little horn *prevails* against the "saints" or "the holy ones." Nowhere in Old Testament history do we find the enemy prevailing against God's people as a nation while they were walking uprightly. This is a further example of how the Lord uses the word "holy ones" to refer to the chosen people's **position** before Him rather than their **character** or purity. The little horn is able to prevail against God's people only because they are not walking in covenant relationship with Him. Later, Daniel shows us that the very purpose of the little horn is to deal with Israel and bring them back to their God. This was always the reason that God raised up enemies to chasten Israel. (See I Kings 8:33-34; 46-48.)

He Prevails Against the Saints Physically, Killing or Maiming Them

The list of Arafat's successes against "the holy ones" (Jews), continually grows. Just a few examples should demonstrate how much he has "prevailed."

At the 1972 Olympic games in Munich, a group of Arafat's men killed eleven Israeli athletes. The PLO group responsible was called "Black September."[49] Arafat's war against the Jews is not limited to Israeli soil. He carries the war to any place in the world where he believes he can kill Jews. Nor is his war against Israel limited to Jews. He is willing to kill or maim people of any nationality, as long as he thinks it will ultimately help his cause against Israel. Unfortunately, too often the resulting international pressure against Israel proves that these perverse tactics work. Of course, there will be no end to killing innocent civilians from any country if the nations continue to yield to the demands of the terrorists. Besides the slaughter at the Munich games, during 1972 Arafat's Fatah terrorist organization also "blew up oil and gas installations in West Germany, Italy, and Holland, hijacked planes, shot American and Belgium diplomats in the Sudan, and a Jordanian in London."[50]

In June 1974, Arafat's Fatah terrorists attacked the Israeli border town of Nahariya, leaving four Israelis dead and six wounded.[51] Then, in March 1975, his terrorists landed on a Tel Aviv beach in two rubber dinghies. They planned on slaughtering youth at the Municipality Youth Center. When a policemen sent out an alert, they chose another nearby target—the Hotel Savoy. When the battle ended, there were eighteen dead—seven terrorists, three Israeli soldiers, and eight hostages.[52]

In March 1978, thirteen of Arafat's Fatah terrorists departed from a large ship in rubber rafts off the coast near Haifa. They murdered the niece of US Senator Abraham Ribicoff as she walked along the beach. Then, they commandeered a bus, killed some of the passengers, and sped toward Tel Aviv where they sprayed bullets into traffic and at the police in a shoot-out. The results of this battle: forty-six dead and eighty-five wounded.[53]

We can add to this list the synagogue worshippers in Istanbul, a child and his pregnant mother in Alfeh Menashe, a mother and her children on a bus in Jericho,[54] seven Israeli buses since the 1993 peace accord, with hundreds dead or wounded, and, we can also add: "whomever Mr. Arafat decides his next victims will be." Some people were certain that Arafat's gangsters would stop the killing once the boss signed the peace accord. Have they? During the eighteen months after the signing of the peace accord, the PLO-Hamas duo doubled the rate at which they were killing Israelis through terrorism.[55] We will see shortly that this increased terrorism is indeed a PLO-Hamas effort, and that the popular idea that Hamas is an enemy to Arafat can be discounted with the facts.

He Prevails Against the Saints Militarily— Their Attacks Cannot Reach Him

The logical question is, Since Israel has consistently proven the ability of its intelligence service and technology to find and destroy one key terrorist after another, why have they never eliminated the much-hated Arafat? This question has, in fact, been discussed often in Israeli circles. One theory is that Israel is afraid that someone worse might seize control of the PLO. However, the facts point to a far more transcendental reason why none of Arafat's phones have ever mysteriously blown up in his face as happened to Ayyash. As we pointed out, even the unbelievers have observed that his "leadership has almost miraculously survived."[56] It has been stated that Arafat seems to be the proverbial cat with nine lives in an eerily uncommon sense.[57] He has had so many "miraculous" escapes from death that one must assume that this cat has *more* than nine lives!

One of his most recent miraculous escapes came on a flight from Khartoum to Tunis when the airplane that Arafat was on crashed in the desert during a sandstorm. It was April 8, 1992. PLO officials assumed that he was dead. However, he had only used one more of his nine lives, because he "miraculously emerged from the aircraft wreck in which three crewmen, including the pilot and copilot, had died."[58]

This sort of escape was nothing new to Arafat. He has escaped death in similar ways so many times that he has the reputation among the Palestinian people for being invincible.[59] On March 21, 1968, an Israeli "armored brigade and two paratroop battalions, supported by reconnaissance units and artillery, attacked the largest Fatah base, located at Karameh in the Jordan Valley... Arafat was forced to flee his besieged headquarters on a motorcycle, dressed as a woman... Arafat reportedly was terrified by his close brush with death."[60]

Then there was Israel's 1982 raid on Lebanon to drive the PLO out of the country. Of course, one principal goal was to kill Arafat. Pilots were informed concerning the building that Arafat was using for his operations room during the battle. They hit the building with a "vacuum bomb" and killed or wounded about 200 who were inside. They were certain Mr. Arafat was dead. Wrong again! Arafat had left hurriedly just moments before.[61] One Palestinian said, "It was only fate that protected him."[62]

It was much more than fate that protected Arafat. One of the most amazing things about Israel's attack on Beirut was that, when they had the PLO surrounded with no way of escape, they decided to allow them all to flee, including Arafat. Proof that Israel literally had Arafat in their gun sites and decided to allow him to live comes from a photograph taken by an Israeli intelligence operative. It shows the full view of Arafat's upper body while he was fleeing Beirut in the back of a truck.[63] The operative himself could have killed him easily. Some attribute Israel's decision to let Arafat escape to the theory mentioned above—that Israel is afraid of getting someone worse. We will see the fallacy of this reasoning in a moment. Others believe that Israel buckled under international pressure. However, given Israel's history of not bending to international pressure when their own survival depends on the neutralization of their enemies, this is unlikely. It seems that Nebuchadnezzar's explanation of what happened is more plausible. He declared that "the Most High rules in the kingdom of men" (Dan. 4:17).

In June 1983, after Arafat and the PLO had been driven out of Lebanon, he met with Syrian President Hafez Assad to iron out their differences. The meetings were not very fruitful. However, Arafat had no idea just how *unfruitful* they had been until it came time for him to leave Damascus. On June 23, 1983, the night before he was to depart in his bullet-proof limousine, he received a warning that the Syrians were planning to ambush his convoy. Of course, when the limousine was attacked the next day, someone else died in Arafat's place because he was not inside.[64]

Another of Arafat's "miraculous survivals" occurred in Tunis on October 1, 1985. There he had established the headquarters of his so-called PLO's "government in exile."[65] Once again, Israel went after him, and bombed the building they knew he was in. They totally leveled the building, but the "cat with nine lives" simply used one more of those lives. He had left the building only seven minutes before.[66] Does this sound like the policy of a nation who wants to keep Arafat alive because they are afraid of getting someone worse? Hardly!

He is clearly being kept alive by someone bigger than he is and bigger than Israel is! That much he recognizes himself. After the assassination of Yitzhak Rabin in November 1995, he was asked if he was concerned that he might face the same end as Rabin. His answer was, "No. I am not concerned, because we all have to reach our destiny." Does he know something about his own destiny, work, and identity that God's own people do not know?

Who is keeping this man alive? Some may say that it is Satan who is doing it. However, Satan seeks to destroy his own people. (See Isaiah 14:12-16,20.) God Himself spares vessels of wrath for His own purposes. The Apostle Paul explains, "Does not the potter have power over the clay, from the same lump to make one vessel for honor and another for dishonor? What if God, wanting to show His wrath and to make His power known, "*endured with much longsuffering the vessels of wrath prepared for destruction?*" (Rom. 9:21-22) We should ask ourselves why God is maintaining Arafat in this world, enduring him with so much longsuffering. He is obviously being used as a very important vessel of wrath to bring repentance to God's people, Israel. Arafat will continue to "prevail against the holy ones" until God decides otherwise!

He Prevails Against the Saints Politically— He Is Uprooting Them From Their Lands

Sometimes physical death is more desirable than extreme spiritual and emotional suffering. Every year hundreds of people throughout the world reach that conclusion and commit suicide. The Bible confirms that life can sometimes be so excruciating that people actually "seek death" (Rev. 9:6a). Yasser Arafat is submitting the Jewish nation to enormous emotional and psychological damage by uprooting Israeli "settlers" from his newly acquired autonomous areas. Jewish immigrants who were willing to expose their families to constant dangers by choosing to live among or near Moslems in places like Hebron, Bethlehem, and many places in Samaria, were once considered to be heroes in Israel. Before he died, Prime Minister Rabin labeled them as a nuisance, whose physical protection was not the responsibility of the Israeli government.[67]

Even though Jews have been willing to live alongside Moslems for decades, Arafat has repeatedly made it clear that the settlers should find other places to live once he is in full control. It is now obvious that the options are well-defined for the settlers—either leave the place they have called home for years or face terrorism and death. Most of the settlers are fervently religious Jews who believe that God has given them the land. This conviction has always been a primary motivation for living on the fringe of the nation's borders and on the fringe of death for years. Abandoning that land for which they exposed their children to many years of constant danger, and suffering the humiliation of now being called "crybabies"[68] instead of being called heroes is not even the most traumatic part of their suffering as Arafat prevails against them. What really shreds their emotions is the government's total disregard for all that is called holy according to their understanding of the Bible. Now, after it seemed that God was beginning to fulfill His covenant anew with the Jewish people, they are being uprooted once again.

This time it is not hate-filled Gentiles who are oppressing them, but Israelis—their own people—as they cooperate with Arafat in his war against God's people. Emotionally, this is more than many are able to endure as Arafat prevails against them! Herbert Zweibon, a member of Americans for a Safe Israel, put into words what is in the settlers' hearts. He declared, "Israel's leaders should be calling for Arafat's trial as a war criminal. Instead—unbelievably, sacrilegiously, they are investing him with legitimate authority over the Land of Israel... A great people prostrated itself before a bankrupt thug. A people priding itself on its moral sensitivity committed an act of ultimate immorality, deliberately bestowing legitimacy on a mass murderer. As long as the Jewish people live, this shame will adhere to them."[69]

* 10. He Shall Be Different From the Other Horns

"The ten horns are ten kings who shall arise from
this kingdom. And another shall rise after them;
he shall be different from the first ones" (Dan. 7:24a).

Could anyone be more "different" than Yasser Arafat? He is not only different from the ten horns, but he is different from just about every other leader on earth! There are several ways in which Arafat is different. One of those differences is unmistakable. The Lord wants us to understand that one of the major indicators telling us that we are correctly identifying the little horn will be that, in some way, this man will stand out from all the other heads of state or "horns." Arafat's personal appearance certainly fulfills this prophetic detail. When he is gathered with other world leaders, he is definitely not just "one of the gang."

In any photograph where he appears with *any* group of world leaders, including Islamic leaders, his difference from them is remarkable and causes him to stand out immediately. Even if all the leaders in the photograph are Arab and are all wearing a kaffiyeh, the Arab headdress, Arafat still stands out. First, he ties his kaffiyeh differently from all other Arabs, forming a little horn on the top. Another difference is that he dresses in military fatigues that are often rumpled, while the other leaders are all dressed in their finest clothes. Furthermore, he is almost always unshaven with a three or four day beard. And he always wears his pistol at his side. Even when he addressed the UN in 1974, he refused to surrender it. It has been said that "Arafat is extremely careful about his careless appearance," so that "he stands out immediately, attracting attention."[70] Just as Daniel said he would be, this little horn is "different!"

An additional, important difference between Arafat and the ten horns is that he has always been a terrorist instead of being a politician, military man, or royalty, as most others have been. More than this, he is a statesman without a state, a chairman without a people, and a king without a kingdom. His so-called "Palestinian people" are nothing more than a race that has been invented by the Islamic world in its insane battle against the God of the universe and His plans for the holy land.

The Palestinian People Are a Creation of the Islamic World

As a result of decades of media hype about the plight of the "Palestinian people," the facts have been almost totally submerged in a sea of lies. A number of honest people have raised their voices to make known the truth, but those voices have been drowned out by waves of hysteria coming from the international news media. The unbelievable and extremely documentable truth is mind boggling—there's never been such a thing as a "Palestinian people" and never in history did the Arabs give a name to the land [of Israel] to which they now lay claim.[71] Yasser Arafat has succeeded in getting huge amounts of financial aid from the world community for "rebuilding damaged infrastructure,"[72] because "all [the Palestinian] infrastructure has been destroyed"[73]—an infrastructure that has never existed in history and that is being "rebuilt" for a people that has never existed either! His subtle wording plays well to the enemies of Israel. It sounds like he has been commissioned to undertake the noble task of rebuilding what Israel has destroyed.

For those who have ears to hear, there are times when Arafat makes his "infrastructure" message clear, comparing "the destruction of the Palestinian territories' infrastructure under Israeli occupation with the total devastation wreaked on Germany in World War II."[74] Although there was no Palestinian infrastructure to destroy, in at least one way, the comparison is quite valid. Most reasonable people understand that Hitler's Germany required forceful intervention in the same way that the hotbed for international terrorist groups in the Palestinian territories has required Israel to intervene forcefully at times.

One of the sane and unbiased voices that has been raised in defense of the truth regarding the so-called "Palestinian people" is that of Joan Peters, former White House consultant on the Middle East and contributor to *Harper's* and other respectable publications. She traveled to the Middle East with the express purpose of writing a book that would expose the horrible plight of the "Palestinians."[75] What she found prompted her instead to write *From Time Immemorial*,[76] a book that exposes the tragic plight of the Jewish people at the hand of wicked Islamic nations and a deceitful international community. There, she strips away the cloak of international deception perpetrated against God's people by the Moslem world through their fabrication of the "Palestinian" lie.

Zuheir Muhsin, late military department head of the PLO and member of its executive council stated, "Yes, the existence of a separate Palestinian identity serves only tactical purposes. The founding of a Palestinian state is a new tool in the continuing battle against Israel."[77] Where, then, did the concept of "Palestine" and "Palestinians" come from? "[The name] Palestine was given to the land of Judea by the Romans in an unsuccessful attempt to purge the land of the 'nationalistic,' obstinate Jews."[78] What about the Arab "Palestinians"? In her research, Joan Peters discovered that "the findings of even those historians most vaunted by the Arab world have been specific in their contradiction of Arab claims to historical right of sovereignty in the land of 'Palestine'... To speak historically of original inhabitants Judah-cum-Palestine as 'Arab' peoples, then, is categorically incorrect. Not only was there no country of 'Palestine,' never a 'Palestinian' Arab rule, there was only an extraordinarily short period of time—a matter of decades—when any Arabs ruled Arabs on that land" in all of history.[79]

The Arabs claim that Israel came into the land of "Palestine" and took it away from the "Palestinians" who had been living there for thousands of years. What is the truth? In 1937, the British Royal

Commission reported something that is an indisputable historical fact, but which has been ignored for so long that history has been changed— at least in the minds of millions in the international community today. In the British report, the Commission stated, "Since the fall of the Jewish state, some Jews have been living in Palestine... fresh immigrants have arrived from time to time and settled mainly in Galilee in numerous villages, spreading northward to the Lebanon and in the towns of Safad and Tiberias."[80] Therefore, contrary to what many believe, an uninterrupted Jewish remnant has existed in the holy land ever since its conquest under Joshua around 1400 BC. Even after the destruction of Jerusalem by the Romans in AD 70, most Jews remained in the land, although not in Jerusalem, which was in ruins. The majority of the Jews did not become scattered among the nations until hundreds of years later.[81] Even when most finally did leave, there were always some Jews living in the holy land from the time of Christ to the present day. It is true that sometimes the Jewish remnant in the holy land was exceedingly small, but in what way does this fact automatically confer ownership of the land on the Arabs? The Arab presence in the land was often even smaller than the Jewish presence and, at times, was almost nonexistent. Mark Twain visited Israel in 1867. After having walked through the length and breadth of the land, he declared that he "never saw a human being on the whole route."[82]

How did so many Arabs end up in "Palestine" and in refugee camps? When the Islamic world realized that world Jewry might again become a state in the Middle East, they began to send a flood of Arabs into the holy land to lay claim to the Jewish homeland. During the British Mandate in Palestine, Britain even helped prepare the groundwork for untold suffering and bloodshed in the coming Israeli-Arab conflict. While they forbade any further Jewish immigration to the holy land, saying that "Palestine had no more places for Jews,"[83] at the same time they were "*importing illegal Arab immigrants* by tens of thousands into Palestine to do 'necessary work'—work and place that they denied to Jews," whom they sent back to Hitler's death camps [emphasis mine]. While studying the Winston Churchill papers, Joan Peters discovered positive proof that Jewish settlement in Palestine did not cause the uprooting and persecution of hundreds of thousands of Arabs as is commonly claimed today. In 1939, Churchill wrote, "So far from being persecuted, the Arabs have crowded into the country and multiplied till their population has increased more than even all world Jewry could lift up the Jewish population."[84] Churchill knew that Britain was guilty of gross wickedness because of its policy and actions designed to appease the Arabs. Regarding this appeasement, he said, "The acts that we engage in for appeasement today we will have to remedy at far greater cost and remorse tomorrow."[85] The historical facts speak for themselves—the Arab states not only invented this new race, called "Palestinians," but they sent in multitudes of new "citizens" into the region for the express purpose of opposing the State of Israel in the Middle East.[86]

Many of the Arab "immigrants" that were sent to the holy land, along with their descendants, became refugees when war broke out between the Arab world and Israel. The Arab leaders themselves informed the new "Palestinians" that they would have to move to camps until the war was over and Islam had finished throwing Israel into the sea. They were promised that afterwards, they would be allowed to return to their homes. However, those same leaders reneged on their promises and decided, rather, to use the despicable condition of the camps as a political tool to influence world opinion against Israel. They never allowed the refugees to return. King Hussein of Jordan is well aware of this wickedness and declared, "Since 1948 Arab leaders have approached the Palestine problem in an irresponsible manner... They have used the Palestine people for selfish political purposes. This is ridiculous and, I could say, even criminal."[87]

During interviews in Damascus in 1977, Syrian officials expressed their need for qualified technical help to develop Syrian agricultural land. It was known that there were "Palestinian" Arabs who had the necessary skills. The Syrians were asked why they did not consider moving them out of the camps and giving them the positions. One of the Syrian officials answered in anger, "We will give the land to anyone—the Ibos, the Koreans, Americans... anyone who comes—anyone but the Palestinians! We must keep their hatred directed against Israel."[88]

Because of Arab intrigue and an almost total lack of concern for human life, they have succeeded in bombarding the world community almost daily with news from the now infamous "Palestinian refugee" camps. The continual message has been that these people were forced to live under subhuman conditions in these camps because Israel stole their land and could not care less about their terrible situation. This is nothing less than Islam's war against the truth. At one point, Israel decided to step in and help the refugees by building them decent housing. However, the Arab-controlled UN passed a resolution forbidding Israel to move the refugees from their camps.[89] The Islamic nations did not want to lose their political weapon. This demonstrates that the Moslems themselves are the ones who couldn't care less about the plight of their Moslem brothers whom they have been willing to condemn to perpetual suffering in refugee camps! No wonder King Hussein said that the Arab treatment of Arab refugees was "criminal"!

In spite of all the facts, Satanic influences throughout the world have succeeded in convincing the unknowing masses that an entire nation of Palestinians lost their land to a parasitic Jewish state. This has been accomplished through a news media that has lent itself to the mystery of iniquity as a tool to manipulate the masses and induce them to believe a lie and hate God's people. When Winston Churchill declared that the actions of Britain would result in a "far greater cost and remorse tomorrow," he was surely speaking prophetically. He probably did not realize that the whole world was being prepared for Armageddon. Because of the hatred against Israel that has been sown for decades in the hearts of the world's nations through the Islamic "Palestinian" lie, the nations of the world will finally agree to march against God's people. Only too late will they discover that they have marched right into Armageddon and God's wrath!

Consider, then, that when Mr. Arafat declares that he is the sole representative of the Palestinian people, he is unabashedly exposing an amazing difference between himself and the other ten horns of the beast—he is a king without a kingdom and a chairman without a people!

* 11. He Will Speak Against the Most High

"He shall speak words against the Most High"
(Dan. 7:25a RSV, NRSV, ASV).

If your version of the Bible states that he speaks "pompous" or "great" words against the Most High, you will probably note that those renderings appear in the text in italics. This means that they are not actually part of the original text.

Although this description of the little horn may not yet be fulfilled in its entirety, Yasser Arafat does mock the God of the Jews and also the God of the Christians—the same God. A saying that he continues to endorse is, "On Saturday we will kill the Jews, and on Sunday we will kill the Christians." This is an open affront to the God who gave His life for His people and who ordained their religious beliefs. An affront to God's people is an affront to God Himself according to Zechariah. He assures God's people that those who come against them are coming against God when he writes, "He sent Me after glory, to the nations which plunder you; for he who touches you touches the apple of His eye" (Zech. 2:8).

We can be certain that Arafat endorses this wicked call to kill the Jews on Saturday and the Christians on Sunday because of the places where this slogan constantly appears. For example, it often appears in Arabic on PLO flags.[90] Possibly the most publicized example of this took place during the visit to Israel of Archbishop Desmond Tutu of South Africa. He is another well-known Nobel Peace Prize laureate. In 1989, he visited Israel, where he publicly denounced the Jews. Behind him, the PLO flag was flying with this slogan written on it.[91] Those who understand Arafat's iron-fisted control over the PLO and over the Palestinian people themselves know that only he could have authorized such a thing during "peacemaker" Tutu's much-publicized visit to Israel. Another example of Arafat's endorsement of the slogan calling to kill both Jews and Christians is demonstrated by the frequent appearance of this slogan as graffiti within the PLO-controlled autonomous areas.[92] The reader might wonder how anyone could presume to link what Arafat stands for with the message given by graffiti. Justification for doing so will be presented later in the form of documented evidence showing the dictatorial power that Arafat wields over the Palestinians. Once we understand that what the Palestinians do is controlled by Arafat's brutal police state, it will be clear that Arafat could eliminate *all* graffiti if he wanted to, but he does not want to do so!

Another example of speaking against God applies equally to Arafat and *all* Moslems. They all place great emphasis on the Temple Mount in Jerusalem. If push came to shove, the Moslems would probably do more to maintain control of the Temple Mount itself, as they do today, than they would do for any other holy site. One reason that Islam places so much importance on the Temple Mount involves the two Moslem mosques located there. The "Dome of the Rock," called the Mosque of Omar, is built on the approximate site of the Jewish temple, and the al-Aksa Mosque is built on Solomon's Porch where Jesus taught. The Moslems point to the fact that those two mosques are built over two of the most important Jewish and Christian sites as proof that the god of Islam is greater than the God of the Jews and also greater than the God of the Christians.[93] These are strong words spoken against the God of the universe!

There is another, more fundamental reason that Moslems place so much importance on the Temple Mount. They do so because of the deep-seated rebellion revealed in Islam. God has chosen the Temple Mount for Himself, so Satan will do anything possible to make it his own. Islam would react in exactly the same way toward Timbuktu if God had chosen it instead. The truth is, the sanctimonious attitude of Arafat and the Moslem world regarding Jerusalem will soon be seen for what it is—deep rebellion and unadulterated hypocrisy. In itself, Jerusalem is not all that important to them as long as God's people are not permitted to possess it. The Bible proves that the Moslems do not really reverence Jerusalem as they feign to do. It reveals that in the last days Israel's enemies will actually destroy Jerusalem. (See Jeremiah 6:1; 9:11; 30:6-7,18 and Lamentations 5:18.) Satanic vessels of wrath will once again leave Jerusalem in a state of ruins as they have already done on 39 previous occasions throughout history. Six days after signing the peace accord with Israel, Arafat revealed his plans for Jerusalem in a speech he gave in a Moslem mosque in Johannesburg, South Africa. During his speech he quoted a verse from the Koran that refers to the total destruction of the city of Jerusalem that occurred when the Romans entered it in AD 70. Immediately following his quote of that verse, he said, "We will enter the city as they did."[94] These are also very strong words against Israel's God since they were spoken against the *city* of Israel's God. (One Scripture that reveals the desolation that will come to Jerusalem in the last days is Luke 21:20. In point number 40, we will see that the Lord's forewarning about the "desolation" of Jerusalem in Luke does not refer primarily to its desolation in AD 70 because He is clearly speaking in the context of the last days.)

* 12. He Shall Wear Out the "Saints" of the Most High

"...and [he] shall wear out the saints of the most High"
(Dan. 7:25b KJV).

Again, "saints" refers to the "holy ones," or Israel, God's people. Of all the English versions for this passage, the King James Version is most accurate. The Hebrew here literally means that the little horn "wears the holy ones [Israel] out mentally."[95] After reading Chapter 1 concerning "The Peace That Brings Sudden Destruction," many probably asked, "Why would Israel make such a peace with its enemies?" Here is one of the key reasons. The Israeli populace has simply been worn out; not so much by war itself or even the threat of war. They have been worn out by Arafat's constant, unremitting, brutal terrorism. Their four principal wars have been scattered over a period of almost 50 years and they have won all of them in most impressive ways. However, Arafat's 50 years of terrorism has hounded the entire nation literally every day of their lives. No one knows when Arafat's next bomb will strike, ripping bodies apart, killing, maiming, and crippling Israeli men, women, and children. Israel has faced terrible wars against Arab nations after which there have been extended times of calm, but Arafat's terrorism has never ceased. The satanic method of terrorists is to terrorize, and Arafat has been a master at it since Israel became a state. He has simply worn Israel down and worn them out. The attitude of Israel has come to be, "Take what you want, but give us peace."

For many years, President Gamal Abdel Nasser of Egypt believed that the only way the Jews could be driven out of the holy land was through a united and overwhelming military effort of the Arab nations. He stood against fanatics like Yasser Arafat and his little group of gangsters, believing that they were powerless to make any real gains. However, after the disastrous defeat of the allied Arab nations in the Six Day War of 1967, he "revised his view... [and] put his faith in the effectiveness of a 'guerrilla war;' not only would it **wear Israel down**, but it would display the efforts of a 'weak people' against an 'oppressive state' and gain sympathy"[96] (emphasis mine). This revelation of Nasser was, undoubtedly, an inspiration that came from the kingdom of darkness, and it has succeeded on both counts!

Most of the world has no idea what pressure the Israeli society has been forced to endure for decades to protect itself from the constant threat of guerrilla attacks. Even though Israel's wars have all been short, and it has been free from all-out war during most of its modern history, it can never lay down its arms. The Israeli defense forces must be constantly well-armed, well-trained, and well-equipped to protect the nation from terrorism. To accomplish this, the burden of time and money to the Israeli society is staggering. It begins with an across-the-board income tax of 52 percent on all wages from the lower middle class on up. Add to that a five or six percent health tax, and a 17 percent value added tax on every expenditure, including rent, along with property taxes that even a tenant must pay, as well as many other hidden taxes, and we still perceive only *part* of the Israeli defense burden.

In addition to this overwhelming financial sacrifice, everyone in Israel must also make an enormous sacrifice of their very lives. It begins with the youth. A young person cannot obtain a passport to travel outside of Israel nor can they attend an Israeli University until they have fulfilled their three-year military obligation. This is only the beginning of the sacrifice. Until 1995, all men had to give 60 days a year to the military until reaching the age of 50. Imagine the burden this has been for every small business owner who has had to leave his business for two months each year—not to mention the burden put upon every company in Israel where the male employees all have to be gone for 17 percent of the year, not counting vacation time. Worse than this, imagine what it is like to leave behind one's wife and children every year for this amount of time! If all the taxes are added up, it becomes obvious that most of one's life is given to the country. However, to this astronomical tax burden must be added this additional burden—17 percent or one-sixth of one's life—which is what two months of military service each year works out to be. Yasser Arafat has been the primary source of terrorist acts against Israel, and is recognized as Israel's worst enemy. Therefore, we can rightfully say that he and the PLO are the main reason Israel has been forced to continue carrying its formidable defense burden. He has definitely worn the nation out.

Daniel's observation that the little horn wears out Israel strongly implies that his dealings with God's people are spread out over a rather long period of time. Could he have succeeded in wearing Israel out and destroying their morale in five or ten years? I believe that the answer is definitely no for two reasons. The first is their general attitude about life. I am personally acquainted with the optimistic and resilient nature of the Jewish people living in Israel. They feel like they have finally come home after 2,000 years of exile, and they are happy to be living in Israel in spite of the crushing defense burden. They are happy to work to build their nation. That is why they and their fathers came in the first place. Second, how could the morale of a nation be destroyed so quickly after they have accomplished so much in such a short time? It would take a long time to totally discourage a people who could come to a worthless desert and see it blossom as a rose. These same people faced the onslaughts of the armies of seven well-equipped Arab nations whose troops were recruited from populations that outnumbered Israel's population by 40 to 1![97] Not only did Israel survive, but they then emerged as the third military superpower on earth (according to the Russian leadership of the former Soviet Union).[98] Yes, it would take a long time to discourage them, but the little horn has *had* a long time—more than 50 years! And Israel has finally been worn out. The nation has had enough! They are willing to try another approach, even if it ends up costing another war and great loss of life. After all, what do they have to lose?

* 13. He Shall Change the Sacred Seasons and Law

*"...and [he] shall attempt to change the sacred
seasons and the law" (Dan. 7:25c NRSV).*

Most versions translate this passage along this line: "And [he] shall intend to change times and law." I have two sound reasons to believe that this passage speaks specifically of *religious* times and *religious* laws. One is that the New Revised Standard Version translates it this way, as quoted above. The second is that my native Hebrew-speaking friends assured me that the words used here, without question, refer to the religious seasons and religious laws of *any* religion, not necessarily of Judaism or Christianity.

The religious laws and seasons that the little horn will change could well refer to those of his own religion. In Yasser Arafat, there has already been a fulfillment of this prophetic revelation of the little horn both regarding a change of religious law and a change of sacred seasons or times. In accordance with the laws of the Islamic Arab League, the mufti of Jerusalem is to be appointed by King Hussein of Jordan.[99] The title "mufti" refers to the top Islamic religious leader who is in charge of any Islamic holy site or mosque. The mufti of Jerusalem has been, traditionally, a very powerful position in the Islamic world, and is a lifelong appointment. He has the oversight of all the Moslem holy sites in Jerusalem, including the Temple Mount. The grand mufti of Jerusalem during the Second World War, Haj Amin al-Husseini, appeared often in world news during and after the War. He was extremely influential and powerful in the Moslem world.[100]

Shortly after Arafat signed the initial peace agreement with Israel in September 1993, the mufti of Jerusalem just happened to die. To demonstrate his authority over Jerusalem, Arafat immediately named the next mufti, and announced that the appointment of the mufti who King Hussein had chosen was void. Arafat "extracted a declaration from the foreign ministers of the Arab League to the effect that the PLO has the sole right to rule in Eastern Jerusalem."[101] He also announced that "henceforth the PLO would be responsible for the Moslem Council and the Wakf" (the religious body in charge of Moslem affairs), thus changing the religious status quo in Jerusalem.[102] Arafat had succeeded in changing the Islamic religious law over Jerusalem and the West Bank!

Next, Arafat and his mufti proceeded to change the timing of Islam's most important "sacred season," or religious holy day. The ninth month of the Islamic calendar is Ramadan. During this entire month,

Moslems fast during the day and feast at night. The first day of the month, and therefore the first day of their fasting and feasting, is determined by the first appearance of the moon. The religious authorities in Mecca are traditionally responsible for announcing when the new moon of Ramadan first appears. Arafat and his mufti changed all that in 1995. Arafat declared, "For the first time in the history of the Palestinian nation, we announce... to the Arab and Islamic world the witnessing of the new Ramadan moon from the Aksa Mosque [in Jerusalem] under the Palestinian Authority."[103]   The Moslems of Palestine duly obeyed their new leader and began the feast one day sooner than Jordanian Moslems. Arafat had succeeding in making his first change in the timing of a "sacred season." To Jews and Christians this means nothing, but to the Moslem world, it is the equivalent of someone in the US deciding that they had the right to determine when Christmas begins each year! This is only the beginning of the changes in Islam that the little horn will make. Later on, we will see some more details about these changes, as revealed in Daniel's prophecy.

14. The "Saints" Are Given Into His Hand for Three and a Half Years

"Then the saints shall be given into his hand for a time and times and half a time" (Dan. 7:25d).

Yasser Arafat has not yet fulfilled this, but there is little doubt that this will take place. In fact, there are clear indicators that this is already *beginning* to happen, which therefore shows us *how* it will happen. There is only one person in the universe who can decide to "give" the holy people into the hand of someone so wicked as the little horn. That person is the Lord Himself. Why would the Lord do this to the Jews? Only because He loves them enough to do whatever He has to do to bring them back to Himself and cause them to fulfill their calling to be a people separated unto Him.

Today, the "holy people" are called "Jews." The word "Jew" in the Bible comes from the word "Judah" and is basically the same Hebrew word.[104]   Judah was also the name of the one who betrayed the Lord— "Judas" is his name translated into English after being filtered through the Greek New Testament. He was known in his day as "Judah," not "Judas."[105]   Judah, the traitor, was prophetic of Judah the nation. It was not only Judah, the man, who betrayed the Lord, but Judah, the nation, betrayed Him as well. "He came to His own and His own did not receive Him" (Jn. 1:11).

We could possibly excuse the actions of Israel's top leaders at the time the Lord was crucified if we attribute what they did to ignorance. While on the cross, the Lord Himself forgave them when He prayed, "Father, forgive them for they know not what they do." However, after the events surrounding the cross, those leaders were left with no excuse. They heard the testimony of the Roman soldiers who guarded the Lord's tomb. Those soldiers were witnesses to what happened at His resurrection when the angel appeared and the Lord arose. Instead of repenting, the leaders paid the soldiers money to deny what they had seen and to propagate a lie. (See Matthew 28:11-15.) They also heard about the testimony of over 500 people who saw Him alive after His resurrection, and they were forced either to repent or to pretend that the 500 were either all liars or totally deceived. (See I Corinthians 15:6.) Later, they witnessed the miracles that were done in His name, turning the city of Jerusalem upside down. They recognized that unlearned and ignorant men were speaking with an authority from heaven that caused people's hearts to burn with a love for God and that caused their own hearts to be convicted of sin. They had to admit that those men were revealing the same glory they had seen resting on the Carpenter from Nazareth. (See Acts 5:28-33 and Acts 4:13.) In spite of all this, they clung to their own honor and position and thereby brought unspeakable tragedy upon their own people.

In Psalm 109, the Lord speaks prophetically through David and describes what Judah, the man *and* the nation, would do to Him. Peter applies this Psalm directly to Judah, the traitor, but it has had, and will *yet* have, an even greater fulfillment in Judah, the nation. (Compare Psalm 109:8 and Acts 1:20.) I am sure that with tears for His people the Lord declares, "They have spoken against me with a lying tongue... In return for my love they are my accusers... They have rewarded me evil for good" (Psa. 109:2b, 4a, 5a). He then prays to the Father, "Set thou a wicked man over him: and let Satan stand at his right hand" (v. 6 KJV). This is precisely what will happen when the "holy people" (saints) are given into the hand of the little horn. It will be Satan himself, embodied in the little horn, whom God will set over Judah. Satan will then manifest his hatred toward the ones God loves.

In the New Testament, we discover God's loving heart and purpose for placing any human being under the hand of Satan—it is for their ultimate salvation. Paul exhorts, "Deliver such a one to Satan for the destruction of the flesh, that his spirit may be saved in the day of the Lord Jesus" (I Cor. 5:5). For thousands of years, Satan has been a vessel of wrath and judgment used to force people to run to the Lord for help and salvation. The Lord's purpose for placing Israel under the hand of the little horn will soon be accomplished—"all Israel will be saved" (Rom. 11:26a). Tragically, Paul clarifies that "all Israel" will only be a "remnant" (Rom. 9:27). Most will not survive what the little horn has planned for them!

One of Yasser Arafat's heroes was Adolf Hitler. There is a published photograph, available for all to see, that reveals the heart and goals of the real Yasser Arafat. It is a photograph of one of his former offices where a Nazi swastika and Arafat's portrait are hanging together behind his desk.[106] It was Arafat's second cousin, Haj Amin al-Husseini, friend and companion of Hitler during the days of the Holocaust, who declared, "Allah has bestowed upon us the rare privilege of finishing what Hitler only began... Murder the Jews. Murder them all."[107] Remember, Daniel explains that the little horn's vision is greater than the vision of his companions. This includes the vision of Haj Amin, who was once one of Arafat's "companions!" Arafat's own clearly-defined goals, which he has constantly stated from his youth onward, as well as his barbarous acts against the Jews for over 50 years, should dispel any doubts about what he will do once the holy people are under his hand!

How, in the name of sanity, could Israel ever find itself under the hand of this wicked man? The nation has been worn down, yes, but they certainly never thought that making concessions to Arafat for the sake of peace would ultimately place them under his hand. How will this happen? The answer for all the world to see is only months away from the time of this writing. The territory that Israel is presently placing under Arafat's control will ultimately place *them* under Arafat's hand! Throughout Israel's modern history, wherever and whenever there has been a terrorist base near the borders of the nation, it has been used continually to rain terrorism of all forms on the nearby Israeli population. This is the reason Israel is so divided today about giving the Golan Heights back to Syria. Too many Israelis have vivid memories of how Syria used that mountain range before the Six Day War—to fire missiles and shoot bullets into the Israeli settlements in the valley below. There is no reason to believe they will not resume their terrorism once they have that territory in their hands again. To the contrary, there is every reason to believe they *will*, because they continue to do precisely the same to this day through their terrorists in Syrian-controlled southern Lebanon.

One of the terrorists' favorite weapons is the Russian-made katyusha rocket. Since the range of these rockets is only 10-15 miles, most Israeli civilians have lived outside the reach of this horrendous form of terrorism since the 1967 war. That is all changing at this very moment. If you refer to map number 6 in Appendix A, you will notice that once Arafat has the entire West Bank under his control, most Israeli cities, towns, and settlements will be well within the range of those rockets, including Tel Aviv and western Jerusalem. Later, we will learn from Daniel that the little horn will practically destroy Israel. How will he get away with systematically destroying and terrorizing the nation while the world looks on? In precisely the same way that he has already begun to do from his newly-acquired autonomous areas. As one terrorist attack after another is launched from the PLO autonomous areas, and as one Israeli after another is murdered, and as thieves from "PLO land" are encouraged to plunder at will, Mr. Arafat washes his hands in innocence as Pilate once did before the Jews of Judah. He declares that he simply cannot control these things. The multitude is out of control! He tells Israel and the world that the Hamas terrorists and other groups, operating from the autonomous areas, are simply doing what they want and that he really cannot stop them from killing the Jews. Pilate acted like he could not stop the mob from killing *the* Jew! Is God reminding His people of what happened in the First Coming of Christ so that He can deal with them and ultimately bring them into a blessing during His Second Coming?

Hamas is no more out of Arafat's control than the conquered Jewish nation was out of Pilate and Rome's control when Pilate washed his hands to declare that he was innocent and could do nothing to control the mob. Before we jump to conclusions, maybe we should allow Arafat and Hamas to speak for themselves. Speaking about Hamas, Arafat declared, "The Islamists are part of the PLO... They are not against the PLO; they are in the PLO."[108] The Hamas Covenant explains it all by declaring, "The PLO, one of the movements closest to the Islamic Resistance Movement, **is father**, brother, kinsman, and friend."[109] If these words were merely idle talk it would be one thing, but they are part of the Hamas written covenant. Surely the authors knew the truth about Hamas if anyone did. If the PLO is the "father" of Hamas, then Arafat had a direct part in birthing it! No wonder Benjamin Netanyahu, the new Prime Minister of Israel, declared before he was elected that the

PLO and Hamas "are operating hand in glove."[110] In March 1996, 13 Moslem nations met with Bill Clinton and other leaders in Cairo, Egypt to condemn terrorism in general and Hamas in particular. Later, on "The McLaughlin Group," a well-known TV panel discussion, one of the panelists asked, "If they [the Islamic nations] are really against Hamas, why don't they cut off the $67 million in annual aid to Hamas, since Hamas would immediately dry up without it?"[111]

In order to bring our understanding of the PLO-Hamas relationship into proper perspective and balance, I would be quick to add that, just as in the case of Satan's spiritual kingdom of darkness, Islam is filled with division, strife, rivalry, and hatred. As I already mentioned, this is one of the reasons that the State of Israel has survived—over the years, the Moslems have been too busy fighting among themselves. Therefore, to say that all the many factions under Arafat's control are living together in blissful harmony would also be a farce. There can be no question that Arafat's organization is filled with rivalry from top to bottom, but this does not mean that he has totally lost control anymore than Satan has lost control of the hordes of demons and fallen angels.

While Arafat continues to slaughter the Jews, the world buys his story about Hamas being out of control and even feels sorry for him, since he is trying *so* hard to bring peace to Israel. The news media and the world will soon feel even more pity for him, as his loss of control begins to cost tens of thousands of Israeli lives. Who knows, they might even add an expression or two of how sad they are to see Israel wiped off the map, and that it is too bad that no one can do anything to control those overzealous "freedom fighters," as they are being referred to frequently these days![112] The four suicide bombs within a nine day period between February 25 and March 4, 1996, is an example of what the PLO and Hamas are able to do at will. It also gives a good indication of how the world will react. The bombers managed to kill or injure over 200 Israelis. The world community reacted by promising to give Yasser Arafat more arms with which to control Hamas![113]

Two questions should arise in every mind: 1) if Arafat is trying so hard to bring peace, why does his security chief, Jibril Rajoub, encourage Hamas men like "The Engineer," Yihye Ayyash, to continue making bombs to kill Jews (as we saw that he did in Chapter 4)? and 2) if things are already out of control, what *ever* will happen when he "controls" the whole area? Israel has maintained control over these areas since 1967. If Mr. Arafat is incapable of doing so, then why is Israel placing them under *his* control, or should we say, under his total *lack* of control? The only answer is that the Sovereign One has decided to *"give* the holy ones" into the hand of the little horn, and He is blinding Israel in order to reach that goal. The glorious side of all this is that Israel will be under the hand of the little horn for only three and a half years. Revelation and Daniel both make it clear that after a "time, times and half of time," or three and a half years, the King will come to save His people and bring ever-lasting righteousness to this earth![114]

Daniel Is Given Further Revelation About the Little Horn

As far as the last-day nation of Israel is concerned, most of the prophetic revelation in Daniel 7, 8, and 11 involves details about the little horn and what he will do to Israel. After the vision of Daniel 7, the Prophet Daniel receives another vision that reveals the geographical origin of the little horn that destroys "the holy people" (Dan. 8:9,24). He also sees many additional details concerning this horn.

Daniel 8:1-8 records Daniel's vision of a ram with two horns who is overcome by a male goat with one "notable horn." The notable horn (king) is broken and in its place four horns arise. Out of one of those four horns comes the "little horn." Daniel then sees many things that this little horn will do, especially with respect to God's chosen people. After seeing these things, Daniel seeks understanding of the vision and the angel Gabriel is sent to interpret it for him (Dan. 8:15-16).

We briefly considered Gabriel's interpretation of this vision in Chapter 2. We will review that interpretation and note some additional key elements. Gabriel begins, "Understand, son of man, that the vision refers to the **time of the end**" (v. 17). Gabriel then emphasizes again that this vision will be fulfilled in the last days, saying, "Look, I am making known to you what shall happen in the **latter time** of the indignation; for at the appointed time **the end** shall be" (v. 19). Gabriel begins his interpretation of the vision by revealing events that were soon to take place in Daniel's day so that Daniel would understand what was about to happen in the world around him. He interprets the ram with two horns as being the kings of Media and Persia (v. 20). This vision was given to Daniel while Belshazzar, the last king of Babylon, was still reigning (Dan. 8:1). Therefore, the angel is giving Daniel understanding that the Medes and the Persians will soon conquer Babylon and become the next great empire. This occurred in 539 BC, when Cyrus terminated his victorious siege of Babylon.

Concerning the male goat that would later come against the kingdom of the Medes and Persians and conquer them, Gabriel continues,

"And the male goat is the kingdom of Greece. The large horn that is between its eyes is the first king" (v. 21). History leaves no room for doubt regarding who the first king of the Grecian Empire was. He was Alexander the Great who did, in fact, conquer the Medes and Persians. No sooner had he finished his conquests of the East than he died at the age of 33.[115] His kingdom was divided into four smaller kingdoms and out of one of those kingdoms the little horn must come. (Compare Daniel 8:8-9 and 8:22-23.)

At this point of his interpretation, Gabriel takes a huge leap forward in history and arrives at the time of the end or the last days. He does this by referring to the latter time of the four parts of Alexander's kingdom, saying, "And in **the latter time of their kingdom**, when the transgressors have reached their fullness, a **king shall arise**..." (v. 23). Who is this king that arises in the last days? Gabriel's explanation here is in the context of the great horn that would be broken and be replaced by four horns (v. 22). By referring back to Daniel's vision at the beginning of Daniel 8, we discover who this last-day king will be. In his vision, immediately after seeing the notable horn replaced by four horns, Daniel writes that a **"little horn" arises** (v. 8-9). Therefore, that "little horn" is interpreted by Gabriel to represent a future king (the biblical term for a national leader[116]).

Note that this little horn or king arises at the "latter time" of the four kingdoms into which Alexander's kingdom was divided. Also, to confirm further that he is speaking about the very last days, Gabriel explains that this will occur when "transgressors have reached their fullness." In other words, when men are as wicked as they can possibly become. This is unquestionably the day we are presently living in. If you have any doubt, read on to discover what kind of an abominable human being the world has honored with the Nobel Peace Prize!

We can be sure that the "little horn" in Daniel 7 is the same "little horn" found in Daniel 8 not only because of his title, but also because in both chapters the "little horn" destroys "the holy ones" in the last days. (Compare Daniel 7:21 with Daniel 8:24. See also Daniel 7:25-28 where the little horn's reign ends with the coming of the Lord.) Let's consider now Daniel's further revelations about this "little horn."

* 15. He Comes Out of Alexander's Former Kingdom

"And out of one of [the four horns] came a little horn" (Dan. 8:9a).

Geographically, there is no question about Arafat's credentials regarding this aspect of the little horn. He definitely was born and raised in the Middle East, which was part of the four kingdoms into which Alexander the Great's kingdom was divided. However, there is additional related evidence regarding Arafat's origin—evidence that he has denied for decades—the place of his birth. Even in this simple matter, Arafat cannot tell the truth! In a number of reference books that I have consulted concerning this, I have been surprised to discover that not only the news media, but even respectable publishers are willing to repeat Arafat's lies. He claims that he was born in Jerusalem, and many print this without concerning themselves with the facts. At other times, he claims to have been born in Gaza, though Jerusalem is his usual claim. It is true that his mother was born in Jerusalem and that his father was born in Gaza.[117]

Arafat has several problems regarding his claims. One is that he belongs to a very large clan, including an immediate family of six children.[118] They are not all dead, nor are they as given to severe memory loss as he is. The fact is, the majority of the members of both his maternal and paternal clans remember very well that he was born and partially raised in Cairo, Egypt.[119] His second problem is that his birth certificate gives Cairo as his birthplace on August 24, 1929.[120] His third problem with his claim is that his University registration form at the Cairo University states that he was born in Cairo.[121] He seems to have had a better memory when he filled out the form. And, possibly the most revealing problem of all, is his Egyptian accent. Try as he may, he has been unable to hide it.[122] The Palestinians know that "Mr. Palestine," as he likes to be called, is really an Egyptian![123] So he is, in fact, from Alexander's kingdom.

It is no secret why Mr. Arafat avoids the truth in this area. After all, how can he pretend to be fighting for his so-called Palestinian homeland, supposedly from which he and others were expelled, if he is more from Egypt than from Palestine? Understanding this brings into focus the truth—he is fighting to kill the Jews, not to find a place he can call home! I should point out here that his father brought the family back to Gaza from Cairo for the express purpose of organizing a group of Moslems who would help destroy the Jews in the holy land.[124] Arafat inherited his hatred of Jews from his father and older brother, Badir, who vowed that he would "devote his life to killing Jews."[125]

* 16. He Grows Great Toward the South, East, and the Glorious Land

"…[he] grew exceedingly great toward the south, toward the east, and toward the Glorious Land" (Dan. 8:9b).

Yasser Arafat has already fulfilled this revelation of the little horn in at least two ways. His growth toward greatness has followed this south, east, Glorious Land sequence at least twice. His growth first began when he was sent **south**—by his father, from Gaza to Cairo. He returned to Egypt to study at the University of Cairo. That's when he joined the Palestine Students' Federation and ultimately became its leader. His work of hatred against the Jews finally earned him the respect of the Egyptian government, where he was enlisted in the army and trained in explosives,[126] which are his specialty to this day! After Egypt, he went **east**—first to Kuwait and then to Jordan. In Kuwait, along with others, he founded the terrorist group known as Fatah, which was later incorporated into the PLO. After Kuwait, where he reportedly became wealthy in a construction company that he began, he moved his Fatah terrorists into Jordan. In 1970, he and his cohorts were expelled from Jordan in a very bloody conflict with the armies of King Hussein. If Arafat is in fact the little horn, we should assume that from Jordan in the **east**, his next stop would be the **"Glorious Land."** This is precisely what happened, though it is not immediately obvious. From Jordan he moved into Lebanon. Though Israel does not yet possess Lebanon, from the beginning it was included by the Lord in the holy land.[127]

Arafat has followed this south, east, Glorious Land sequence again in the last few years since the Oslo accord. After Arafat was expelled from Lebanon by the Israelis in 1982, he moved his headquarters to Tunis. In the Oslo accord, Israel agreed to give him territory within the holy land on which he is now founding his Palestinian government. The sequence in which he has taken possession of this land has been the south, east, Glorious Land sequence. He started with Gaza in the **south** and Jericho in the **east**, and now, he is well along the way to occupying what Orthodox Jews would call the **glorious part** of the holy land. In what sense is it glorious? The land that he is being given includes the most sacred cities of Judaism and Christianity. They include: 1) Hebron, the place where Abraham lived and was buried; 2)

Bethlehem, the birthplace of David and the Messiah; 3) Shechem (modern-day Nablus), the place of Jacob's well; and, it seems certain that he ultimately will enter 4) the Old City of Jerusalem (which is the "Jerusalem" of the Bible). If there is such a place as the **"Glorious Land"** within the holy land, Jerusalem is certainly the place!

* 17. He Grows Up to the Army of Heaven and Casts Some Down

"And it grew up to the host of heaven; and it cast down some of the host and some of the stars to the ground, and trampled them" (Dan. 8:10).

For those who might be tempted to believe that I am trying to discover more specific details about the little horn in Daniel than actually exist, please note that this verse really contains four details and not one. For the sake of brevity I am treating them all together.

Although "stars" can refer to angels in the Bible as in Revelation 12:4, and although this detail about the little horn may well have a spiritual fulfillment, it seems that Daniel's vision is primarily concerned with the natural events that surround the natural people of Israel in the last days. I believe that this detail could be giving us insight into a spiritual battle surrounding the rise of the little horn, but I will limit myself to discussing the documentable natural fulfillment found in Yasser Arafat rather than getting into speculation.

In order to understand the natural fulfillment, we must understand how the Bible uses the words found in this verse. The word "host" actually refers to armies and is translated that way in reference to the "armies" of Israel many times.[128] In the biblical context, the phrase "host of heaven" (meaning the "armies of heaven") does not *necessarily* refer to the supernatural armies of God (although it could mean that). God refers to the armies of Israel as "His armies," and He has often fought with the armies of Israel, and will do so again in the last days.[129] If they are considered the armies of the God of heaven, they could also be considered "the armies of heaven"—armies that heaven fights with and commands. Finally, we are told in Daniel that the little horn casts down "some of the stars to the ground." We must not forget another way in which the Bible frequently uses the word "stars." The Lord told Abraham that his children would be as the stars. In the Book of Daniel itself, Daniel compares the righteous to the stars (Dan. 12:3). Stars are also used to refer to the **sons of Israel** in Joseph's dream of the sun, moon and stars in Genesis 37:9. Finally, in Deborah's song, she compares the soldiers of Israel to stars who fought in Judges 5:19-20.[130]

Daniel's thought of the little horn "growing up" until he reaches the armies of Israel, might have a humorous side. After all, God has a sense of humor—even in the context of the vessels of wrath. They are so insignificant to Him that He can actually laugh about them—Satan included! (See Psalm 2:4.) From childhood, Arafat had such a hatred of the Jews instilled in him that he wanted to start killing them immediately. In November 1947, at eighteen years of age, he traveled from Gaza to Jerusalem and offered his services as a fighter to Abdelqadir, deputy to the grand mufti, Haj Amin. Abdelqadir was commanding Haj Amin's terrorist activities against the Jews. When Yasser appeared on the scene, Abdelqadir gave him a pistol and told him to kill as many Jews as he could with it.[131] Yasser immediately rushed out and tried to find a Jew to kill. It wasn't until the next day that he got his first opportunity while attacking a Jewish shop. However, when he pulled out his pistol to shoot, instead of shooting the "enemy," he shot himself in the thigh, and became the laughing stock of the organization. When Abdelqadir found out about it, "he took the pistol away from him, patted him on the head, and said, 'No more fighting for you, young man. From now on you will stay in the headquarters and make the coffee.' "[132] He had to grow up before he could reach the host—the armies of Israel!

The wicked side of this "growing up" most likely refers to his growth in followers, equipment, financing, and in the knowledge of the perverse methods of terrorism needed to reach his goals. This, in fact, required a tremendous amount of patient growth, as his life's story demonstrates. Once he had matured physically, he spent many years growing in these areas. Part of his problem was that Israel had learned how to keep the terrorists at bay through their tight security. Arafat finally had enough men and enough knowledge of Israeli security to be capable of bringing death to "some of the host," and to cast down to the ground some of the "stars" (soldiers of Israel's army). His growth in this area was so slow that his first attempts at terrorizing Israel were a total failure, even with Syrian backing.[133] His growth in manpower was even more dismal. He tried to find recruits for his small company of followers, but few were interested, and he had no name that attracted followers.[134]

Finally, when the Syrians saw his lack of experience and almost total inability to find recruits, they came up with a plan. They told him that he should spend his time in the Palestinian refugee camps getting recruits, and that they would stage terrorist attacks against Israel in the name of Arafat's almost non-existent Fatah terrorist organization, publicly giving his group "credit" for the attacks.[135] Suddenly, people had heard of Yasser Arafat and of his mighty guerrilla army that did not even exist. Soon he was able to find more recruits and to begin growing in manpower until he ultimately was able to reach the armies of Israel and kill some of the soldiers (stars). Once he could reach the "stars" and "some of the host," he "trampled them under foot" every time he had the opportunity. He revealed his total disrespect for human life that is characteristic of the satanic nature of Daniel's fourth beast, as we discussed in Chapter 4. He had finally grown and was reaching his lifelong goal and ambition to kill the Jews!

* 18. He Exalts Himself as High as the Commander of the Army

"He even exalted himself as high as the Prince of the host" (Dan. 8:11a).

All serious students of the Bible should be aware of the fact that written Hebrew does not have or use capital letters—such things do not even exist in Hebrew! Therefore, any time we read the Old Testament and find capital letters in our English translations, such as the "P" on the word "Prince" in this passage, we should immediately understand that this is strictly the interpretation and opinion of the translator. The translator of the **"Prince of the host"** in the above passage, was obviously convinced that the little horn would be so proud that he would place himself on the same level as the Prince of heaven, the Lord Jesus Christ. Later, we will see that he will, in fact, do this. However, there are strong reasons to conclude that this is *not* the thought of Daniel in this particular passage.

I offer three sound reasons for concluding that this passage is not speaking about the Lord. First, we should look at how the Old Testament Hebrew uses these two words, "prince" and "host," together. Of the 44 times these two words are used together, 38 times they are used to mean the "general" or "captain" of the "army" or "host." For example, Phichol is called the "captain of the host" of Abimelech (Gen. 21:22). Joab is called the "general of the army" of David (I Chr. 27:34). My second reason for believing that this passage is not speaking about the Lord is that my native Hebrew friends even thought it was humorous when I told them that my English translation applied it to the Lord. They assured me that this word is used to refer to a governmental position and is commonly translated into English as "minister." The phrase translated as "Prince of the host" is common in Hebrew and simply means the top leader of a nation's army. Israel's Prime Minister is the commander in chief of the nation's armies. Third, we have just observed that the context of the preceding verse is the army of Israel, and the sons of Israel or "stars" who are killed by the little horn. We should keep in mind that Daniel is being shown what will happen to his people, Israel, in the last days.

If my native-born Hebrew-speaking friends are right, then what Daniel is saying here is that the little horn, through his own efforts, actually succeeds in reaching the same level of honor accorded the Prime Minister of Israel—the commander in chief of the armies of Israel. Is it possible that Daniel was seeing the perverse day in which Yasser Arafat would stand at the side of Israeli Prime Minister Yitzhak Rabin, and that together, they would receive the highest international award offered on this planet—the Nobel Peace Prize? Did that scene in 1994 cause something to stir in you? Can we begin to imagine what the attitude of heaven was at that moment? Consider what it *must* have been. To be in a position to comprehend, we must review the basic events that heaven had witnessed—events that led up to that moment.

Israel's Last 2,000 Years of History Summarized

For much of the last 2,000 years God's people lived as a people scattered among the nations, under the heavy dealings of God. He designed these events to bring them back to Himself. The nations misunderstood God's purposes and considered His chastening of the Jews to be a divine license to oppress His people. (See Jeremiah 33:24 and Ezekiel 28:25-26.) Obviously, the nations did not understand that God had spoken to Israel, saying, "Though I make a full end of all nations whither I have scattered thee, yet will I not make a full end of thee: but I will correct thee in measure, and will not leave thee altogether unpunished" (Jer. 30:11). The Jews were despised, rejected, ridiculed, mocked, cursed, tortured, and killed. Some claim that the Jews are such vile people that they deserve it, as if the accusers could claim to be above the same verdict themselves. Others point out that *many* peoples have suffered just like the Jews. The Just Judge who weighs our sins in His balance and "repays [the wicked] to his face" (Deut. 7:10) has declared that Israel has "received from the Lord's hand *double* for all her sins" (Isa. 40:2).

In the Crusades, beginning around the year AD 1000, an oft-heard slogan in Europe was "Kill a Jew and save your soul."[136] During the Spanish Inquisition of the fifteenth century, Jews were faced with one of three options: 1) they could convert to Catholicism, 2) be tortured and killed, or 3) leave behind everything they owned and flee for their lives.[137] In the pogroms of Russia and Eastern Europe during the nineteenth century, they were starved, tortured, and killed. In the death camps of Hitler, six million died. Many of those who tried to escape from Hitler by traveling to the holy land were turned back by the British, who knew that they were sending them back to die in the death camps of Europe. "Not even the confirmation of the destruction of most of Europe's Jews and the photographs from the death camps could melt the stone hearts of British policy makers."[138] Britain was determined that no Jewish state would ever again exist in the holy land.[139] They faced just one obstacle to their plan of permanently hindering Zionism—God! It was God Himself who covenanted that He would gather His people from among the nations in the last days and give them back the land that He deeded to Abraham forever (Ezek. 11:16-17). Anyone who resists Israel's right to the land resists God Himself, and history teaches us about who always wins when man resists God. Britain's demise has subsequently confirmed that fact. In a few short years, she has lost one of history's greatest empires, and now sits on a political, economical, social, moral, and spiritual ash heap.

Before Israel was ever scattered, even before they had entered Canaan the first time, God promised them that after they were scattered, He would bring them back to their land so that His name would be glorified among the nations. (See Deuteronomy 30:1-9 and Ezekiel 36:23-24.) As He began to gather Israel, He sovereignly moved the UN to vote to give the Jews a tiny sliver of land on which to form their new little nation. And little it was! Much of it was only 10 miles across. In 1922, the British "with one stroke of the pen lopped off nearly 80 percent of the land promised the Jewish people [in the Balfour declaration of 1917], closing this area to Jews to this day."[140] Later, in November 1947, the UN was *barely* persuaded (by one vote) to allow the Jews to have a homeland. Their decision was to give the Jews just half of the remaining 20 percent, and to give the other half to the Palestinians.[141] The Jews finally got just 10 percent of what Britain had once promised them. (See Maps 3-5 in Appendix A.) The price they paid for this land was the highest price ever paid for a homeland in the history of humanity—the lives of 6 million Jews in Europe whose suffering and death was *barely* enough to convince the world that the "scattered people" should finally be gathered again!

Of the land originally promised by Britain, 90 percent was dedicated to a homeland for the Palestinians of the Middle East. That land finally became the new nation of Jordan. Yasser Arafat has constantly made declarations concerning the right of the Palestinian people to have a homeland. King Hussein of Jordan has often responded to Arafat's claim saying that the Palestinians already have a homeland. Both to the Arabs and to the world he has stated, "Palestine is Jordan and Jordan is Palestine. There is one people and one land, with one history and one destiny."[142] But today, no one remembers that minor historical fact, nor considers that God's people might also have a right to exist as a free people with a homeland.

The uninformed as well as the biased sometimes ask, "But what about all those poor Palestinian refugees living in camps? What can they do?" The truth is, the refugees have been abused by their own Arab brothers, who have turned them into political pawns. The world never talks about the approximately 800,000 Jewish refugees who lost everything they owned by being forced out of their homes and businesses in Arab lands when the Arab-Israeli conflict boiled over.[143] They landed on Israel's doorstep with nowhere else to go and no money. They were absorbed into a poor nation that had been given about 8,000 square kilometers of land by the UN, and had a total of 650,000 citizens in 1948. These facts are almost universally ignored when the international community and the news media bring up the subject of the Palestinian refugees. Depending on which estimate one chooses to use, there are between 300,000 and one million Palestinian refugees as a result of the Middle East upheaval. They live in camps only because the UN, through an annually renewed UN resolution, has forbidden Israel to build them formal dwellings.[144] The sane question should be, "Instead of forcing them to remain in refugee camps, why can't their extremely rich Arab brothers absorb them into their own nations, given the fact that they possess over 12,000,000 square kilometers of land between them?" The Arab nations possess 1,500 times more land than the UN gave Israel in 1947, and they are so wealthy that they have been able to invest $1 trillion in arms during the last 30 years, yet they have not been able to absorb a few refugees. Two things should be pointed out. First, they have invested this absurd sum of money in arms in order to destroy Israel and take away the little land that the Jews have. Second, most of the refugees were in the holy land only because these same nations sent them there with British cooperation to oppose the formation of a Jewish state. Even many refugees see through the mystery of wickedness that has turned them into pawns. They declare, "We left our homeland on the strength of false promises by crooked leaders of the Arab States."[145]

Zuhayr Muhsin, a former top leader in the Palestine Liberation Organization, actually denied the existence of a separate Palestinian people. He said, "We speak about a Palestinian identity only for political reasons, because it is in the Arabs' interest to encourage a separate Palestinian existence."[146] He considered the Palestinian revolution to be nothing more than a part of the Arab war to take Palestine.[147]

Instead of demanding more land from the UN in 1947, the Jews joyfully accepted what they were given for their new homeland, and David Ben Gurion formally announced the rebirth of the State of Israel on May 14, 1948. The next day seven Arab nations declared war on the new infant.[148] At the beginning of the conflict, the total Israeli "army" consisted of 18,400 soldiers.[149] Among them they possessed 10,000 rifles,[150] two tanks, a few unarmed piper cubs, and a small number of other weapons.[151] The seven nations they faced had massive superiority in firepower, including twin engine bombers, spitfires, tanks, heavy guns, and armored cars.[152] They also had the supervision and even direct involvement of British officers in the battle.[153] There was only one thing that could offset these impossible odds—God Himself supervised Israel! He also did for His people what He had often done for the nation under King David—He fought for them. Within a few months the people of Israel had miraculously defeated all their foes.

Eight years later, when Egypt nationalized the Suez Canal and forbade Israeli shipping, the nation was forced to go to war again or be strangled. Once again, the victory was quickly given to Israel. In 1967, Israel was forced into a third major war that lasted only six days. Then, in 1973, the nation was attacked again on Yom Kippur, the holiest day of the year for believing Jews. Nearly the entire army was with their families observing this biblical feast. In the north, 1,100 Syrian tanks came rolling into Israeli territory where the only resistance they faced was 157 Israeli tanks.[154] In the south, the only resistance that hundreds of Egyptian tanks and 8,000 Egyptian soldiers met was three Israeli tanks and 436 Israeli soldiers.[155] On both fronts, it looked like the end had come to the State of Israel. Once again, God fought for Israel in awesome ways. God so turned the tide for Israel that within a few days, the Israeli armies were just hours away from conquering Cairo and Damascus, the capital cities of their enemies. How is it that Israel not only survived her wars but came through to glorious victory in every one, each time taking possession of more of the land that God had promised them?

Numerous reports came out of Israel after both of her last two wars describing supernatural experiences and visions that Israeli soldiers had on the battlefield. Although the various versions of some of those events differ in detail, they do not differ in basic content. Why didn't the Syrian tanks simply keep advancing until they rolled into Jerusalem? The reason I have heard on numerous occasions is that God saved Israel then in the same way He had often done in the past—by bringing the fear of the Lord upon their enemies. When Syrian tanks had penetrated well within Israeli territory without resistance, suddenly the Syrians became afraid. They said to themselves, "Israel would never do this! They couldn't possibly be this unprepared. They are too smart to permit this. Obviously, they are allowing us to enter so deeply into Israeli territory because they have planned an ambush against us. Quick! Let's retreat!" On the southern front, there are stories of Egyptian tank commanders surrendering because they were afraid of the huge men dressed in white they saw standing behind the pathetic Israeli defense. I personally talked with an Israeli tank commander who found himself behind enemy lines for two days. He told how they attempted to destroy his tank with mortar fire. As the line of fire approached his tank, he was certain that his end had come. He knew that God had done a mighty miracle when a mortar fell in front of his tank and the next one fell behind it—without ever touching his tank!

It is not really important whether or not all the reports of what happened in Israel's wars are precise. What really matters is that there are sufficient, undeniable, military facts available to demonstrate that God fought with the armies of Israel! He was, and still is, showing the world that He is a covenant-keeping God, and that He still has a plan for Israel. He did great things for His people and for the general who led the forces in the Six Day War—Yitzhak Rabin. Instead of recognizing God's hand, the world's military analysts called Rabin one of the greatest military tacticians of all time! He became internationally famous. Honored by Israel and the world, Yitzhak Rabin, the general of the "armies of the Lord," went on to become the Primer Minister of his nation.

Back to the Little Horn

What does all this history have to do with Yasser Arafat and the little horn? It is impossible to understand just how abominable Yasser Arafat's claims to the holy land really are without being aware of the historical facts.[156] We can now perceive something of the wickedness involved in the self-exaltation of the little horn, of which Daniel observed, "He even exalted himself as high as the Prince of the host."

At the same time in which God was revealing His glory by fighting for Israel, there was a young man in the Middle East who was seeking his own glory—a glory of his own making. Instead of gaining international fame because of divine intervention in his battles, he gained international infamy by guiding his terrorists in vicious attacks against innocent civilians like elderly Leon Klinghoffer whom the great "freedom fighters" threw overboard from the *Achille Lauro* in 1985. He also became the leader of his people, the Palestinians. He did so not because of the great honor they bestowed upon him, but because of the great fear he instilled in them—fear of his brutal treatment of any fellow Palestinian who refused to collaborate with his cowardly path to glory. One of Israel's loved and respected defense ministers, Ariel Sharon, pursued Arafat for years. He gives the true story of how Arafat attained the "support" of his people—"he ordered innocent Arabs in Nablus hanged by their chins on butchers' hooks until they died; by [his] orders the bellies of pregnant Arab women were split open before the eyes of their husbands and the hands of Arab children chopped off while their parents looked on."[157]

This is the man who stood beside Prime Minister Yitzhak Rabin, and together with him, received the greatest honor that the international community can bestow upon an individual—the Nobel Peace Prize.[158] This man had "exalted *himself* as high as the commander in chief of the armies," armies with which God Himself had fought. As the cloud of witnesses in heaven looked upon this pitiful day in human history, and the blasphemous sham of the mystery of iniquity that calls evil good and good evil, they must have turned their heads! Daniel, too, must have felt the impact of that moment. He looked ahead in time to the last days and saw the vilest of men—a little horn—reaching his goal of self-exaltation until he was recognized as being on the same level as the commander of Israel's divinely-led armies.

Someone else who simply could not bring himself to countenance this blasphemy was Kaare Kristiansen. For years, he was a respected voting member of the Nobel Peace Prize commission in Norway. In spite of all his efforts and arguments to avoid it, the commission made the decision to award the Prize to Arafat. On December 10, 1994, Mr. Kristiansen met with 2,000 Israelis in Jerusalem to explain that he was forced to resign from the commission because he was unable to place his approval on awarding the Prize to a man who had dedicated his life to killing others.[159] He explained that one of the justifications that the commission gave for choosing Arafat was that they felt it was legitimate to use the Prize to motivate men like Arafat to improve his record in the future. Mr. Kristiansen could not agree with that concept and so resigned.

19. He Takes Away the "Continual"

"...by him the daily sacrifices were taken away" (Dan. 8:11b).

The way in which this phrase has been translated has resulted in a number of serious doctrinal errors among Christians. One of those errors is to assume there is a connection between the so-called "daily sacrifice" in this verse and the "sacrifice and offering" of Daniel 9:27a, where Daniel writes, "Then he shall confirm a covenant with many for one week; but in the middle of the week he shall bring an end to sacrifice and offering." In fact, this is such a common assumption that the editor's notes for Daniel 9:27 in some Bibles declare that it is the "little horn" who brings an end to sacrifice and offering.[160] Daniel 8:11 is then offered as the proof text where the little horn takes away the "daily sacrifice." This misunderstanding stems from two sources: 1) the misleading translation from Hebrew to English of the phrase "the daily sacrifices" in Daniel 8:11-13, and 2) an apparent unfamiliarity of some Bible commentators with the biblical religious ritual of the Jewish nation and their sacrifices in the temple. Let's look at both these problems.

The Misleading Translation
Concerning the "Daily Sacrifice"

By referring to any interlinear Hebrew-English Bible or to one of the several Hebrew-text computer programs now available, it will be observed that the phrase "daily sacrifice" has been translated from one single Hebrew word—the noun "tamiyd."[161] (In the *Strong's Hebrew Dictionary* it appears under #8548.) Just as many Hebrew nouns are derived from verbs, this noun also comes from a Hebrew verb that means "to stretch." Note that the phrase "daily sacrifice" does not even appear in the original Hebrew. It was added to many English versions by the translators. It is not a translation of the text, but rather an interpretation based on the personal understanding of the translators. Some of those versions do, in fact, inform the reader that the word "sacrifice" does not appear in the Hebrew. They do so by printing it in italics to indicate that it is a word that has been added by the translators. By examining other places in the Old Testament where the Hebrew word "tamiyd" is used, we can conclude that it is also employed as both an adjective and an adverb for which an accurate translation is simply "continual." The American Standard Version translates it somewhat more precisely as "the continual *burnt-offering*." Note that "*burnt offering*" is italicized, meaning that it is not in the Hebrew. From this we understand that the *literal* translation of Daniel 8:11b is, "By him **the continual** was taken away." Although this literal translation of the Hebrew does not produce good grammar in English, for the sake of clarity I will use "the continual" to translate "tamiyd," especially since "tamiyd" is accompanied by a Hebrew article corresponding to "the" in English. I choose to use this literal translation because this is exactly what any Hebrew-reading person understands from this passage, although there is something deeper that they understand as well.

So what is Daniel referring to? If we allow ourselves to be led by the Old Testament usage of this word instead of our preconceived ideas, it is less likely that we will err. The first time this word is used is in reference to the showbread being **continually** before the Lord in the Tabernacle (Ex. 25:30). It is also used to refer to the fire that was to be burning on the altar **continually** (Lev. 6:13). Very often it refers to the **continual** burnt offering, also known as "the morning and evening sacrifice" explained in Exodus 29:38-42. There we see that the sacrifice Israel offered in the morning was identical in every way to the sacrifice offered each evening in the Temple. For this reason, the translators took the liberty to add words to the text, calling it the "continual burnt offering" or "daily sacrifice." However, the full understanding of the "continual" does not come from Exodus and certainly not from a translation. It must come from the context of the entire Bible.

Before the Book of Daniel was ever written, King David gave a deeper meaning to the "continual" than is immediately understood from the translators' rendering of "daily sacrifice." In many ways, King David is a pattern for the New Testament Believer. For example, David's throne is the throne that Christ inherited. (See Luke 1:32.) Therefore, it is a revelation of the New Testament throne or Kingdom. According to James, the New Testament Church is actually a rebuilding of God's eternal dwelling place that David discovered as he spent time in the presence of the Lord. (See Acts 15:13-17.) James said that the experience of the early Church was a fulfillment of God's promise to "rebuild the tabernacle of David, which has fallen down" (Acts 15:16). Obviously, the "tabernacle" that James was speaking of was not the literal tent that David pitched in his backyard for the ark of the covenant. Rather, it was the very life of a true worshipper that David prepared for the Lord as a dwelling.

The Church becomes the Lord's tabernacle or dwelling place only as it becomes a place of praise. David discovered that God dwells in the praises of His people, not in a tent made with hands, as revealed in his declaration that God "inhabits the praises of His people" (Psa. 22:3 KJV).[162] The intimate relationship between David and the New Testament is revealed in other ways also. The New Testament actually begins and ends with David—his name is the first and last *human* name found there. He was a man who experienced the blessing of New Testament forgiveness— something found in the age of grace, but that the law could not provide. (Compare Hebrews 10:28, II Samuel 12:13, and Romans 4:6.)

One other glorious truth found in David's life helps us understand what the "continual" is in *God's* mind today—even if it is not what the translators or we have in mind when we see the word "continual." Since David's tabernacle[163] did not have the brazen altar on which the **continual** burnt offering could be offered, he was forced to seek God and discover what the spiritual New Testament fulfillment of this Old Testament shadow is.[164] David reveals the *spiritual* way to offer the Lord the "continual" or the morning and evening sacrifice. That revelation is found in Psalm 141:2 where he prays, "Let my prayer be set before You as incense, the lifting up of my hands as the evening sacrifice." Since the evening sacrifice was identical to the morning sacrifice, then prayer and the lifting of David's hands became his "**continual**." David clarifies and emphasizes this before he dies by commanding the Lord's priests "to stand every morning to thank and praise the Lord, and likewise at even" (I Chr. 23:30). Morning and evening prayer and praise is not only *David's* "continual;" it is also the continual of the New Testament age. Hebrews exhorts us, "By him therefore let us offer the sacrifice of praise to God **continually**, that is, the fruit of our lips giving thanks to his name... for with such **sacrifices** God is well pleased" (Heb. 13:15-16).

The Difference Between the "Continual" and the Sacrifices of Daniel 9:27

An in-depth study of the Old Testament Levitical offerings is outside the scope of this book. However, for those who are interested in more details, refer to Leviticus 1-7 where the five principal offerings are explained, including the laws that govern each. Using the *Strong's Hebrew Dictionary* again, any English reader can confirm that the "sacrifices and offerings" of Daniel 9:27 refer to specific offerings—the "peace offering" of Leviticus 3 and the "meal offering" ("meat" in King James Version) of Leviticus 2. Note that Leviticus 1 gives the details of another offering—the "burnt offering." The "continual" in Moses' tabernacle was always a "burnt offering." (See Exodus 29:42.) A Hebrew-reading student of the Bible simply never makes the mistake of confusing the sacrifices in Daniel 9:27 with the "continual" of Daniel 8:11. Never once in the entire Old Testament did the Spirit of God ever confuse the different offerings. We, too, must be careful not to confuse them, especially since many of the popular interpretations of Daniel frequently heard in the Church today have confused them.

How Will the Little Horn Take Away the "Continual"?

Throughout our reading of Daniel it is helpful to keep in mind that Daniel's message is for his people, Israel, in the last days. As anyone who has visited Israel knows, the Orthodox Jews are extremely faithful in offering the "continual" of King David—prayers and praise to Jehovah. Every morning and every evening they gather at the Western Wall, often called the Wailing Wall, to pray and to offer their God thanksgiving and praise. Of course, Orthodox Jews throughout the world offer to God their "continual" regardless of where they are—even when they are flying on a commercial airline flight they pray and praise at the indicated time. However, for Jews, the holy mount in Jerusalem is simply the most desirable place to do so. They do not yet know their Messiah, but they still offer sacrifices of prayer and praise to the same God we know and love.

Yasser Arafat has already revealed what he plans to do about this continual offering of prayer by the Jews. On August 5, 1995, Arafat called on Moslems to converge on the Temple Mount to prevent Jews from praying there. A large group of Moslems camped on the Temple Mount to physically prevent Jews from entering.[165] Is this a harbinger of things to come? What can we expect Mr. Arafat's attitude to be about the "continual" when he gets total control of the Temple Mount? Arafat has already taken total control of the Wakf (the religious body in charge of Moslem affairs in Jerusalem).[166] On April 25, 1995, that governing body declared, "Jewish worship on the Temple Mount will not be tolerated... The entire area is a mosque, and according to Islamic law it is forbidden for non-Moslems to pray at a mosque... what the Jews call the Temple Mount, is... **defined as both the mosque structure, and the walled area around it**."[167] The "walled area around" the mosque includes the Western Wall, or Wailing Wall, where the Jews have been praying daily since 1967. Arafat was doing more here than "tipping his hand." With one sweep, he was both reconfirming his control over the religious law governing the Temple Mount and notifying the Jews about what to expect. Once he is in total control of the holy mount, he will inform them that there will be no more "continual," not even at the wall surrounding the area—he will take it away by force as Daniel is about to tell us!

On April 5, 1996, a political cartoon appeared in *The Jewish Press* which definitely reveals what Mr. Arafat has in mind regarding the continual prayer of the Jews at the Western Wall. He is shown standing before a sign that reads, "**By Order of Palestine Authority: Rachel's Tomb Forbidden to Jews; Cave of the Patriarchs Forbidden to Jews**." He has almost succeeded in establishing these prohibitions for the Jews who live in Israel today. However, as he stands before the sign, Mr. Arafat is looking off into the distance and his mental vision is depicted in the cartoon. He sees the Western Wall where the Jews pray, and he also sees a sign in front of the Wall revealing another of his ambitions: "**By the Order of President of Palestine: Forbidden to Jews**."

20. Because of Him, the Place of God's Sanctuary Is Cast Down

"...[by him] the place of His sanctuary was cast down" (Dan. 8:11c).

This is one of the most tragic portions in Daniel's entire description of the little horn. Some Christians today actually believe that, after Christ's First Coming, God changed His plans regarding the physical land of Israel and is no longer interested in it. However, the Lord warns the nations in Joel 3:2 that He will bring them into judgment in the last days because of what they have done to His people and to His land.[168] Specifically, the nations have divided God's land, giving huge portions of it to Palestinians who claim it as their own. The land was given to Abraham's descendants as an *"everlasting* possession," not just for the years before the coming of their Messiah! (Gen. 17:8) To the Lord's way of thinking, have you become a collaborator with the nations that are dividing God's land? Those who agree in their hearts with the decisions of the nations have placed themselves on the side of those nations who are opposing God's will.

Of all the land of Canaan, there is no question that the Lord speaks more longingly and lovingly about His "holy mount," the place of His temple, than any other place. Due to the wicked maneuvering of Yasser Arafat, along with the willingness that the Israeli Labor government manifested to make peace at any price, the **place of the Lord's sanctuary**, the Temple Mount, has almost been literally cast away at this very time in history. Since Israel conquered the Old City in 1967, they have permitted the Moslems to continue their activities in their two mosques on the Temple Mount. However, until recently, the Israeli government maintained supervisory control over the mount through the police and military. Today, they possess the key to only one of the nine gates that lead to "the place of His sanctuary."[169] The Arafat-controlled Wakf has total control over all the gates except one. That gate would have almost certainly been cast away also if the "peace-at-any-price" syndrome that views the heritage of the Lord as something worthless would not have been interrupted by Israel's election of Benjamin Netanyahu as the new Prime Minister of a very conservative government.

One of the most difficult hurdles for Mr. Netanyahu may simply be staying in office. Assassination is only one of several possible challenges he faces. Another will be to hold together the shaky coalition that the Likud has formed. This could prove to be a formidable task. Assuming he meets these challenges, the next question is whether or not the new government will be able to hold onto the Old City of Jerusalem. Whoever governs Israel at this point will almost certainly find themselves forced to give the Old City of Jerusalem over to the PLO. There are at least two possible scenarios that could very well force Israel to capitulate on this issue. I consider the first scenario to be very plausible in the present world political climate. It would be an all-out attack against Israel by one or more Arab nations. Such a war could very well force Israel to take drastic military measures just to survive, including the use of nuclear weapons. During such a war, Arafat could gain control of East Jerusalem through the force of his armed terrorists. Any use of nuclear weapons by Israel would drastically turn world opinion against them. This would give Mr. Arafat even greater moral support to continue his terrorist attacks and reign of terror on Israel long after the end of the war. Arafat's oft-stated goal—the total liberation of Palestine—would then seem much more plausible.

A second possible scenario does not involve all-out war at the beginning. In this case, such a war would come at the end. This scenario would start with Arafat directing his cronies to unleash a horrendous onslaught of terrorism against the Israeli populace. Arafat would blame the renewed Hamas terrorism on the new hard-line Israeli government that will not give him everything he has asked for. This exponential increase in terrorism would then cause a public outcry among the Jews demanding that the Israeli government give Jerusalem to the PLO just as the former government apparently promised to do. However, even though Israel might be suffering more terrorist attacks than ever before, it is almost inconceivable that Prime Minister Netanyahu would actually turn Jerusalem over to Mr. Arafat. He would first have to lay aside his oft-expressed faith in God's covenant with Abraham. He is a man who believes in that covenant and believes it is still valid today. It is more likely that he will find himself pressured into accepting some sort of international government over East Jerusalem.

Once a Gentile government of any type takes control of the Old City, it will mark the beginning of the last 42 months before Christ returns. At that time, we can also expect Yasser Arafat to increase the PLO police force that has already been functioning in Jerusalem ever since the former government permitted its deployment there. It would be an easy matter for him to simply and effectively take control of Jerusalem as the newly installed "international government" looks on helplessly. In the present climate of goodwill that the world leaders manifest toward the "former" terrorist, it is unlikely that anyone would attempt to resist Arafat's total control of East Jerusalem. His armies will then take control of the Temple Mount and remove the continual just as Daniel 11 reveals will happen. We will see this later in points 57 and 58.

The *Place* of the Temple is Given Up—*Not* the Temple

Before we continue, please note that Daniel 8:11c does *not* say that Israel will be casting away the **sanctuary**. It specifies that it is giving up the **place** of His sanctuary. There is obviously a huge difference. Although the reader's viewpoint concerning the last days may be in conflict with my next statement, I believe that as we continue considering the details of the little horn, what I am saying will become very clear.

This passage in Daniel is a very strong indication that during the last three and a half years, when the little horn and the Gentiles have control over Jerusalem, there will be no physical Jewish temple present in Jerusalem. A Jew would never talk about giving over the "**place** of His sanctuary" if, in fact, they were giving over the sanctuary itself. To the Jews today, the most holy place on earth is the Temple Mount—the place of His sanctuary. However, if there were a temple there, then the temple itself would be the most holy place, and they would speak of losing the temple, not merely its "place." I am aware of the mental conflicts this causes in the minds of those who have envisioned a temple being rebuilt with the help of the antichrist when he makes peace with Israel. I am also aware of the Scriptures used to support this teaching, but the teaching actually creates more problems with Scripture than it solves. We will discuss this theme further as we go along.

21. An Army Is Given to Him Through Wicked Means

"And an host was given him against the daily sacrifice
by reason of transgression" (Dan. 8:12a KJV).

This is a difficult passage to translate from Hebrew into English as seen by comparing the variations between one English version and another. Actually, if we remember that "host" means "army," the King James Version comes the closest to how my Hebrew-reading friends explained this verse to me. In a little simpler English, it means that "through wickedness an army is given to the little horn to oppose the continual." The idea is that he obtains an army through wicked means. We already discussed how the Syrians originally helped Arafat get his first recruits. While they were attacking Israel and giving the credit to Arafat, he was recruiting new terrorists. That was only the beginning of how he obtained an army through wickedness, which will ultimately give him power over the Temple Mount and the continual prayers there.

Yasser Arafat's army continues to be formed through very wicked methods. He has ways of "convincing" the Palestinian people to accept him as their commander. News of the infamous "intifada" (the Palestinian uprising) against the State of Israel has appeared somewhere almost daily on TV and in newspapers around the world, showing pictures of rock-throwing, screaming Palestinians. It was consistently reported to be an expression of the anger and exasperation that the Palestinians felt toward the harsh Israelis who governed them. No one doubts who started the intifada—Yasser Arafat. Rarely is the whole truth told. He had a dual purpose for starting it—to resist Israel and at the same time gain control over the Palestinian people themselves. This, too, is common knowledge in Israel. The story that the media almost never mentions is Arafat's almost continual brutalizing and terrorizing of his own people through his PLO and Hamas henchmen. One of Arafat's terrorists appeared in action on Israeli TV as he administered "justice" to the Palestinians in the city of Nablus. He was shown shooting the Palestinians whom he considered to be Israeli "collaborators." Some were only shot in the knees to permanently destroy their knees, while others were shot in the head. The Arabs under Arafat's rule are forced to accept his orders and to participate in the uprising, often against their own will. Ariel Sharon only touched the tip of the iceberg when he spoke of Arafat hanging men on meat hooks to die in the marketplace and cutting off children's hands in front of their parents.[170]

By December 1992, at least 700 Palestinian Arabs had been executed by Arafat's intifada tribunals and over 4,000 wounded, with "evidence of unspeakable brutality."[171] To gain a true perspective of these numbers and the percentage of families affected, keep in mind that we are speaking only of the Palestinians who live in the West Bank and Gaza—no more than 2 million people. If someone were permitted to brutalize almost 5,000 people in a city like Detroit, Michigan, most of the populace would think twice before doing or saying anything that might cause them to become the next victim. The victimized include young men, teenage girls, the middle-aged, and the elderly. Arafat has boasted that "the executions were the culmination of democratic due process; that all the condemned were first afforded an opportunity to recant and mend their ways; that only if they refused to repent were they tried by intifada tribunals... He even bragged that every case had to be approved personally by him, if not before the execution, then after."[172]

On December 4, 1992, *The Jerusalem Post* published photographs of one of the many "executions" in Gaza. The victim was a young man named Fadda, who was 31 years old. I quote from the *Post* of that day:

"By now 700 Palestinian Arabs, mostly innocent of any wrongdoing, have been 'executed' by their brethren. If lucky, they were murdered swiftly, like Fadda, with a bullet in the head. Others were tortured, often for days, in ways reminiscent of the Spanish Inquisition or the torture chambers of Syrian intelligence... On a recent American television program, [PLO] spokeswoman Hanan Ashwari declined to condemn the killings; she attributed them to Palestinian 'pluralism,' to differences of opinion. She was probably close to the truth. The victims are seldom 'collaborators'... Mostly they simply disagree with the intifada methods, or lead a life of which the 'activists' disapprove. Yet world governments watch these systematic killings—now increasing in number even as the peace process progresses—... with utter equanimity. Nor do the media pay them much attention. The horrible Gaza pictures... have failed to enter most of the leading newspapers in the United States. Ironically, most of the press roundly condemns not the Arab killers, but the special [Israeli] army units which apprehend them. The lesson is plain: No one cares about the sufferings of the Palestinians unless Israel can be blamed for it."

The article continues, "The photographs, testimony... to the killers' boldness... do not bode well for peace. The murderer not only committed the 'execution' in broad daylight in the middle of a crowded street. He played to the cameras, stepping on the dead body and waving his gun in triumph."

In another interview, Arafat insisted that "the bulk of the death-squad killings were fully under PLO control."[173] He went on to declare, "The PLO is the sole legitimate representative of the Palestinian people. We are a democratic society... we are democrats and came to our positions by the will of the people... Palestinians of the West Bank and Gaza or anywhere in the world are one people. And all are an indivisible part of the PLO."[174] The truth is, not one of those Palestinians have any choice. If they express any misgivings about the PLO's brutal terror, they are the next victims to be tortured and killed. That is Arafat's definition of "democracy." One Palestinian living under Arafat's new "democracy" lamented over the brutal injustices and said, "God should chop off our hands which threw stones at the Jews. We brought this disaster on ourselves. Now there is no law and no justice."[175]

Neither the Palestinians nor the Jews have yet experienced the dregs of the cup of wickedness that this man will finally serve them. One last example of how the PLO treats those who are under its dominion should demonstrate what awaits the holy people. "Susan S. was at home with her parents when a number of PLO officers broke in... The PLO men killed Susan's father and her brother, and raped her mother, who suffered a hemorrhage and died. They raped Susan 'many times.' They cut off her breasts and shot her. Hours later she was found alive, but with all four limbs so badly broken and torn with gunshot that they had to be surgically amputated. She now has only the upper part of one arm... She has asked [those who care for her] to let her die, but they have consistently replied that they cannot do that."[176]

The national and international world leaders know these things, yet instead of exposing Arafat and bringing him to trial as the vilest of criminals, they have recognized his claim to be the sole representative of the Palestinian people, and even honored him with the Nobel Peace Prize! It should be shouted from the housetops that, in the eyes of God, the Western governments are full-fledged collaborators with one of the most brutal, wicked men who has ever lived on this planet. God holds the nations responsible for their actions! When we know this is the way Mr. Arafat's army is wickedly being "given" to him and how he keeps it "loyal" to himself, and yet we honor him, how can we escape the judgment of God?

God's judgment on the Western media will be even worse, because they know what is really happening and not only hide it, but systematically warp what they *do* report to make the wicked look righteous. Their concern for the poor Palestinians is hypocrisy and the stench of it reaches to heaven. If they had sincere concern for the Palestinian people, they would not continue to support Arafat and cover his tracks so that the international community permits him to bring these people under one of the most brutal reigns of terror in history. One goal of a free press is to expose injustice so that it cannot infect society unchecked. This goal is not served by a media that dictates the kind of stories it will air. It seems that the principal reason for the media's twisted reporting on the Middle East can only be a satanic hatred of God and His people, Israel.

* 22. He Casts Truth Down to the Ground

"...he cast truth down to the ground" (Dan. 8:12b).

It is one thing to lie, but this statement refers to something far more sinister. This refers to an active attack on the known truth. The Apostle Paul refers to those who "turn the truth of God into a lie" (Rom. 1:25). For such people, truth becomes a target. Simply advancing their lies is not enough to satisfy them. They also want to destroy truth in the earth. Arafat and his proxies are masters at turning truth on its head and then slaying it. We have seen one example where Arafat's spokeswoman, Hanan Ashwari, turned Jesus into a Palestinian. Arafat has been calling Jesus a "Palestinian prophet" for many years, placing

Him alongside Mohammed.[177] Jesus *is* the Truth, and look what they have attempted to do with Him!

Arafat claims that the seeming stain on the Israeli ten-agorot coin is a map depicting Israel's expansionist goals to have a nation that extends from Egypt to Iraq.[178] The design on the coin is nothing more than a reproduction of the remnants of an ancient Israeli coin that was partially destroyed and whose ragged edges form what Arafat calls a map.[179] No one can tell him otherwise, because his goal is to cast truth to the ground and destroy it.

Arafat never could have received the Nobel Peace Prize without renouncing terrorism. However, in so doing, he presented a convenient inversion that completely redefined the word "terrorism." In Geneva, on December 13, 1988, he announced: "I, as chairman of the Palestine Liberation Organization, hereby once more declare that I condemn terrorism in all its forms... I also offer a reverent salute to the martyrs who have fallen at the hands of terrorism and terrorists, foremost among whom is my lifelong companion and deputy, the martyr-symbol Khalid al-Wazir [Abu Jihad], and the martyrs who fell in the massacres to which our people have been subjected in the various cities, villages, and camps of the West Bank, the Gaza Strip, and South Lebanon."[180] We should not be reassured by a change of terms masquerading as a change of heart. The only "terrorists" he condemns are Israeli security forces. The war of terror his inhumanly, ruthless followers wage against innocent civilians through random acts of violence is deemed legitimate, even holy. His is a religion that can sanctify torture, lynchings, bus-bombings, assassination of Olympic athletes, the murder of women and children by any means possible, and then make martyrs out of those who are thwarted in these crimes. Thus, he defines terrorism as Israel's retaliation against Arafat's holy war against the Zionists who, he claims, have stolen his land. Everyone knows what terrorism is and who the master of modern terrorism is, but once again he has cast truth down to the ground!

* 23. He Prospers In Everything He Does

"He did all this and prospered" (Dan. 8:12c).

This same Hebrew phrase is repeated in Daniel 8:24. It actually means that the horn "prospered in everything it did" (Dan. 8:12c NIV), or that he succeeded in everything he did.[181] When we combine this revelation of the little horn with the fact that he has a mouth that speaks great things, we understand that Israel faces a formidable enemy. What this little horn decides to do, he will succeed in doing.

If we review the history of Yasser Arafat, it becomes evident that he is the epitome of the fulfillment of this description of the little horn—albeit, in an extremely perverse way. Speaking even of mundane things, he is reportedly a wealthy man because of his successful construction business in Kuwait. But, aside from that, how could anyone in history ever equal Arafat for having succeeded in such abominable ways? Anyone who has a conscience should shake their head in wonderment at the mystery of iniquity revealed in this man.

This is a man who has dedicated his life since childhood to torturing, maiming, and killing innocent men, women, and children throughout the world. Ironically, *this* man ended up being called a "man of peace" when he received the 1994 Nobel Peace Prize, the highest international honor the West bestows. He is now considered to be an international statesman. He was honored at the UN in 1974 by being allowed to address the entire assembly. He was honored as a very high dignitary on the White House lawn in September 1993. Israel has been giving him huge tracts of the holy land. The former Israeli government called him their "peace partner." Leah Rabin, the widow of Israel's slain Prime Minister, said that she considered Yasser Arafat a better friend than Benjamin Netanyahu, who was one of Israel's top conservative political leaders at that time and who became the new Prime Minister in the May 1996 elections.[182] The international community now calls him and his terrorists "freedom fighters."[183] Can anyone deny that this is "success"? It is both one of the greatest and one of the most perverse success stories of all time. The Lord warns us, "Woe to those who call evil good, and good evil; who put darkness for light, and light for darkness; who put bitter for sweet, and sweet for bitter!" (Isa. 5:20) This divine pronouncement of judgment against such wickedness was surely meant for the present generation more than any other.

* 24. He Tramples Under Foot the Holy Land and the Armies of Israel for 2,300 Days

"Then I heard a holy one speaking; and another holy one said to that certain one who was speaking, 'How long will the vision be, concerning the daily sacrifices and the transgression of desolation, the giving of both the sanctuary and the host to be trampled under

*foot?' And he said to me, "For two thousand three hundred
days; then the sanctuary shall be cleansed" (Dan. 8:13-14).*

I have no desire to find fault with the translators of Daniel, but I do
have a desire to find the truth. I have never found the perfect translation and am quite sure that it will never exist, simply because of what is
involved in translating. Anyone who speaks more than one language
knows that it is impossible to translate from one language to another
without our own interpretations entering into the translation. This
happens because it is often impossible to translate literally from one
language to another. For example, in English we say, "Bill jumped
down Joe's throat this morning." If that were to be translated in its literal form into another language, it would only produce wonderment—
at the size of Joe's throat or else at the smallness of Bill! A translator
would not only have to **translate** this into another language, but he
would also have to **interpret** this phrase to mean, "Bill got angry with
Joe." Therefore, we should recognize the impossible task translators
have, and be thankful that someone has attempted to make God's message available to us as accurately as they possibly could.

Notwithstanding all the problems involved in translating, I am
amazed at what the translators have almost universally done with
Daniel 8:11-14. In this short passage the word "sanctuary" appears
three times in all the major English versions. What is amazing is that
none of them explain to the reader that they are translating two totally
different Hebrew words as "sanctuary," and that, in two cases,
"sanctuary" is an interpretation rather than a translation. The first
word, which appears in Daniel 8:11, is "miqdash" (*Strong's Hebrew
Dictionary*, #4720). This word definitely means "sanctuary." However,
the second word, which appears twice in Daniel 8:13-14, is "qodesh"
(*Strong's Hebrew Dictionary*, #6944). This word is from the same Hebrew root as the word "holy" found in Daniel 7:21, and also in the
phrase "then I heard a **holy** one speaking; and another **holy** one said..."
(Dan. 8:13). We already discussed why it should be translated as the
"holy ones" in Daniel 7:21 instead of the "saints" of the so-called
"Gentile Church." Likewise, the word "qodesh" is primarily translated
as "holy" by all the major English translations. In fact, although the
translators have sometimes rendered it as "sanctuary," the *Strong's Hebrew Dictionary* does not even give that as an alternative meaning.[184]

What happened, then, to the translators in Daniel 8:11-14? Some
were surely applying this to the desecration of the holy land by Antiochus Epiphanes around 170 BC, as well as his desecration of the temple.

However, as Biblical Hermeneutics tells us, most prophecies have at least two fulfillments—one which is historical and another which is related to the last days. (Hermeneutics is simply the study of the almost universally accepted biblical principles needed to interpret the Bible properly.) We should expect that this prophecy concerning 2,300 days would have some fulfillment in the last days also. It would appear that many translators of the Book of Daniel were so convinced that another Jewish temple would be built before the Second Coming of Christ, that they used this passage to confirm it, even though "sanctuary" does not appear in verses 13 and 14. Putting together what we have learned, Daniel 8:13-14 should be translated in the following way (my changes are in bold letters): "Then I heard a holy one speaking; and another holy one said to that certain one who was speaking, 'How long will the vision be, concerning the **continual** and the transgression of desolation, the giving of both the **holy** and the **army** to be trampled under foot?' And he said to me, 'For two thousand three hundred days; then the **holy** shall be cleansed.'" What does the word "holy" refer to then? In the context of Old Testament Hebrew, it refers to any *holy* place—the holy land, the holy city, the holy mount, or yes, even the holy temple.

Is Arafat and the PLO presently fulfilling this prophecy? They have definitely begun to fulfill part of it. Note that there are three aspects involved: 1) the "continual" is taken away, 2) the "holy" is trampled under foot, and 3) the army is trampled under foot. We are told that this vision concerning these three things all take place in a period of 2,300 days. Most students of prophecy will remember that Daniel 12:11 explains that from the time that the "continual" is taken away and the abomination of desolation is established, there will be 1,290 days remaining. Putting both revelations together, we understand that there will be a period of 2,300 days in which the holy and the army are trampled underfoot. During the last 1,290 days of that period, the continual will be taken away and the abomination established.

In the sight of God, one of the most vile aspects of the initial accord that Israel signed with Arafat on September 13, 1993, was the surrender of a large portion of the holy land to him to form a nation within the nation. He would literally be "trampling under foot" the holy. They were giving *God's* land to one of the most vile men that has ever breathed! Anyone with ears to hear what was being said also knew that Mr. Arafat would use his new foothold in the holy land to launch attacks against Israel's army and civilian population as he and other PLO officials have often declared. For anyone with doubts about his true intentions, those doubts should have been dispelled by Arafat's own words during the afternoon of September 13, 1993, on the *very day* he signed the initial agreement with Israel. On that afternoon, he was interviewed live from Washington on Jordanian TV. In that interview, he revealed what his monumental agreement with Israel meant to him. Among other things he told the Arabs of Jordan, "Since we cannot defeat Israel in war we do this in stages. We take any and every territory that we can of Palestine, and establish a sovereignty there, and we use it as a springboard to take more. When the time comes, we can get the Arab nations to join us for the final blow against Israel."[185] The ink was barely dry on the contract Israel signed with Arafat, when twice as many Israelis (military and civilian) were already dying at the hands of Arafat's terrorists.[186]

Translational questions aside, Arafat is definitely "trampling under foot the holy and the army" precisely as the Hebrew text says the little horn will do. In light of this, we should ask ourselves if it is nothing more than coincidence that there will be 2,300 days between the infamous September 13, 1993, signing and the first day of the new millennium—January 1, 2000! Please note that I am *not* predicting that any special event will occur precisely on January 1, 2000. Arafat and the PLO did not actually enter Palestine and begin trampling the land until some months after September 1993. However, it certainly seems significant that this date was exactly 2,300 days from the new millennium. Could it be that the Lord was trying to call our attention to this passage in Daniel and its impending fulfillment through this "coincidence"?

Besides the death of so many more Israeli soldiers since the "peace process" began in earnest, the army is being "trampled under foot" in another way. From the day Israel became a nation, the IDF (Israel Defense Forces) has gone from victory to victory. They have literally conquered the holy land through incredible military successes in wars that were fought defensively, not as unprovoked campaigns of aggression. In the process, the IDF became one of the best trained, best equipped, and most formidable armed forces in the world. They have always moved forward against their enemies and prospered. Today, they are literally turning their backs on their enemies and leaving in shame as they surrender one city and town after another to the PLO. On at least one occasion, they have literally *run* away from their enemies to avoid the shame of the Arab rock-throwers and the accompanying scoffing and scorning. When it came time to withdraw from Nablus, one of the principal cities, they decided to leave a day early and sneak out before any Palestinians realized what was happening.[187]   In their haste to avoid further shame, they forgot the Israeli flag that was still flying over their former headquarters. Of course it was desecrated the next day when the Palestinians discovered that their "oppressors" had fled during the night.[188] How sad! What shame! And they only have to go through this in 450 cities, towns, and villages in the holy land! Not only are their physical bodies being trampled under foot through terrorist attacks, but also their very souls and spirits are being trampled as they face the shame of surrendering. To add insult to injury, the news media's coverage of events frequently makes the real, live Philistine, Yasser Arafat, seem like a righteous "David" who has slain the uncircumcised, wicked, Israeli Goliath.

There is at least one other way in which Arafat and the PLO are trampling under foot not only Israel's land but also its people and army. Through years of battles, ambushes, and skirmishes, Israel has succeeded in capturing literally thousands of Arafat's trained terrorists who have murdered hundreds of Israelis. Part of the peace accord calls for the release of all those terrorists, including all the proven murderers. Israel has already released thousands, and the numbers in Arafat's Palestinian police have swelled enormously as a result.

These murderers are now the honored police force of the Palestinian Authority.[189] In one city after another, they are the ones who move into the IDF headquarters as the Israeli soldiers are leaving. Two terrible examples are the new chiefs of police for Nablus and Ramallah, two of the largest cities being turned over to the PLO. The police chief in Ramallah is Abu Firas, one of the terrorists involved in killing the eleven Israeli athletes in the 1972 Munich games.[190] Mahmoud Aloul is the chief of Nablus. He was in charge of the PLO killing of Jews in Samaria.[191] Would you feel "trampled under foot" if you were forced to surrender your office to a uniformed murderer who had killed your wife or children or a fellow soldier? Would you be able to walk out meekly as he enters amid the applause and shouts of the multitude while you leave with rocks and insults being hurled at you? Has this actually happened? It happens in the hearts of thousands of Israelis every time there is a new withdrawal. Remember, until recently, every able-bodied male in Israel has been a reserve soldier until he reached 50 years of age. In their hearts, they are all together in every new withdrawal. For some, it would be easier to be physically trampled under foot than to be trampled under the foot of unspeakable injustice and humiliation—brought on by their own government in the name of peace! Yes, Arafat and the PLO are trampling under foot the holy land and the holy people in a most perverse way. It is much like a continual repeat of a scene that took place in Israel 2,000 years ago, when a wicked murderer was released while the Just One was scorned, mocked, and crucified. The Lord seems to be reminding Israel of that time when they asked that Barabbas be released instead of Jesus. Surely, He is lovingly calling the nation to repentance so He can bless them again!

* 25. He Shall Have Fierce Features

"A king shall arise, having fierce features" (Dan. 8:23b).

Is there any need to discuss Arafat's "fierce features"? The word "features" here actually means "face" in Hebrew.[192] I am quite certain that if we could place all the political leaders on earth together in a world-wide contest to decide who has the most fierce facial appearance, Arafat's percentage of the popular vote would make any politician jealous!

* 26. He Understands Sinister Schemes

"...[he] understands sinister schemes" (Dan. 8:23c).

A more precise description of Yasser Arafat could hardly be found than what we get by combining the various translations of this phrase given by the major English versions of the Bible. They tell us he is, "a master of intrigue" (NIV); "a king... who understands riddles" (RSV); "a king... skilled in intrigue" (NRSV); "a king... understanding dark sentences" (KJV); and "a king... who understands sinister schemes" (NKJV). The Hebrew word used here actually means "a parable, a riddle, an enigmatic saying, a perplexing saying, an obscure utterance, or double dealing."[193] In other words, an expression that has hidden meaning.

Arafat's ability to say things with hidden meaning is well-publicized in Israel. He is also known to be a man who understands the hidden symbolism behind words and events. That is, he understands parables. One of his most recent utterances that had hidden meaning came six days after he signed the peace accord with Israel. He was in a mosque in Johannesburg, South Africa, speaking to a gathering of Moslems there. He thought he was free to speak openly about his intentions. He did not know that a reporter had entered the mosque unnoticed with a tape recorder! His speech was later published for the world to read.[194]

During his Johannesburg speech, Arafat declared, "This agreement [Israeli-PLO Peace Accord]—I am not considering it more than the agreement signed between our prophet Mohammed and the Kuraish tribe—a despicable truce."[195] Arafat was referring to a time when Mohammed was militarily weak and, therefore, signed a truce with the Kuraish tribe who did not accept Islam. The truce was to last ten years, but after two years Mohammed was strong enough to betray them and to break the truce. He attacked and killed every male in the tribe.[196] Islamic law has taken Mohammed's truce as the model and precedent for all peace agreements with infidels—never permanent and never to last more than ten years.[197] Moshe Sharon, a recognized expert on Islam, declares, "Arafat's allusions to these particular events in the history of Islam was not accidental... He was speaking in well-known codes and symbols."[198] Here is a man who understands parables whose meanings are hidden from most of the world! Sharon goes on to write, "Islam is not permitted to stop its war against non-Moslems for more than [ten years]... The fact that Arafat took this agreement as the model for the agreement with Israel is very significant. He wanted to tell Moslems (including Hamas) that he regarded the agreement as not only despicable, but temporary."[199]

In his Johannesburg speech, Arafat also used another "parable" or utterance with hidden meaning. He alluded to "Omar and Sophronius." Omar was Mohammed's close friend and companion and became the second Caliph of Islam.[200] Moshe Sharon explains, "Not wishing to confiscate the Holy Sepulchre, Omar made an agreement with the [Christian] Patriarch [Sophronius], in which both agreed that Jews would not be allowed to return to live in Jerusalem."[201] Again, Arafat was giving a secret message to both Jews and Christians. In his speech, he had already declared holy war against the Jews for Jerusalem, so they were to understand that they would be defeated and that he would take the city. The Christians in Jerusalem were to understand that they would become subjects and slaves of Islam as they were when Jerusalem was under Omar. Sharon concludes, "In some cases, words uttered in the Middle East are worthless. In others, they possess a magic power. To be on the safe side, the Jews of Israel should take Arafat's intentions, plans and dreams seriously."[202]

Arafat is constantly demonstrating his understanding of both symbolism and veiled speech. Just before the peace process was in full swing, he used another hidden message to warn Israel and to alert the Moslems, saying, "The PLO offers not the peace of the weak, but the peace of Saladin."[203] The interpretation of Arafat's enigmatic saying was given by Benjamin Netanyahu, the head of the Likud at that time. He explained, "What is not stated but what the Arab audiences understand well in its historical context is that Saladin's peace treaty with the Crusaders was merely a tactical ruse that was followed by Moslem attacks, which wiped out the Christian presence in the holy land."[204]

In recent speeches, Arafat has been exhorting his Moslem listeners, "Do not abandon the mountain as in the battle of Ouhud." Does this sound like an "obscure utterance" or "dark saying" to you? This is the way Arafat talks, just as the Prophet Daniel said the little horn would do! The "mountain" in this statement refers to the holy mount or the city of Jerusalem, and the battle of Ouhud refers to an historical battle in which the Moslems, certain of victory, lost because they laid down their arms too soon.[205] When a teacher uses parables, he usually explains their meaning to his close disciples. Jesus' disciples understood His parables, but the Lord explained that He was speaking to the multitudes in parables so that "hearing they do not... understand" (Matt. 13:13b). Many Jewish people can see through Arafat's tactics. As long as he speaks in veiled sentences and parables, he cannot be accused of saying anything inflammatory. After all, a parable can be interpreted any way you like. Only the author and all his close followers know the real meaning!

* 27. His Power Shall Be Mighty

"His power shall be mighty" (Dan. 8:24a).

Along with others, I used to laugh at the ridiculously grandiose plans and claims that Arafat often expressed. He certainly has had a "mouth that speaks great things." One reason I laughed was I simply did not understand the tremendous power this man has managed to accumulate over the last 50 years. An entire book could easily be written on the extent of this little man's power!

For many years he has had tremendous **economic power**. Few people realize that since 1969, Mr. Arafat has been collecting approximately 6 percent tax on the salaries or incomes of every Palestinian worker throughout the entire Islamic world.[206] Even before this, the Khartoum Arab summit of 1967 pledged sixty million dollars to fund Arafat's Fatah and PLO.[207] These multiplied millions of dollars that Arafat has had at his disposal in the past to wage terrorism throughout the world and buy influence are "small potatoes" at this point in his

long career of terrorism. As a result of having been internationally declared a wonderful peacemaker, his coffers are now receiving *billions* of
dollars of aid from the nations of the world to help him organize his
new nation and police force.

Coming to the subject of his **political power,** if Arafat has not had
a personal audience with a world leader, it is probably because that
leader does not have enough influence or power himself to be granted
an audience with Arafat! It could almost be said that if Arafat hasn't
met with them, they aren't worth meeting with. This man has met with
everyone from the Pope, the President of the US, Russian and Chinese
leaders, on down. How many world leaders address the UN General
Assembly with as much fanfare and publicity as Arafat did in 1974?

Arafat not only has friends in high governmental positions, but he
has political clout and friends in very high places within the news media. Consider the fact that his official spokesperson, Hanan Ashwari, is
called "the darling of the media."[208] According to *U.S. News and World
Report,* she has had a dating relationship with Peter Jennings, the news
anchor of ABC-TV.[209]   Could that relationship have given Arafat even
more clout with US public opinion through Jennings? Whether or not it
has, one thing is certain—Peter Jennings is one of Arafat's greatest
promoters! A Peter Jennings report in May 1989 gives us a glimpse. He
began his news broadcast with, "A young Arab was nearly lynched today in Jerusalem."[210] The viewers then had to wait for the rest of the story
until after a commercial, while they simmered about Jewish mistreat-
ment of Arabs. After the break, he continued, "In Israel today, the government tried to use a Palestinian act of violence to discredit the PLO."
He finally finished the story—the young Arab hadn't done anything
more serious than to stab to death two elderly Jewish men who had been
waiting for a bus. He was then chased, subdued, and beaten by enraged
onlookers.[211] Wouldn't most politicians in the world just love to have this
kind of political power through the TV that Mr. Arafat enjoys?

Let's come to Yasser Arafat's **power in education**—even among
the children of America. A program called "Reminding the World" is
part of a weekly current events series telecast on educational channels
throughout the US for children in grades 4-6. It tells the story of "a
young Palestinian boy named Rahman."[212] Here is the story:

> "Long before Rahman was born in 1929, Jews and Arabs had
> been fighting over his country. When the Jewish nation of Israel
> was established in 1948, Rahman was only a teenager; but he

had long been active in promoting the cause of the Palestinian people.

In the 1960s, the Palestine Liberation Organization was formed to try to win back the land. Within the PLO, small armies were created to attack the Israelis. Rahman helped to form one such army [called Fatah].

Fatah members preached that the Palestinians must rely on themselves—not on other Arab nations—to fight the battle against Israel. Often it seemed to be a hopeless cause. The Israelis had the strongest military in the Middle East. They had proved it time and time again against the Arab armies. As a result, Fatah's message drew little attention from the Arabs or the rest of the world, until the battle at Karameh in 1968.

The Israelis suspected that Palestinian terrorists lived in refugee camps in Karameh, a village in Jordan. The Israelis planned to wipe them out.

Refusing the advice of his allies, Rahman led an army of several hundred Palestinians against Israeli tanks and paratroopers. He inspired his soldiers by saying, 'We will not withdraw. We will fight and we will die.'

Rahman did not die. The fight ended with both sides withdrawing. It was far from a conquest for the Palestinians, but by their courage the world finally recognized their determination to win a homeland of their own.

Today, Rahman is the most prominent of all Palestinian leaders. The world knows him by the nickname Yasser and one of the names he was given at birth—Arafat."[213]

And you didn't think that Mr. Arafat has "mighty power?" He is educating the children of the US with his version of history! Aside from numerous historical errors in this teaching, which serves to demonstrate the low level of academic preparation of its author, it is slanderous. It claims that the holy land was "Arafat's country" and that the Jews came in and took it away from them. The *unrevised* edition of history tells us that there have been more Jews than Arabs in the holy land since the early 1820s![214] As we have seen, the issue has never been territorial, but rather religious and spiritual. Remembering that the Palestinians already received 90 percent of the land that Britain promised the Jews, we should again ask the question, Are the Jews the only ones who have no right to a homeland? The PLO was supposedly formed to "win back the land." From its inception, it was formed to eliminate the Jews of the Middle East by killing them all! Then, the clear implication is that Israel was not even sure if the refugee camps had terrorists, when, in fact, they were only attacking Arafat's Fatah, and they knew exactly where they were. It is made to sound as if Israel planned to "wipe them out" whether they were innocent civilians or not.

Arafat must have written the last part himself during one of his frequent memory lapses. The fact is, this was one of those times when Arafat should have died but escaped with his life. He fled on a motorcycle dressed like a woman and left his troops behind to die. What valor little Rahman displayed! This story does not tell of the Arafat who, along with his men, raped their host nation, Jordan, until King Hussein had to send in his own *Arab* troops to drive them out of his country. It does not tell that Hussein, a fellow Arab, was the one who finally decided to drive Arafat and his men out of Jordan because they were such brutal terrorists. It does not tell that for decades Hussein has openly declared that the Palestinians already have a homeland—Jordan. Arafat turns out to be the David-like hero and Israel is the big, bad Goliath. Anyone who has the power to rewrite history to this degree and then succeed in feeding it to the grade school students in the US is a very powerful man!

Finally, Arafat has great **military power** and that power is growing daily. For decades he has received military aid in the form of arms and money from the other Islamic countries. He has also received military aid from Russia and China. His Russian-made katyusha rockets are one of the many weapons in his arsenal. Of course, with his new multi-billion dollar budget, he can afford to build up a much bigger army and equip it, which is precisely what he is presently doing. His so-called "police force" is nothing less than an army of terrorists. A PLO official saw no need to hide the organization's plans when he declared, "The Palestine Liberation Army forces will be transformed into security police, with an aim of bringing in thousands of PLO guerrillas outside the camp in stages."[215] The PLO "police force" is one of the few police forces in the world where having served time in prison for previous terrorist activity will help get a new applicant hired![216] For years Arafat's power to bring death and destruction throughout the world has been far greater than was immediately apparent and that power is now increasing enormously.

Arafat not only has many friends in high political positions and in the press, but he has great influence among the world's terrorist organizations. Most of them are his former students who came from all over the world to learn from the master terrorist. He has trained most of the major terrorist organizations on earth including the German Red Army Faction (Baader-Meinhof Gang), the Japanese Red Army, the Irish Republican Army, Italy's Red Brigades, the Turkish Liberation Army, the Armenian Secret Army for the Liberation of Armenia (ASALA), France's Direct Action, and a host of Latin American terrorists, including representatives from Colombia, El Salvador, and Nicaragua.[217] Even Sandinista Interior Minister, Tomás Borge, spent a short time in a PLO training camp.[218] Such connections give Arafat a powerful influence in the world of terrorism throughout the globe because many of the terrorists are his former pupils. He is, indeed, a *very* powerful man!

* 28. His Power Is Not His Own

"...but not by his own power" (Dan. 8:24b).

The power that Yasser Arafat possesses today has come from a variety of sources, including the Islamic nations, communist nations, the Western news media, and the direct help of the United Nations. Ironically, a great measure of his power, and one reason he has had so much success for decades, comes from Israel itself. Israel's unwillingness to attack civilian centers has provided Arafat with a very effective shield for himself and his men. He hides behind civilians. That is why he has frequently chosen hospitals and public buildings to house his terrorists and to store his weapons.

Obviously, the true source of Arafat's power is Satan himself. He sold his soul to Satan in order to take God's land from God's people. In an interview with the Lebanese newspaper *Al-Sayyad* in 1969, Arafat exposed his willingness to make a deal with Satan. He declared, "I want that homeland even if the devil is the one to liberate it for me."[219] Apparently, he is getting his wish and has received power that does not come from himself or from any other human being.

Daniel's declaration regarding the little horn's source of power almost certainly refers to an earthly, literal source as well as to his spiritual source. We have already seen that, from the beginning of his rise to influence, Arafat depended on others in every way. First, the Syrians gave him the military and financial aid he needed to get recruits. Then, the Arab world supported him in similar ways. His power came from others. Yet, the mystery of iniquity that made Arafat who he is today has roots that run far deeper than mere Islamic political soil. The international community has helped create this monster.

The United Nations Became a Source of Power for Arafat

We need not resort to obscure, insignificant examples to demonstrate the wickedness that has been openly manifested against Israel by the world's nations in giving Arafat the power he has. The help that the United Nations has given to Arafat and the PLO is a glaring example. In May 1950, the United Nations Relief and Works Agency (UNRWA) was established for the sole purpose of caring for Palestinian refugees (*not* other refugees in the world).[220] As funds came in, the Palestinian refugee camps took on a very rudimentary order, and schools were formed by UNRWA. Even before the PLO had arrived on the world scene, UNRWA "taught hatred of the United States as well as of Israel and Jews in general."[221] From 1968, these schools were controlled by the PLO with continued UN financial support. In the school at Siblin, near Sidon, one room was reserved for Yasser Arafat, and his portrait hung on the wall above a swastika.[222]

Article 10 of the PLO Charter explains, "Fedayeen action forms the **nucleus** of the popular Palestinian war of liberation" (emphasis mine). The word "fedayeen" comes from an Arabic word that refers to fighters that are willing to give their lives for the cause. Even before he founded his Fatah terrorist group, or had gained control of the PLO, Arafat emphasized to his gunmen that every one of them were fedayeen and must be willing to die. No wonder there are so many suicide bombers—this is the **nucleus** of their method of fighting according to Article 10! One may ask, But what young person would be willing to join such a fanatical gang? At one time, the answer was, Anyone who wanted to graduate from a UNRWA school![223] It was a requirement to graduate that every student had to join one of the PLO's fedayeen groups, yet the nations of the world continued to pour in money to educate the future PLO gunmen!

Today, Arafat no longer needs this help from the UN because the Palestinian populace has now been "trained." They know better than to reject the "privilege" of fighting for their homeland as a fedayeen under Arafat! Thanks to the help of the UN and others, Arafat now has enough gunmen to "convince" the Palestinian youth that it is a good idea to give their lives to Arafat's cause. Later, we will see that Arafat not only makes war with the "chosen ones" (Israel) but also with the Palestinian Arabs themselves. Not all of them are as excited about Arafat's dream as he is, but a little "persuasion" usually convinces them that being a fedayeen is better than being tortured!

Arafat Has No Real Military or Political Power of His Own

There are at least two other ways in which Arafat has never had any power of his own—militarily and politically. The foundation of real **military** power is measured by the size of a leader's army and whether or not it can win battles. Arafat has never won a battle. How could he have? He has never had a real army or military power of his own. By constantly killing or injuring children and adults alike, he has simply "worn out the holy people," as Daniel said the little horn would do.

The foundation of real **political** power in today's world depends on the politician's ability to garner votes through popular support. History teaches that *usually* even a ruthless dictator does not die of old age unless he enjoys a good measure of *genuine* popular support. Arafat does not have this power base. Some may point to his recent landslide victory in the Palestinian elections on January 20, 1996, as proof of his power base. Historically, the elections in communist countries produced overwhelming landslides also, but no one took them seriously.

The First "Democratic" Palestinian Election

The Palestinian election was a sham, put on for international consumption and validated by the international community who sent important people, like the former president of the US, Jimmy Carter, who supposedly guarded against fraud. Consider what really happened. The unbiased observers "did not even bother 'observing' the two procedures in the voting process most susceptible to irregularities: They failed to ensure that the ballot boxes be transported under guard, and that the counting of the ballots be supervised... So much for the credibility of the international community."[224] The result was that not only did ballot boxes disappear—for example, 40 in Hebron alone—but there were more votes counted than the number of registered voters. As the final votes were being counted, those who were declared winners at first suddenly lost their majority and were later declared losers.

What Arafat did even before election day to ensure himself victory demonstrated just how uncertain he was himself of winning in fair elections. Candidates who had a strong showing in the primaries were removed from the ballot by none other than Mr. Yasser Arafat himself.[225] Also, the local press was intimidated constantly before the elections through Arafat's normal methods of operation, and he ran for president against a "nonentity" whose candidacy Arafat himself had arranged.[226] The only wonder is that eleven percent of the people would have actually dared to vote for the other almost unknown candidate with Arafat's police standing by every polling station physically helping the voters cast their ballots! The picture on the front page of *The Jerusalem Post* for January 21, 1996 (the day after the election), was of a Palestinian policeman and a Palestinian woman with her child. The policeman was not only standing beside the polling station, but he was helping a Palestinian woman put her ballot into the box. I cannot imagine her having voted for someone other than Arafat with so much "help" on hand!

After the dust had settled, even the Palestinian Domestic Monitoring Committee (PDMC), made up of the Palestinians themselves, called for new elections, admitting that "the voters were assisted by... agents of the candidates who... did not 'respect the wishes' of the voters they were helping!"[227] But there is no cause for concern. New elections were, in fact, held in certain selected areas on January 31, 1996.[228] We can all rest assured that everything was done in strict adherence to proper voting procedures—especially since the international community could not interfere this time, having long since returned home! Most surely the second voting was done with the purest of motives—to correct the worst of the anomalies; certainly not to change the final results even further! The world will almost certainly never know what really happened in those new elections. Just how far will the international community let this man go without raising the slightest objection, all the while, pouring billions of dollars of aid into his coffers?

In spite of the rampant election fraud, the principal complaint about the whole procedure came from Jimmy Carter and was leveled against Israel, not the Palestinians. He complained that Israel had an "intimidating police presence" *near* the Jerusalem polling stations![229] Apparently, it was "intimidating" to have any other observers around who would see, first hand, the sham that the international community happily validated by means of their presence and assurances to the world that everything had been done in order. It did not seem to bother Carter that Arafat had *his* police *at* the polling stations and not just near—helping the voters decide! Nor does it seem to trouble the international community that Arafat is the "sole representative of the Palestinian people" today because he has terrorized them into submitting to his demands and wishes, and no one else has ever been allowed to challenge him. Most Palestinians feel compelled to collaborate with him once they have carefully considered their options!

Why Arafat Has World Influence Through the News Media

A great degree of Arafat's influence and power with the international news media has been obtained in the same way he has become "popular" with the Palestinian people. His influence is not because he is a powerful politician, and certainly not because he is likable. The media has often presented Arafat's version of events because he is a brutal terrorist who strikes fear into the hearts of the news correspondents themselves. So much has been written on this subject that the facts can hardly be ignored. A senior Palestinian journalist from Ramallah in the West Bank wrote about what the Palestinian press can expect under Palestinian rule. He warned, "Every journalist who wishes to interview a senior Palestinian official must be equipped with the following items: a casket, a burial plot for himself and his family, and a will prepared well in advance."[230] This would be humorous if it were not true. Unfortunately, it is so true that, because of Arafat's intimidation of Palestinian journalists, they wrote very little or nothing concerning the recent Palestinian election. One Arab editor said that he did not cover the election at all "because it was the only way to be sure not to be arrested."[231]

It is understandable how Arafat could wield influence over the Palestinian media, but his successes in controlling the Western news media as well have been both astounding and sickening. When we consider the next aspect of the little horn that Daniel gives us, we will look at Arafat's reign of terror for almost seven years throughout Lebanon. It was beyond human comprehension, yet what Arafat and the PLO were doing to an entire nation went almost totally unreported by any news media in the world even though most of them knew about it. Why? To begin with, all visas to enter Lebanon had to be approved by the PLO.[232] They had literally taken control of the country. They screened the newsmen who sought to enter Lebanon. Once a correspondent arrived, the rules of the game were explained to them. The rules were really quite simple under Mr. Arafat's "democracy"—report only what Yasser wants or be tortured and killed.[233] In fact, at least seven Western journalists were murdered during this period because they reported things that displeased him.[234] Of course, the PLO, being the patient organization that it is, usually gave an uncooperative journalist a "warning" before taking action. On a number of occasions these warnings were delivered to their doorsteps—"human limbs in plastic containers with warnings that unless they toed the mark editorially, they, too, would 'wind up wrapped in plastic.' "[235]

One of Beirut's news editors, Salim El-Lawzi, refused to obey orders. He was the owner of the independent Lebanese Arabic weekly, *El Hawadess*.[236] After repeated warnings, the building that housed his newspaper was destroyed by a bomb. He then moved his paper to London and continued to print his anti-PLO news. During a visit to Lebanon for his mother's funeral,[237] his car was stopped as he was on his way to the airport for his return trip to London. He was taken to a PLO torture chamber. "The fingers of his hands were cut off joint by joint. He was subsequently dismembered and his remains turned up scattered about the village. Horrifying photographs of El-Lawzi's mutilated body spread terror throughout the capital's journalistic colony."[238]

Ze'ev Chafets, the director of Israel's government press office writes, "I was in close contact with many of the foreign correspondents in the Middle East. Some of them who visited Jerusalem... admitted that there were now subjects that they would not report."[239] He concludes, "But at one time or another over a period of some seven years, Reuters, *Time*, *Newsweek*, *The New York Times*, *The Washington Post*, CBS, ABC, the Associated Press—to name only some—played an active part in hiding from the public many of the facts about what was happening in Lebanon in general and, in particular, the way in which their newsmen were being subjected to intimidation and violence there."[240]

Freelance journalist Kenneth R. Timmerman, was held in a PLO underground prison for 24 days during Israel's siege on the PLO in Lebanon.[241] He states, "Terror, intimidation, and the law of silence: these are the basic tools used by the Palestine Liberation Organization to manipulate the international press. Most of the sins committed by Western newsmen under PLO constraint were sins of omission [against Israel]: showing bombed buildings but not the arms stockpiled in their basements; describing bombed hospitals but not the PLO fighters whose bases of operation were inside; and so forth. The list is infinite, [and] the effect unmistakable: the reversal of international opinion on the moral equation of the Middle East conflict."[242]

But alas, Yasser Arafat is a new man today! After all, he has received the Nobel Peace Prize, and no longer threatens newsmen. The Prophet Jeremiah asks, "Can a leopard change his spots?" (Jer. 13:23) The answer is an obvious no, and little innocent "Rahman" has not changed either. On December 25, 1995, Maher Alameh, editor of the Jerusalem Arabic newspaper, *Al-Quds*, was arrested by the "Palestinian Preventive Security" agents.[243] He was taken from Jerusalem to Jericho to talk directly with Arafat, who was angry that the editor had not placed a story comparing him to the seventh century Arab conqueror, Omar, on the front page. The story that praised Arafat was placed on the inside since there was no room left for it on the front, since Arafat's photo and the election advertisements took up all the available space. The editor was finally released six days later.[244] This arrest was made in Jerusalem, a city that is theoretically not even under PLO jurisdiction. That was fortunate for Mr. Alameh, because otherwise it is doubtful that anyone would have heard from him again. In fact, Arafat himself said, "I released him only because Shimon Peres contacted me. He was going to be taken to the courts."[245] Anyone acquainted with Arafat's "courts" well understands this not-so-veiled message! After his release Mr. Alameh said, "Democracy is not something that you just talk about, it is also something you must practice. Palestinian society is not yet practicing democracy."[246] Reporters around the world understand that Mr. Arafat's very long arm reaches beyond the Palestinian lands. They know that the power he seems to have is not inherently his own, but must be exacted from others through threats, torture, and death. Most of them have elected to avoid Salim El-Lawzi's end if possible!

* 29. He Shall Destroy Fearfully

"He shall destroy fearfully" (Dan. 8:24c).

"Hundreds of motorists, halted in a traffic jam in Beirut, Lebanon, witnessed the execution of a man by the PLO. The captors and their victim stood on a piece of open ground at the side of the Avenue Sami al-Solh... Round his neck the PLO militiamen tied sticks of explosives... The victim stood still, 'with strange quietness and dignity,' as one witness said, while the fedayeen prepared literally to blow his head off. They set a fuse, and ran back from the man, who continued to stand where he was, quite still, until the explosion came. Not only was he decapitated, but the rest of his body was blown to pieces."[247] This is what Daniel means when he says that the little horn "shall destroy fearfully." In the Hebrew, this word "fearfully" actually means to destroy in such a way that afterwards the victim cannot even be identified.[248]

A Lebanese surgeon, Dr. Khalil Torbey, with a degree from Harvard Medical School, was frequently called upon to attend to victims of PLO torture sessions.[249] He states, "I know of cases of people being thrown into acid tanks and reduced to unrecognizable masses of porous bone... I treated persons with arms severed by shelling, and men whose testicles had been crushed by torturers. I saw men—live men, mind you—dragged through the streets from fast-moving cars to which they were tied by their feet."[250]

Frederick El-Murr, a 54-year-old civil engineer and prominent Lebanese industrialist, tells of how Arafat and his men destroyed fearfully. He explains, "A favorite method of ridding themselves of political opponents was to tie the feet of the male victims to separate cars speeding off in opposite directions. One such incident was witnessed by my 17-year-old daughter, Nada."[251]

In 1970, after Arafat and his PLO were driven out of Jordan by King Hussein, the other Arab states were unwilling to open their doors to them. Finally, Lebanon made the fatal decision to provide them sanctuary.[252] By 1975, the PLO had succeeded in taking control of the Lebanese population "through coercion, intimidation, and force of arms."[253] For the next seven years, until Israel drove Arafat and his mobsters out of Lebanon in 1982, that nation experienced a reign of terror that few people in history have experienced. In the news media, it was called "Lebanon's civil war," but it was called the "Seven-Year Rape of Lebanon" by those who witnessed it.[254] Peter Grace describes Lebanon's sorrows in his book entitled *The Rape of Lebanon*.[255] By referring to the atrocities as a "civil war," the media was able effectively to hide the truth from the world— that the "war" was between Arafat's PLO and Lebanon.

On September 19, 1976, in his farewell radio address to the nation, the outgoing president of Lebanon, Suleiman Franjieh, told the nation what had gone wrong. He said, "They (the Palestinian Arabs) came to us as guests. We awarded them every possible hospitality but eventually they turned into savage wolves. They sought to kill their hosts and become masters of Lebanon. Indeed, our guests have already sabotaged Lebanon's executive, legislative and judicial authorities, as well as the nation's regular army..."[256] By 1976, the entire nation had become hostages to the PLO and Beirut had become "the most savage and uncivilized place on earth."[257]

The seven-year period of sorrow that came upon Lebanon has been referred to as "the carnival of death."[258] The description is heartrending and reveals the abomination that the PLO really is. Those who witnessed this abomination that caused desolation wrote, "... a certain illicit excitement in the freedom to kill with impunity filled the streets... The parasitic PLO 'state' in Lebanon was a subversives' honey pot. Here they had license to shoot and kill in an alien world, with no consequence to themselves... playboys and playgirls of terrorism... came to dress up, strut, blow up, gun down. The adventure required the suffering and dying of multitudes of helpless people. It was a carnival of death."[259]

The story of one of the adventures of Mr. Peace Prize's future Palestinian police is typical of what happened throughout Lebanon. One of the few survivors of the ordeal for the people living in Damour, Lebanon writes, "The attack took place from the mountain behind. It was an apocalypse. They were coming, thousands and thousands, shouting, 'Allahu Akbar! God is great! Let us attack them for the Arabs, let us offer a holocaust to Mohammed!' And they were slaughtering everyone in their path, men, women and children."[260] The description of what they did continues, "Whole families were killed in their homes. Many women were gang-raped, and few of them left alive afterwards... In a frenzy to destroy their enemies utterly, as if even the absolute limits of nature could not stop them, the invaders broke open tombs and flung the bones of the dead into the streets."[261] Tragically, Israel can be sure that the same thing will happen to many of their dead one day soon. Jeremiah's endtime message actually foretold of Israel's enemies going to the same depths of perversion and hatred against them—not in Lebanon but in Jerusalem itself. He prophesied, "At that time, saith the Lord, they shall bring out the bones... of the inhabitants of Jerusalem, out of their graves: and they shall spread them before the sun" (Jer. 8:1-2a).

In case there is any doubt about who had control of all these abominable acts in Lebanon, the story of Mansour Labaky, the priest of Damour, Lebanon, dispels those doubts. When the PLO entered his town, he called the Moslem sheik of the district and asked him what he could do. The sheik's words were most comforting. He informed him that he could do nothing to help since they were Palestinians. He concluded by saying, "They want to *harm* you."[262] Mansour Labaky then called Kamal Jumblatt—a government official that backed Arafat—pleading for help. Kamal's reply was, "I can do nothing for you, because it depends on Yasser Arafat." Kamal then gave him Arafat's phone number.[263] Arafat's aide, however, would not pass the call to his boss, but like the sheik, was very reassuring. His comforting words were: "Father, don't worry. We don't want to harm you. If we are destroying you it is for strategical reasons."[264] At least everyone knew who was in charge—Mr. Arafat, the future man of peace. His people did not want to *harm* anyone; they simply wanted to *destroy* them for strategical reasons!

It was very understandable that no one wanted to get involved in any way to help the PLO's victims lest they be branded a collaborator with the enemies. What the PLO did just for amusement thoroughly convinced the populace that doing anything actually to upset them was not a healthy idea. One of the more desirable ways to die at the hands of Arafat's henchmen was to have the hands and legs chained to four different vehicles. At the signal of an officer, the drivers would race away in four different directions, ripping the victim's body apart. The pieces were then dragged through the city behind the vehicles.[265] Every time this happened, an echo of the words of young Mr. Arafat must have been heard in many hearts—the words he spoke to his young terrorist companions when he killed innocent Rork Hamid— "Let this be a warning to you all!"

Dying behind four vehicles was definitely more desirable than facing another favorite method the PLO used to deal with their victims—the chain saw treatment. They "dismembered live human beings with chain saws. First the fingers, joint by joint; the toes; hands; feet; lower arm; lower leg; and so on. A witness to the barbarity is still tormented by the memory of the terrible screams of her 21-year-old friend. 'Why don't you kill me,' she screamed. 'We will, we will,' the animals replied."[266] The little horn indeed "destroys fearfully."

* 30. He Shall Destroy the Mighty and the Holy People

"[He] shall destroy the mighty and the holy people" (Dan. 8:24d KJV).

What were the final results of Yasser Arafat's rule over Lebanon? In addition to opening the door to Syrian control of the nation and the entrance of the Iranian terrorist organization, Hizbullah, there were at least two other major results. First, he left behind a nation in almost total desolation. Some estimates of the innocent civilians who died in the carnival of death are as high as 300,000.[267] Something just as tragic was the approximately 100,000 young girls who were pregnant because of the PLO—they had been raped by Arafat's future Palestinian police force.[268] Then there was the tragedy of the 50,000 orphans who were left behind by the innocent and noble Rahman who is presented as a hero to the schoolchildren of the US![269]

When Israel finally went into Lebanon to remove the PLO, they were welcomed even by the Moslem population as the saviors of the nation. On March 2, 1983, Robert Fisk described what he saw during Israel's invasion in *The Times*. He writes, "I witnessed the welcoming of the Israelis to come and drive the PLO and Syria out of Lebanon... Citizens of Marja'yun told me they had stood together cheering when the Israelis bombed Beaufort to 'soften up' the target before the infantry took it."[270] After the Israeli invasion, Walid Azzi, a 27-year-old Lebanese man, said, "The Israelis are our friends, and I hope they stay some time with us."[271]

Of course, the news media turned the whole story around and made Israel look like the villain. On June 20, 1982, *The New York Times* published a full-page ad with statistics from the International Red Cross entitled "Death and Devastation."[272] The ad accused Israel of attacking Lebanon and of causing there to be "40,000 killed or wounded" and "700,000 homeless." Where did the Red Cross get their numbers? From the PLO, of course![273] After all, the PLO should have been an unbiased source—they had no reason to lie about how Lebanon ended up in such utter destruction! Or did they? By falsely blaming Israel's short military intervention in Lebanon for so much carnage and destruction, they successfully enraged the international community against Israel. At the same time, the grossly inflated statistics they provided helped to reduce the enormous number of dead for which they would be held responsible. After reading the Red Cross report we can be sure that many were much less interested in hearing about what had been happening during the previous seven years of PLO terror. Besides, the news media had successfully convinced much of the world that those hundreds of thousands of deaths were caused by Lebanon's "civil war." The tactic was to make Israel look like a foreign adversary who was guilty of unprovoked military intervention in a neighboring country and that they had caused untold suffering. After all, "civil wars" are internal affairs of a nation and, generally, no one is condemned by other nations for the tragedy, so the reputation of the PLO escaped unscathed.

There was another major result of Arafat's rule over Lebanon. He obtained valuable experience on how to govern a democracy! The reader might think that I am being sarcastic or funny. The truth is, I am only quoting Mr. Arafat. It is commonly believed that he has never had any experience in governing. During a press conference, he was reminded of this and asked how he planned to govern Palestine. He assured thos present that he had received twelve years of experience governing Leba-non.[274] Before assuming power over Gaza, "Arafat boasted that the PLO could run it expertly. 'We acquired our experience in Lebanon,' he said."[275] In other words, Lebanon was the training ground, and he plans to govern Palestine just as he governed Lebanon. At least he is being truth-ful. Woe to the Arabs who are already under his rule, and woe to the Jews when they are finally "given into his hand" for three and a half years! (Dan. 7:25) No wonder an Arab woman from Gaza, said, "God should chop off our hands which threw stones at the Jews. We brought this disaster on ourselves. Now there is no law and no justice."[276]

It is too bad that the world still does not care about how Arafat governed Lebanon. Sadder still is what the Palestinians and Israelis face once his police state is *fully* established in the holy land! The de-struction that Arafat has brought on Israel, the "mighty" and "holy" people, for the last 50 years is nothing compared to what is soon to come. The PLO-induced Israeli death toll is still counted in the hun-dreds, but it will soon be counted in the thousands. Arafat has been destroying the mighty and the holy people for over half a century, but he has hardly begun! The day that Jeremiah foresaw—"the time of Ja-cob's troubles"—is at the door (Jer. 30:7). Israel has never known de-struction like that which the little horn and Islam will soon bring upon the nation. Jesus and the prophets declared this to be so. (See Daniel 12:1 and Matthew 24:16,21.)

* 31. Because of His Cunning He Will Cause Deceit to Prosper

"Through his cunning he shall cause deceit to prosper under his rule" (Dan. 8:25a).

When Yihye Ayyash, known as "The Engineer" who made bombs for terrorism, was killed by a bomb that had been placed in his cellular phone, a political cartoon of Arafat and two of his cohorts appeared in *The Jerusalem Post.*[277] (Seen on previous page.)

This is a graphic demonstration of a characteristic found in the little horn that Daniel saw in his vision. The cartoonist was in no way presenting an exaggerated viewpoint of reality. Arafat is a very cunning man, and through his cunning he causes deceit to prosper in both the Arab world and the Western world. Did Arafat do anything similar to what this cartoon depicts? Consider how he reacted to Israel's success in exterminating Ayyash—a man who was planning, with the PLO's knowledge, further terrorism against Israel.

Arafat declared that Israel had violated the Oslo peace accord by coming into Gaza and killing Ayyash. How cunning! Few Palestinians know what the Oslo accord says and, like Arafat, they couldn't care less what it says! Remember, Arafat called it a "despicable truce." Far from violating the Oslo accord, Israel has the right to enter the autonomous areas in hot pursuit of criminals, and Arafat has the obligation to extradite terrorists.[278] Therefore, it was, in reality, Arafat who had violated the peace accord since Rabin had personally requested that Ayyash be extradited.[279] Arafat's cunning causes deceit to prosper among the Arabs.

To the international community, Arafat declares that the Hamas terrorists operating within the PLO autonomous areas are out of control and that he is unable to stop their terrorism against Israel. In fact, he is so cunning that when Hamas attacks Israel, the world community even feels sorry for Arafat because of how much "damage" Hamas is doing to him and his wonderful peace initiative! If Hamas is such a danger to him, why does he repeatedly demand that Israel release the top leader of Hamas, Sheik Ahmed Yassin, whom he calls his "brother," along with the thousands of other Hamas terrorists who are still in Israeli jails at this writing?[280] This, along with many similar declarations and actions, reveals the true nature of his relationship with Hamas. Yet the horrendous deception regarding Hamas prospers in the international community—the world believes that Hamas is really his enemy. This allows Hamas to attack Israel while the world looks the other way and even feels sorry for Mr. Arafat! To see this hypocrisy, consider a few revealing circumstances in which we find this cunning fox before and after Ayyash's funeral.

Before Ayyash's funeral, Arafat went to the home of Dr. Mahmoud Zahar, a senior Hamas leader, and offered condolences.[281] In his anguish, Zahar let the truth slip out. He lamented to Arafat, "Hamas has paid with martyr after martyr for the liberation of Palestine. I remind you of your remark that we are all potential martyrs."[282] Arafat sat on the couch in Zahar's living room, held Zahar's hand, but said nothing.[283]

After Ayyash's funeral, Arafat held a rally of thousands of Palestinians. In his speech he declared, "We have made the peace of the brave. We are committed to it. We ask the other side not to violate this peace, to enter Palestinian territory in Gaza and kill and assassinate the struggler, the martyr, Yihye Ayyash."[284] He also called for "iron-clad national unity between Fatah [PLO terrorists] and Hamas."[285] Ayyash was a member of Hamas![286] If Arafat believes what he tells the world—that Hamas are the bad guys—why would he mourn one of their deaths and afterward have a huge rally to speak about Israel's violation of the peace accord? Why would he "arrange a 21-gun salute for Ayyash"?[287] Why would he "cite the 1974 plan to destroy Israel in phases in every speech"?[288] Why would he "publicly lionize suicide bombers and other terrorists" continually?[289] Furthermore, sitting in the living room of a principal leader of Hamas and holding his hand to comfort him for the loss of one of his prime terrorists is not the reaction of an **active peacemaker** who is doing everything he can to thwart rebellious saboteurs. Rather, this is the reaction of an **active terrorist** who is taking full advantage of the deception that has prospered through his cunning! Is it any wonder that Jeremiah's endtime message ends with a great lamentation for the condition of Jerusalem, saying that he saw it to be "desolate, with foxes walking about on it"? (Lam. 5:18)

If Arafat is not controlling Hamas, then who is? Many believe that Arafat has simply changed his tactics so that Hamas is the terrorist arm and the PLO is the peace-making, political arm of his war on Israel.[290] This suspicion has been strengthened since his much publicized meetings with the Hamas leadership in Egypt during the third week of December 1995. There, he and Hamas decided that terrorist attacks on Israel would be restrained until after the full Israeli withdrawal from the territories that Israel is handing over to the PLO.[291]

Amazingly enough, even before the PLO-Hamas agreement was reached in December 1995, the last quarter of 1995 saw very little terrorist activity in Israel.[292] The almost total lack of terrorist attacks during those three months is proof that Hamas does not operate independently of Arafat's wishes. Does the Western news media remember that they have been trumpeting the theories that Hamas terrorists are trying to sabotage the peace agreement and that Arafat cannot control them? If either of those theories is correct, why did Hamas suspend its terrorism during the last months of 1995 while Israel was withdrawing from the West Bank? That period provided Hamas with an unbelievable opportunity to sabotage the peace accord. Israel almost certainly would have discontinued its withdrawal from one city after another during the last months of 1995 if Hamas had launched just a few attacks during that period. Either Hamas is not trying to sabotage the plan, or it is not operating without PLO approval—both are probably true. The little horn is so cunning that deceit continues to prosper! A very logical observation was made recently in *The Jerusalem Post* that further proves that Hamas is not trying to end the peace process. The *Post* commented, "Had [Hamas] really wanted to end the [peace] process, they would have blown themselves up near Arafat and his entourage, not in downtown Tel Aviv."[293]

Something else should be mentioned regarding Arafat's cunning that causes deceit to prosper. In the Hebrew "deceit" can also be translated as "treachery."[294] Arafat is not only a very cunning deceiver, but he's also a cunning terrorist that has caused treachery to prosper. His terroristic cunning has allowed him to set many records in the field of terrorism, many of which still stand. He has set records for "the largest hijacking (four aircraft in a single operation); the largest number of hostages held at one time (300 passengers); the largest number of victims killed or wounded by a single booby-trap bomb (15 killed, 87 wounded); the largest number of casualties in a terrorist raid (38 killed, 70 wounded); the largest number of people shot at an airport (31 people); the largest ransoms ($5 million paid by Lufthansa; $15 million ransom demanded but not paid due to armed intervention by special forces in Mogadishu); and the greatest variety of targets (two-thirds of which were against countries other than Israel) which include 40 civilian aircraft, five passenger ships, 30 embassies or diplomatic missions, and about the same number of economic targets, including fuel depots and factories."[295]

* 32. He Will Consider Himself Superior

"...he will consider himself superior" (Dan. 8:25b NIV).

It is understandable why Yasser Arafat considers himself superior to others. Remember that, beginning at the age of seven, his Uncle Yusuf drilled into him that he was a supernatural child on whose mind the Koran had been imprinted before birth. This would tend to make any child feel somewhat superior to their companions in an Islamic society! One of the best-known biographers of Arafat's life is Thomas Kiernan. In his secular biography, he was definitely not attempting to link Arafat to Daniel's little horn or to anything spiritual, yet he wrote that by the age of ten his Uncle Yusuf "had already instilled in [Rahman] a strong sense of superiority."[296] His uncle was convinced that young Rahman had a very special call in the world of Islam. Whether Yasser Arafat is Daniel's little horn or not, it turns out that Yusuf was right; the more so since a "call" for the family of Rahman was generally viewed as a call to kill Jews. The family dedicated themselves to this "call" for years, but Rahman excelled them all.

Concerning Arafat's later life, Kiernan writes, "He looked especially on members of his family with contempt, but he was also abrupt and superior to those who were close to him."[297] One of his fellow University students recalls, "In my opinion, winning the presidency of the PSF [Palestine Students' Federation] turned Yasir into a power-maniac. Just the way he behaved after his election—he suddenly began to thrive on his position... He became pretentious. He used to say that he could no longer have close friends because there might be times when he had to discipline or dismiss or even punish someone, and if he was a friend..."

Young Mr. Arafat repeatedly demonstrated that he considered himself so superior, that to his way of thinking, even the lives of those closest to him were of very little worth. A willingness to destroy someone else's life for no greater purpose than to give an object lesson has always been standard practice for this great teacher of the ignorant. One example of this abominable trait was seen in how Arafat treated a young man whose parents had sent him out of Palestine to live with relatives in Cairo during Israel's War of Independence in 1948. He became one of Yasser's closest friends. The boy's parents remained behind in Palestine and ended up living under the new Israeli government. When Yasser Arafat discovered this, he ordered the boy to denounce his parents publicly for remaining in Israel. Although the boy worshipped Yasser, he could not bring himself to denounce his parents. The superior wisdom of Yasser determined that the boy had to be disciplined. He declared, "My Arab brother cannot bring himself to be a true *feday*, so he must be taught." He then ordered one of the other members of the PSL, a totally ruthless boy that the group called The Scimitar, to castrate the boy. The day following this operation the boy was found dead. He had apparently killed himself.[298] The "superior one" had taught him and all the rest of his unworthy, inferior students a lesson.

Arafat's superiority complex is also manifested in his treatment of journalists and reporters. On a recent occasion, an Arab journalist asked him if he was concerned about Hamas and others opposing the peace process. Arafat's reaction was typical. He shouted, "Who are you anyway? How dare you ask me such a question. Don't you know who I am? I am Yasser Arafat, the leader of the mighty Palestinian people. You apparently don't belong to this people. Our mighty people can destroy conspiracies by dwarfs like you!"[299] At least, in his great pride, he revealed how patently easy he considers controlling Hamas to be if the world would only listen!

A Western journalist, who interviews Arafat frequently, said that he has learned the technique for interviewing him. He explains, "You cannot provoke this man. You have to remind him constantly that he is the greatest leader in the world and that the world would have been destroyed long ago if not for him. He expects questions like, 'Mister President of the State of Palestine: As a great and mighty man, as the undisputed leader of a nation no less mighty, as a man beloved by his people and the world, a man who has neither competitor nor substitute, as a distinguished president, generous and democratic, as a veteran and honored freedom fighter, what is your response, Mister President, to...' "[300] In light of this journalist's method of interviewing Arafat, could we say that even the world's news correspondents recognize that Arafat fulfills Daniel's description of the little horn by being one who considers himself superior?

Arafat's unwritten demand that everyone grovel and bow before him in honor, recognizing his superiority is even respected by the international community, amazingly enough. The Geneva based International Commission of Jurists, wrote him a letter before the January 20, 1996, Palestinian elections, requesting that he consider postponing them to "switch to a more democratic election process." The Commission expressed "concern whether the proposed Palestinian electoral code conforms with democratic and human rights values." They wrote, "In the meantime allow us, your excellency, to request that the Palestinian National Authority not proceed with elections until proper preparations are made."[301] Arafat surely condescended to read the letter once he realized that the Commission was calling him by a title used for great leaders—"your excellency." (How ironic that former president of the US, Jimmy Carter, went along with Arafat's farcical adherence to a "democratic process" during the Palestinian election, in spite of the fact that this recognized international body knew it was a sham from the outset!)

* 33. Through Peace He Destroys Many

"...by peace [the little horn] shall destroy many" (Dan. 8:25c KJV).

"**Peace** for us means the **destruction** of Israel."[302] These are the words of Yasser Arafat. They were not invented by this author to prove that Arafat is the little horn! The Apostle Paul reveals that when Israel declares, "Peace and safety," then "sudden destruction will come upon them" (I Thess. 5:3). This word "safety" in the Greek can also be translated as "security from enemies"[303]—Israel's longing. This is also what the Hebrew word translated as "peace" means in this detail that Daniel gives us about the little horn. In fact, other English versions translate it as "security" or "secure." For example: "In their **security** shall he destroy many" (Dan. 8:25c ASV), and "when they feel **secure**, he will destroy many" (NIV). Although the precise meaning of this Hebrew word is not "peace," yet the translators of the King James Version probably provided the best possible translation by rendering it "peace." The goal in translation is to convey the *concept* and not simply give a *literal* translation, which often would make no sense. The *literal* meaning of this word is "quietness,"[304] but my Hebrew-reading friends confirmed the accuracy of the *concept* that the King James gives us by translating it as "peace." They assured me that this word refers to the atmosphere and attitude that prevails as a result of making peace or a peace treaty. Quietness and tranquillity are what Rabin and Peres thought had come to Israel through their peace agreement. Rabin promised that now we will have "a time without worries, nights without anxiety, the end of death." Peres added: "The agreement has inaugurated a new, violence-free era."[305]

If we combine Daniel's revelation with Paul's revelation, we discover *how* this "destruction" referred to by Paul will come upon Israel at the precise time they are seeking peace and security. It will come through the little horn. The little horn uses the "security" of a fictitious peace as an occasion to destroy many. Yasser Arafat has already begun to fulfill this prophetic word with precision. As mentioned previously, immediately after he had signed the peace accord, twice as many Israelis began dying as a result of terrorist attacks than at any other time in the nation's modern history.[306] Arafat's plan calls for the rate of Jewish murders to increase from dozens to thousands until the Jews are exterminated!

There is one thing that Israel will never be able to say—that the nation was never warned. They have been warned repeatedly; not only by Daniel, Jeremiah, and other biblical prophets, but by Arafat himself! He has never stopped declaring in unmistakable terms what his plans are for the Jewish state—total destruction—and that these plans remain unchanged in spite of the new atmosphere of "peace and security." Can Israel ever say they did not know that Arafat considered his peace accord with them as nothing more than the peace of Mohammed—"a despicable truce"—that can and will be broken at his earliest convenience?

Can Israel pretend they never heard what Arafat said in the interview he gave live on Jordanian TV, transmitted from the US on the very day he first signed a peace agreement with Israel? As we already mentioned, he explained, "We take any and every territory that we can of Palestine, and establish a sovereignty there, and we use it as a springboard to take more." Arafat continues to shout before Moslem audiences, "With blood and spirit we shall redeem thee, O Palestine." Everyone knows that his definition of "Palestine" includes the entire Jewish state. The former Israeli government even made excuses for him, saying that he was just playing to the crowd, but one day, when thousands of Israelis are dying, they will have to admit that his game was deadly serious and that he was also speaking truth that they were unwilling to hear! Then, even the unbelieving Israeli politicians will understand why Daniel said that "by peace [the little horn] shall destroy many."

* 34. He Shall Stand Up Against the Prime Minister

"...[he will] take his stand against the Prince of princes" (Dan. 8:25d).

The word "prince" here is the same word we discussed in point 18 above, and can mean "prince, captain, chief, general, or minister." Again, the capital "P" is strictly the translator's interpretation. The phrase "prince of princes" can be translated as "minister of ministers," and is almost certainly referring to the top **political** leader of the nation, or the Prime Minister, whereas the "prince of the army" refers to the top **military** leader of the nation.

Arafat does not hesitate to stand up against Israel's Prime Minister and to challenge him and the whole nation. In a speech given in the city of Tulkarm, the Palestinian Authority secretary, Taib Abd Alrahum, said, "We chose the way of peace in order to achieve our aims" (of taking Jerusalem and then all the holy land).[307] Arafat brought clarification to this statement by saying, "But if the Israelis think we have no alternative, I swear by Allah they are wrong."[308] For Arafat, choosing the way of peace is a viable option (with an honorable precedent set by Mohammed himself) so long as he gets what he wants from Israel's Prime Minister every time he stands up to him. Arafat not only stood up to Rabin and won, but ultimately made Rabin pay an enormous price. Later in Daniel, we will see that Rabin's so-called "peace initiative" cost him his life.

Arafat has been standing up against the Prime Minister of Israel in the most amazing and provocative ways, and he seemingly wins every confrontation. Consider a few examples: 1) In Israel's peace agreement with him, the land involved in the negotiations was divided into three categories labeled "A, B, and C areas." As part of the initial agreement, Israel gave the "A areas" to the PLO. However, Arafat has been creeping into the "B areas" even though they have not yet been given. This has been an open violation of the accord.[309] **The Prime Minister has had two choices**—either oppose it and face a confrontation with Arafat, or yield and avoid the conflict. So far, Israel's Prime Minister has yielded. 2) Arafat was not supposed to establish Palestinian government offices in Jerusalem, but he did so anyway.[310] **The Prime Minister had the same two choices**, and again, he chose to yield. 3) In the peace accord, Arafat promised to change the PLO Charter calling for the destruction of Israel. As the deadlines for it to be changed came and went, Israel kept giving him more time as the Prime Minister yielded once and again. More than two years after signing the initial peace agreement, the Charter had not yet been changed, and Arafat even declared publicly that he would not change it.[311] Finally, Israel established one more deadline—two months after the Palestinian elections which were held on January 20, 1996. That deadline came and went also and meant no more to Arafat than the other deadlines. In this last case, **the Prime Minister actually had *three* choices**—either give him another deadline, oppose him and face a confrontation, or stop asking that the Charter be changed. As mentioned previously, it was the pressure of risking the loss of US aid that finally caused Arafat to convene a meeting to discuss the issue of possibly writing a new Charter. If the Prophet Daniel's little horn is, in fact, Yasser Arafat, we can fully expect him to continue standing up to Israel's Prime Minister. This could also happen under a Likud government, especially if Arafat were to apply pressure through increased terrorism.

35. He Will Be Destroyed Supernaturally

"Yet he will be destroyed, but not by human power" (Dan. 8:25e NIV).

This promise concerning the little horn brings a ray of hope in the midst of darkness for the people of God, and it is a sure hope that will not fail. Israel need not question the final outcome. The end of the little horn is coming and God Himself will bring it about! This could refer to something that men will relegate to an "act of nature." Whatever men call it, and however it comes, his end will be the result of divine intervention, probably not by a car or airplane accident nor because of a bullet or a bomb. These methods seem to be too closely related to and controlled by "human power." No wonder he has walked away from so many brushes with death, including an airplane crash. For many types of crimes, God has ordained that men bring vengeance on the criminal and bring justice to those offended. (See Romans 13:1-4.) However, after this wicked man completes everything that he will ultimately do to God's people, and after having taken so many lives throughout the world, it appears that God has reserved His own vengeance for this man, and that no one else will be used to bring it. Surely the words of the Lord through Paul apply to this man: " 'Vengeance is Mine, I will repay,' says the Lord" (Rom. 12:19).

The Angel Continues to Interpret
Daniel's Vision With More Details

We go now to Daniel 10 and 11 to find that the angel of the Lord gives Daniel many more details about what the little horn will do in the Middle East during the last days. (Note that some believe that the "angel" who appears in Daniel 10:5-11 is the Lord Himself. That could be. However, please allow me to refer to him as an "angel" just in case this one who was "sent" to Daniel in Daniel 10:11 was still Gabriel who was sent to him in Daniel 8:16-17.)

The angel explains to Daniel, "Now I have come to make you understand what will happen to your people in the **latter days**, for **the vision** refers to many days yet to come" (Dan. 10:14). The angel's declaration here concerning the purpose of his visit is very similar to the purpose for which Gabriel visited Daniel in chapter 8. There he declares, "Understand, son of man, that **the vision** refers to the **time of the end.**" By comparing the interpretation of "the vision" that the angel now gives in Daniel 11 with the interpretation given in Daniel 8, we discover that the angel is interpreting the same vision in both places—the vision Daniel received in chapter 8. In Daniel 11, he is simply giving greater detail of what will happen to God's people, Israel, in the last days.

We observed that the angel made a huge leap forward in history during the interpretation he gave in Daniel 8, and he does the same in this expanded interpretation. That leap forward occurs between verses 20 and 21 of Daniel 11. There the angel begins to give further details of the little horn. Although he does not call him the "little horn" in Daniel 11, there are enough details given there to allow us to identify him positively as the same little horn described in Daniel 7 and 8. The little horn is the main character revealed in the last half of Daniel 11 between verses 21 and 45. He is introduced as a "vile person" in verse 21. This vile person is unmistakably linked to the little horn because he is the man who takes away the "continual" (translated as "daily sacrifice") just as the little horn does in Daniel 8.

In order to avoid cluttering the text here, I have provided a fuller explanation of the interpretation given in Daniel 11 in Appendix B. It has been provided for those who would like more biblical background and justification to be sure that the vile person of Daniel 11 is the little horn of Daniel 8. We continue now with the rest of the details Daniel gives about this wicked leader.

* 36. He Is a Vile Person

"And in his place shall arise a vile person" (Dan. 11:21a).

Most of the world still remembers Nicolae Ceausescu, the dictator of Romania from 1965 until December 1989. He is remembered mostly because of how he died—at the hands of angry Romanian people who killed both him and his wife for crimes against the state. For some time after his death, the reports of just how exceedingly wicked his reign of terror had been came oozing out of the cesspool he had created. We can only begin to imagine what the people were like who surrounded him and helped him in his perversity. Proverbs tells us, "If a ruler pays attention to lies, all his servants become wicked" (Prov. 29:12). Likewise, if a ruler is a vile criminal, that is the kind of people that surround him.

One of the people who was near to Ceausescu was Lt. Gen. Ion Mihai Pacepa. He acted as Ceausescu's personal advisor and was the chief of the Romanian foreign intelligence service[312]—a position in communist countries that is not generally associated with the nicest of people! Another was Gen. Constantin Munteanu. He was a Romanian "Department of Foreign Intelligence Service (DIE) General [who] was transferred to Beirut as a head of a group of advisors who were to teach the PLO how to run deception and influence operations in order to get recognized by the West."[313] Both these men knew Yasser Arafat well, because he was a close friend of Ceausescu, and Arafat visited him often in Romania. In his book, *Red Horizons*, Pacepa describes Ceausescu and Arafat as being like twin brothers who not only looked alike but who also thought and acted alike.[314] Ceausescu considered Arafat to be his best friend and called him his "clever fox."[315] Munteanu said of Arafat, "I've never before seen so much cleverness, blood, and filth all together in one man."[316] Remembering that Munteanu and Pacepa were themselves collaborators in one of the most vile governments on earth, imagine just how vile Arafat really is, when Pacepa himself would say of him, "I felt a compulsion to take a shower whenever I had been kissed by Arafat, or even just shaken his hand."[317] Just how vile would a person have to be to inspire such a reaction from the personal advisor to a man like Ceausescu? It would appear that few people in history have so totally fulfilled Daniel's description of the little horn as being a "vile person" like Yasser Arafat does.

* 37. He Does Not Receive the Honor of the Kingdom

"...to whom they will not give the honor of royalty" (Dan. 11:21b).

"...to whom they shall not give the honour of the kingdom"
(Dan. 11:21b KJV).

Obviously, no one looks on Yasser Arafat as one in whose veins royal blood flows. Therefore, no one gives him the honor of royalty. If this is the only significance to this observation of Daniel regarding the little horn, then we can rightfully assume that not only Arafat fulfills this, but just about everyone else on earth. It seems likely that there is something a little more substantial to this observation of Daniel. The Hebrew word translated as "kingdom" in the King James Version and as "royalty" in the New King James Version (as well as in other versions) appears 91 times in the Old Testament. Of those 91 times, the Kings James Version translates this word as either "kingdom, reign, realm, or empire" 78 times and 13 times as "royal" (almost exclusively in Esther), but never as "royalty."

If Daniel is revealing that the honor of the **kingdom** is not given to the little horn, then Yasser Arafat's life is an amazing fulfillment of this in ways possibly unheard of in history. In fact, this issue is presently at the forefront of Arafat's concerns and is one of the great frustrations of his life, and with good reason. His PLO has some degree of diplomatic relations (often ambassadorial) with all of the major countries of the world, including the US, where the opening of PLO offices in Washington, DC has been authorized.[318] In spite of the PLO's attack on the 1972 Olympic Games where they killed 11 Israeli athletes, the Olympic Games Commission decided to treat the PLO and the Palestinians in the holy land as a sovereign state. As such, they were invited to send athletes to the 1996 Olympic Games.[319] In addition, a Palestinian delegation is sent to the UN.[320] All these things bring great honor to Arafat, the PLO, and the "mighty Palestinian people." There is just one little problem—the State of Palestine does not even exist and never has! Israel has given parts of the holy land to Mr. Arafat and his "Palestinian Authority" over which he presides and which are called "autonomous areas." However, Israel has not given him the honor of the kingdom. They have not given him the honor of real statehood.

This is a great humiliation for the little horn! How often has the world been willing to deal with a people as though they were a nation when that nation does not even exist? It is understandable why Arafat will almost certainly declare soon, without Israel's consent, the independence of the "State of Palestine." Of course, Israel will have no moral obligation to respect the boundaries of that state, but the international community will very likely insist that it does. They will not countenance Israelis crossing the borders into Arafat's newly formed "sovereign state." Such actions, even when done for national security reasons, will surely stir up greater anger against Israel within the world community.

* 38. He Shall Come In Peaceably

"...he shall come in peaceably" (Dan. 11:21c).

Daniel has shown us that the little horn has no kingdom, no army, and no power of his own. A logical question would be, How does he ever amount to anything? And how is it then possible that he would ever pose a problem for God's people, Israel? The answer is that he comes in peaceably. "Peaceably" is the same word we discussed in point 33, where it is translated as "peace" (KJV) or "security" (RSV). Daniel is revealing that the little horn will come into his position in some way that is related to peace or the security that peace brings. He will not come in by war or by the force of arms. Has Yasser Arafat fulfilled this prophetic word?

The world knows that Mr. Arafat and his PLO were politically "on the ropes" just before September 1993.[321] Even the enormous financial backing for the PLO was beginning to dry up because Arafat had backed Saddam Hussein during the Gulf War.[322] Much of the international community saw him as the ringleader of the worst butchers on earth and the murderer of thousands of innocent children and adults worldwide. If he had set foot on US soil, he would have been imprisoned immediately for his multiple crimes against US citizens. How in the world did he not only avoid political oblivion, but end up coming into an incredible degree of recognition by the nations of the world as an international statesman,[323] a respectable national leader who should be permitted to establish diplomatic relations with the world, a companion of President Clinton at the White House, a "true friend" of Israel, Prime Minister Rabin's "peace partner,"[324] a "father" to Leah Rabin's children,[325] and a Nobel Peace Prize laureate?

This is surely a once-in-history phenomenon. Daniel tells us that when he saw this happening, along with the other aspects of his vision, it made an incredible impression on him. He writes, "And I, Daniel, fainted and was sick for days; afterward I arose and went about the king's business. I was astonished by the vision" (Dan. 8:27). Who wouldn't have been "sick for days" if, while living in the more sane days of Daniel, they had witnessed what we have actually seen happening in these last days? Arafat came into all this glory by making peace. He was transformed before the world's very eyes when he decided to take the peaceful approach. Before his death, Arafat's friend Ceausescu, the Romanian dictator, gave him counsel that he has obviously followed. He said, "How about pretending to break with terrorism? The West would love it... The West may even become addicted to you and your PLO."[326] Ceausescu must have understood the deception that fills the human heart, and how man will blindly run after a false peace because he rejects the Prince of Peace, the Lord Jesus Christ. Arafat took his counsel, and it has certainly brought a harvest beyond his wildest dreams!

* 39. He Shall Seize the Kingdom By Flatteries

"...[he shall] obtain the kingdom by flatteries" (Dan. 11:21d KJV).

Some translations render this as, "He shall seize the kingdom by intrigue" (NKJV). If we resort to the definition given by the *Strong's Hebrew Dictionary*, we get a good idea of the meaning of the Hebrew word used here—"flattery, slipperiness, fine promises, smoothness." Is this a description of Yasser Arafat? A better question might be, Does anyone on earth fulfill it as well as he?

Let's talk about Arafat's "flattery." If only a fraction of the hatred he has expressed toward Jews since his childhood is actually in his heart, how could his deep expression of appreciation for Yitzhak Rabin, the very leader of Israel, be anything more than flattery at its worst?[327] Remember that he imbibed the vision of his second cousin, the grand mufti Haj Amin al-Husseini, who rejoiced that the god of Islam had committed to his followers the task of finishing what Hitler only began—to murder *all* the Jews. He worked directly with and for the grand mufti to bring about the fulfillment of their common vision.[328] Even though that "vision" has been a controlling factor throughout his entire life, when he received the Nobel Peace Prize, Arafat flattered the Jews in order to turn many hearts of the world toward him. He declared, "[peace will allow] Arab consciousness a deep understanding [of] the European Jewish tragedy."[329] He also stated that the suffering of Jews had created a "tortured Jewish soul," and that "no one is capable of understanding torture more than the tortured."[330] How could he call the Holocaust a "tragedy" or commiserate with the suffering of the Jews when he believes that the will of his god is their total destruction? How could he engage in such blatant flattery when a great portion of the suffering that the Jews have endured for the past 50 years has been brought on by none other than Mr. Arafat himself? Is this flattery or is this flattery? Something far worse, is what he meant when he referred to giving the "Arab consciousness a deep understanding of the European Jewish tragedy." Through his "peace that brings destruction," Arafat's plan is to give the Arabs this "deep understanding" through a Jewish Holocaust in their own midst as he works to fulfill Haj Amin al-Husseini's vision of slaughtering the Jews—at the hands of the Arabs themselves! How else could making "peace" possibly give the Arab world a deep understanding of the Jewish tragedy in Europe? What is there about Mr. Arafat's "peace" that could suddenly cause Arab's to understand what the Jews suffered in Europe? True peace for Israel would tend to make the

Arab's even *less* conscious of what the Jews actually suffered 50 years ago! If we remember what Mr. Arafat said about his "peace" with Israel, we are suddenly able to understand his enigmatic saying here. He said, "Peace for us is the destruction of Israel."

What about "slipperiness"? The definition of this word is, "Not trustworthy; elusive or tricky."[331] For a graphic example of Arafat's slipperiness, please refer back to the political cartoon that accompanies point 31. Is he tricky and cunning? There must be some reason that Ceausescu liked to call him a fox.[332] Is Arafat untrustworthy? Need we go any further? As the joke I have often heard would explain, "Arafat is so untrustworthy that when you look up 'untrustworthy' in the dictionary, you find Arafat's picture next to it!"

Is Arafat guilty of making any "fine promises," or promises that he did not plan on keeping? What he did after promising to change the PLO Charter calling for the elimination of the State of Israel is one glaring example. In January 1995, Yasser Arafat and Nabil Shaath, the PLO's chief negotiator at the time, said that it was "impossible to change the Charter."[333] This declaration showed that, for him, it had been a "fine promise." Why did he, in April 1996, call a meeting of the PNC to supposedly change the Charter? When he risked the loss of $500 million in US aid, he called this meeting to give the appearance that the Charter was being changed. Even though nothing was changed, the world was satisfied by the fanfare, and the US aid was assured. Israel is the only one who loses when the little horn makes "fine promises" that he doesn't plan on keeping. The world fully expects and demands that Israel keep its promises regardless of what Arafat does. After all, who in this world would ever be so foolish as to expect the little horn to keep his?

Finally, we come to "smoothness." The story of how elderly Leon Klinghoffer was shot in the head by Arafat's men and then thrown overboard from the *Achille Lauro* in 1985 just won't die. The Klinghoffer family and their travel agent have been fighting a legal battle against the PLO ever since.[334] Arafat sent a message to the Klinghoffer children saying that he couldn't have possibly been responsible for the death of their father because his religion does not permit him to kill people! He then invited the two daughters to come and talk with him. Apparently, he wants to teach them more about his religion. Smooth?

40. An Overwhelming Army Is Swept Away Before Him

"Then an overwhelming army will be swept away before him" (Dan. 11:22 NIV).

In the Middle East, there is only one truly "overwhelming army," and that is the army of Israel. After the Arab nations have suffered four humiliating defeats in four major unsuccessful attempts to destroy the Jewish nation, they tend to agree with Daniel's military assessment! If the surrounding Arab nations did not continue believing this, they would attack Israel again almost immediately to reach their goal of bringing about its total and final demise. It would seem that over 250 million Arabs[335] pitted against 5 million Israelis should be sufficient to swing the balance of power in favor of the Arab nations. However, Israel has several "equalizers" in its arsenal that are so effective that the military balance still favors Israel.

Israel's first and most important "equalizer" is the God of Abraham who keeps intervening in man's affairs to fulfill His counsels and to frustrate the plans of the wicked. When the God of the universe fights against the god of Islam or any other god, the biggest job always comes after the battle—hauling away the spoils, like the 4,330 truckloads of arms that Israel found stashed in Lebanon during the Israeli invasion in 1982![336] This sounds like the events of the Old Testament are being relived. In those days, Israel often faced a lot of work in gathering the abundant spoils of war after their battles. We are told, "And when Jehoshaphat and his people came to take away the spoil of them, they found among them in abundance both riches with the dead bodies, and precious jewels, which they stripped off for themselves, more than they could carry away: and they were three days in gathering of the spoil, it was so much" (II Chr. 20:25).

Up until now the world has done its best to hinder Israel from taking the spoils of war. Israel's annihilation seemed certain in 1973 during the sudden and vicious attack of the Arab nations while all of Israel was celebrating its most solemn biblical holy day, Yom Kippur (the Day of Atonement). However, within a few days, Israel had not only recovered from the attack, but went on the offensive. Suddenly, to the world's surprise, they were a few kilometers from Cairo on the southern front, and on the northern front they were only a few kilometers from Damascus. In a matter of hours, Israel's spoils of war would have been two entire nations—Egypt and Syria.

The same world that held its peace as long as it appeared that the Arab nations would wipe Israel off the map, began to demand that Israel stop the war at once when it looked like they would take possession of their enemies' lands! Once again, Israel had to return the spoils, including the Sinai peninsula. The saga has not yet ended—another day and another battle is soon to come! The day is near when *all* the nations of the world will try to destroy Israel. (See Zechariah 12:8 and 14:2-3.) God will fight once again, and Israel will defeat them all. Then there will no longer be any nations in a position to keep Israel from taking the spoils the Lord has promised them—the entire earth! (Rom. 4:13) I trust that the reader will understand that I am not speaking here about a rebellious nation that continues to reject their Messiah. I am speaking about the nation that will turn to their Messiah in the midst of what looks like their final hours; a nation that will be "born in a day" (Isa. 66:8); a nation for which the Lord will fight, not because of their righteousness but because of the gross wickedness of the world, because of His covenant with Abraham's children, and for the sake of His own reputation as the King of heaven and earth.

Israel possesses another "equalizer" that helps maintain the military balance of power in the Middle East. During the Persian Gulf War, the US and the UN pressured Israel to stay out of the conflict and not to retaliate for the scud missiles that were striking Tel Aviv. Israel submitted to this pressure until it had suffered the punishment of 39 scuds. Those 39 scuds actually gave proof that the Father always disciplines in mercy. Although they damaged 5,000 homes, only two lives were lost as a direct result of the missiles![337] How merciful the Lord was to Israel! The Israeli government most likely did not have in mind the biblical punishment of "40 stripes save one" (II Cor. 11:24), but maybe the Lord did. For whatever reason, Saddam's thirty-ninth scud finally exhausted Israel's patience.

A report circulated in Israel that the Israeli government informed the US that if one more scud fell on Israel, then Damascus and Baghdad would disappear, and that if the Arab nations wanted to attack Israel, they were ready for them.[338] They let it be known that they possessed military technology that no one else in the world even knew about, and that it would be used to defend the nation if necessary.[339] Surprise! No more scuds fell on Tel Aviv. No one has ever doubted Israel's resolve. The nation has the reputation of doing exactly what it says it will do and a whole lot more. Nor does anyone doubt that Israel has the nuclear capability to remove Damascus and Baghdad from the world map. Apparently, Saddam decided it was not yet his time to go. He might have correctly suspected that the US would not take him out, but he certainly knew that Israel would not play war games with him. Israel's answer to his fortieth scud would have been just one well-guided Israeli missile, delivered to Baghdad with love—love for Israel, that is!

Does Israel really have military technology that no other nation possesses? The world might have to wait a little longer to find out. However, a brief review of recent world history should help to dispel doubts. During the First World War, Britain's only supply of acetone, needed to manufacture explosives, was cut off by Germany. Britain turned to Dr. Chaim Weizmann, a Jew, for help. He developed a way of producing acetone synthetically and saved Britain from almost certain defeat. The result was the Balfour Declaration that promised the Jews a homeland, a promise Britain later broke and even ardently fought against. They forgot that a Jew had saved them and probably the rest of the world along with them.

Many years later, partly because of the work of another Jew, Albert Einstein, the atom bomb was developed, which put a definite end to the Second World War. Is it only a coincidence that Jews played key scientific roles in the development of weapons that helped decide the outcomes of both World Wars? If we look at the intellectual track record of the Jewish people, it quickly becomes apparent that God's blessing has been on His people. One simple barometer is sufficient—the Jews represent two tenths of one percent of the world's population, yet have received ten percent of all the world's Nobel Prizes in the various intellectual fields.[340] That is an average of 50 times more Prizes than any other people on earth have received. No wonder Hitler wanted to eliminate the Jews! If he was ever to attain an earth filled with the German superior race, he would first have to eliminate *the* superior race—God's people!

Since Jewish people were instrumental in saving the world from the domination of dictators in both World Wars, does it not seem reasonable to suspect that God has endowed them with sufficient intelligence to save themselves from the domination of the world in these last days? It is a fact that Israel possesses the best military tank in the world. Perhaps they also possess other arms that the world does not yet have!

It is hard to believe that Israel's army could be swept away by the little horn. Yet Daniel not only witnesses this happening through his prophetic eye, but he states in unmistakable terms that this will definitely occur. He prophesies, "And when the power of the holy people has been completely shattered, all these things shall be finished"

(Dan. 12:7c). The total crushing of Israel's military capability will bring the end and the return of the Lord. Israel will no longer be able to trust in its own arm to save the nation. The nation will turn to their Messiah in repentance, and He will save them.

How could Yasser Arafat and the PLO sweep away this overwhelming military machine? He could not possibly do so by waging an all-out war. What he *could* do, however, is continue his war of terrorism against Israel, hiding behind international support for the oppressed Palestinian people. He already has that support, and if Israel ever attempted to turn back the clock on their peace accords with the PLO, they would almost certainly face the wrath of all the nations of the world. It appears that Israel's future attempts to defend itself, added to other Israeli "provocations" related to the city of Jerusalem will bring about Armageddon very soon when the nations will march against Israel. If Israel were to lose most or all international support, it could not wage war for very long without exhausting its military resources.

What could Israel do if Yasser Arafat's mobsters were slowly but systematically destroying one Israeli military installation after another? What could Israel do if Arafat significantly weakened its armed forces by slowly wearing away the number of Israeli troops. He could accomplish this in two ways: 1) by continuing to increase the number of terrorist attacks against the Israeli civilian and military populations, and 2) a reign of terror so horrendous that Israel's immigration numbers would turn around—more people leaving Israel than entering.

Are these my own idle theories? Unfortunately for Israel, these two scenarios are exactly what Jesus said would happen to Israel in the last days. It is Daniel who tells us that the little horn will play a major role as a vessel of wrath that God will use to bring these things to pass. Speaking of the last days and specifically about Israel itself, Jesus warns, "But when you see **Jerusalem** surrounded by armies, then know that its desolation is near. Then let those who are in **Judea** flee to the mountains... For these are the days of vengeance, that **all things** which are written **may be fulfilled** [including Daniel 12:7b—the total destruction of Israel's military capability]... For there will be great distress in the land and wrath upon this people. And **they will fall by the edge of the sword, and be led away captive into all nations**. And **Jerusalem will be trampled by Gentiles** until the times of the Gentiles are fulfilled... Then they will see **the Son of Man coming in a cloud** with power and great glory" (Lk. 21:20-27).

In this passage, we find that both of the above scenarios will happen to Israel—falling by the sword and becoming captives in other nations. These events will certainly be factors in causing Israel's overwhelming army to be swept away. Note that being "led away captive into all nations" does not necessarily mean that they become slaves or are led away by force. Circumstances can lead people into captivity just as the famine in Abraham and Sarah's day "led" them into Egypt. That trip into Egypt also resulted in a very literal captivity for Sarah in the house of Pharaoh. Later, Jacob and all his household were led by God and circumstances (a famine again) into what became a very literal Egyptian captivity. Through famine, Elimelech and Naomi and their sons were also "led" into a captivity in a foreign nation (Moab) in Ruth 1. There seems to be a difference between being "carried away captive" as slaves—Israel's experience in Jeremiah's day—and being "led away captive." (See Jeremiah 13:19.) How can we be sure that being "led away" captive does not necessarily mean to leave one's country and home as a slave or captive? Obviously, the Lord's discourse, quoted above from Luke 21, had at least a *partial* fulfillment in AD 70. And contrary to what many believe, only a few Jews actually departed the holy land as a result of Jerusalem's fall in AD 70.[341] In the case of those who did, history tells us that they departed of their own volition.[342] Since the days of Jesus' prophetic word concerning the scattering of the Jewish people, there has never been a time when they were *forcibly* scattered among the nations. As we mentioned earlier, the majority of the Jews did not leave and become scattered among the nations until hundreds of years after AD 70.[343] To choose to go into "captivity" of their own volition was, in fact, God's counsel to Israel through Jeremiah before their first captivity. He declared that those who would choose Babylonian captivity would be saved and that the others would die. (See Jeremiah 21:8-9 and 24:5-10.)

Israel Will Be Scattered Among the Nations Again and Then Gathered Again

It is commonly taught that the Lord's reference in Luke 21 to the Jews being "led away captive into all nations" was totally fulfilled when Rome destroyed Jerusalem in AD 70. That is tragically inaccurate because another "captivity" awaits the Jewish people, albeit a very short one. Many Christians are also ignorant of this, even though the prophets clearly foretold that a *second* scattering **throughout the nations** awaits Israel in the last days. During the last 50 years, the Lord has miraculously gathered Israel back to their land from all the nations of the earth. A question that begs asking is, As a nation, does Israel's immediate future hold nothing but one victory after another, even though they continue to reject their Messiah? Secular Israel today so *totally* rejects their Messiah, that, by a Supreme Court ruling, any Jew who believes in Yeshua (Jesus) cannot immigrate to Israel and cannot become a citizen. What will the Lord do to open Israel's eyes? We learn the answer from the Book of Revelation where Babylon rises again. God used Babylon to deal with Israel once and He will do so again.

Babylon and Jerusalem are the two principal cities in the Book of Revelation. They seem to have something in common—they are both natural cities on earth that are symbolic of spiritual cities. In the case of Jerusalem, it is seen to be a natural city in Revelation when an angel refers to it as the city where "our Lord was crucified" (Rev. 11:8). It is also revealed to be a spiritual city when one of the seven angels refers to Jerusalem as the worldwide Body of Christ, calling it "the Lamb's wife" (Rev. 21:2,9-10). Babylon, today, exists again as a natural city which is being rebuilt by Saddam Hussein of Iraq. However, the description of the Babylon found in Revelation 17-18 demonstrates that it is also a worldwide, abominable, spiritual influence that will unite the nations of the world against God's people.

With an endtime Babylon in mind, we can understand Micah's prophecy about Israel going into a Babylonian captivity again in the last days. The prophet speaks of the pains that will seize Israel "as a woman in travail" (Mic. 4:9 KJV). Paul links the concept of Israel travailing with the last days when Israel will be saying, "Peace and safety." (See I Thessalonians 4:15-5:3.) Micah then explains that Israel's travail has to do with them going into a Babylonian captivity, at which time Israel will be redeemed from the hand of her enemies (Mic. 4:9). This cannot be speaking about the captivity in Babylon around 600 BC for at least two reasons. First, the Babylonian captivity referred to in Micah 4:10 will actually result in Israel's *deliverance* from the hand of her enemies. It would be difficult to apply this to Israel's historical captivity in Babylon. Second, at this time the nations of the earth will gather against Israel, but all those nations are defeated and their riches are given over to the Lord according to Micah 4:11-12. This certainly never happened in Israel's historical captivity.

Two other points should be mentioned here to confirm that Israel will go into an "international Babylonian captivity" in the last days. First, as we have seen, Jeremiah tells us that his prophetic message is specifically for God's people in the last days. If we could sum up Jeremiah's message in one sentence, it would be that he promises God's people that they will go into Babylonian captivity. If Jeremiah's message is for the last days, then this *must* have an endtime fulfillment besides the historical fulfillment. Second, Isaiah assures Israel that the Lord will gather them from among the nations two times, and not just once. He promises, "It shall come to pass in **that day** that the Lord shall set His hand again **the second time** to recover the remnant of His people who are left, from Assyria and Egypt, from Pathros and Cush, from Elam and Shinar, from Hamath and the islands of the sea. He will set up **a banner for the nations**, and will assemble the outcasts of Israel, and gather together the dispersed of Judah **from the four corners of the earth**" (Isa. 11:11-12). To understand when this second gathering from among the nations will take place, note that Isaiah tells us it will be "in that day." The preceding verses in Isaiah tell us when "that day" will be—when Christ's Kingdom has finally come to the earth and the wolf dwells with the lamb; when "the earth shall be full of the knowledge of the Lord as the waters cover the sea" (Isa. 11:6-10). Ezekiel 39 confirms that, after Armageddon, the Lord will gather every single Israelite from among all the nations and that not one will be left in the nations any longer. (Compare Ezekiel 39:17-21 with Revelation 19:17-21. Note that it is *after* this battle in Ezekiel 39 that Israel and the nations will know who the Lord is; it will be at *that* time that He will bring back all the captives of Israel, according to verses 25-29.)

Jesus Reveals Israel's Endtime Scattering

Returning now to Luke 21:20-27, there are several reasons why this passage cannot be speaking *primarily* about the destruction of Jerusalem in AD 70. First, Jesus explains that the days of which He speaks are days of vengeance in which the entire prophetic message of the Bible will be fulfilled. That did not happen in the days of AD 70. Second, it is during these events that the Son of man will come in the clouds. This is the time of the Second Coming, not AD 70. Third, Jerusalem is trodden down by the Gentiles in this context *until* the time of the Gentiles comes to an end and the Son of Man comes in the clouds. Jerusalem has been under Jewish dominion for the last thirty years. Only now, in the end, will it be placed under Gentile dominion again for 42 months as Revelation 11:2 reveals.

Tragically Jesus is revealing that in the last days, those who are in Judea (there is only one Judea) will "fall by the edge of the sword, and be led away captive into all nations." This is how Yasser Arafat and the PLO will at least begin to reduce the armies of Israel. Of course, we must not ignore Arafat's continual call to the other Arab nations. As we have seen, he openly tells them that he is counting on their help to destroy Israel once he has the West Bank fully under his control. Jesus confirms that other nations will be involved in the slaughter of Israel when He tells us that Jerusalem will be "surrounded by armies" (Lk. 21:20). We can be sure that Arafat and the PLO will not be alone in Islam's final efforts to crush God's people. Arafat has repeatedly called on the other Islamic nations to help him in the final push to destroy Israel. That call will one day be answered and many armies will gather around Jerusalem.

* 41. A Prince of the Covenant Shall Be Destroyed Before Him

"Then an overwhelming army will be swept away before him; both it and a prince of the covenant will be destroyed" (Dan. 11:22 NIV).

Was This Fulfilled By the Death of Yitzhak Rabin?

In October 1995, while taping a course on Arafat and the little horn for our video and audio correspondence Bible courses, I declared, "The 'prince of the covenant' would be the leader of the nation. Mr. Rabin is apparently going to face his end because of his dealings with Arafat." In less than a month, this prophetic detail from Daniel was fulfilled when Yitzhak Rabin was assassinated. I believe that just as surely as this detail was fulfilled, so, too, all the remaining details concerning the little horn will be fulfilled by Yasser Arafat and/or his PLO. Prime Minister Rabin, one of Israel's princes, was definitely destroyed as a direct result of Yasser Arafat. How?

After the death of Rabin, many commentators frequently declared that Rabin died for peace. Unfortunately, a good number of Israelis agreed with this assessment even though this is simply not the *real* reason Rabin died. If we analyze what is being said, it is actually just one more direct attack against the people of Israel. As a result of Rabin's peace initiative, the nation ended up totally and almost equally divided. About half the population endorsed his peace plan and the other half remained strongly opposed to his plan as long as it involved giving away the land that God had promised Israel. The feelings ran so deeply that a group of ultra-Orthodox rabbis got together and pronounced a seldom-used powerful curse against Rabin in front of his house in September 1995.[344] One report reads, "According to several news accounts, [a rabbi] organized a minyan of supporters outside Rabin's residence... on the eve of last Yom Kippur and invoked the 'angels of destruction... to kill [Rabin]... for handing over the land of Israel to our enemies.' "[345] The report goes on to say, "The curse was to have been effective within about 30 days. Rabin was murdered 33 days later."[346]

To say that Rabin died for peace gives the distinct impression that the reason the Israelis were so violently divided on Rabin's peace plan is because they do not want peace. I live in Israel and I do not know a single Israeli who does not want peace. After 50 years of turmoil, how could anyone want to continue this way? Rabin did not die because he was making peace. No Israeli would have shot him because they sincerely believed that he was bringing the nation into a period of peace. Rabin died because he was giving away the land, and because about fifty percent of the nation was convinced that, by giving the land to Israel's very worst enemy, he was actually bringing Israel into war, not peace. Rabin was somehow convinced by Yasser Arafat and others that together they would bring peace to Israel. Rabin happened to be in Arafat's path toward taking possession of the holy land, and his dealings with Arafat ultimately cost him his life—he was "swept away before him" as Daniel said a prince of the covenant would be. How tragic! It is tragic not only because a man of Rabin's caliber lost his life, but because he lost it for a cause that will ultimately bring the greatest suffering and death to Israel that the nation has ever known. Rabin himself probably understands this by now, though woefully too late!

Because Arafat succeeded in extracting concessions from Rabin that were unheard of in Israel's past, much of the Israeli populace was very discontent. Rabin's life ended when he was gunned down by Yigal Amir, an Orthodox Israeli Jew who was convinced that giving away the holy land was an assault on all of God's people and in open violation of God's Word. In no way am I condoning what Amir did. I am simply presenting the facts, and making clear that, for one reason or another, the hearts of many in Israel are divided over the implications of what happened. The division is not so much over whether or not Amir should be condemned—for the vast majority in Israel, that goes without saying. The division is over the political issue of whether Rabin should have been allowed to continue giving land for "peace." God Himself declares, "I will enter into judgment with them there on account of My people, My heritage Israel, whom they have scattered among the nations; **they have also divided up My land**" (Joel 3:2). Here, the Lord promises judgment on those who divide His land.

At least two interesting details surrounding the assassination of Rabin seem to indicate that God chose Yigal Amir as a vessel of wrath to reveal His displeasure with Rabin for having given away His land. I do not see these details as proof that Amir did what was right because, throughout the Bible and history, vessels of wrath are finally brought into judgment also. Babylon is a clear example. That kingdom was used to bring death and destruction on Israel because of the nation's sin, but then God promised that afterward He would bring judgment on Babylon for what they had done to Israel. This is one of the main messages of the Prophet Habakkuk, and is also revealed clearly by Jeremiah, who tells Israel that they will go into Babylonian captivity for their sin but then ends his message with the promise of judgment on Babylon. (See Jeremiah 21, 50-51.)

The first detail surrounding the assassination of Rabin is related to Rabin himself and has to do with an amazing "coincidence" found in the biblical Hebrew passage that Jews throughout the world were reading the week he was murdered. Since before the time of Christ, Orthodox Jews throughout the world have had the custom of all reading the same designated portions of Scripture each week. To understand the "coincidence," we must understand several details about written Hebrew. First, there are no written vowels; all the written letters are consonants. Second, there are no capital letters or punctuation. Third, in the original Bible there were no spaces between one word and the next. The text was just one continuous string of consonants. Rabbis added spaces for the convenience of the Hebrew reader. Fourth, many times there is more than one possible way to divide the consonants into words in a given passage. Many Rabbis believe that all of the possible ways to divide a passage into separate words reveal truth as long as the divisions form legitimate words with a logical meaning.

If English were written as Hebrew is, the following string of letters would be an example of a sentence with two possible meanings—"heisnowhere." By changing where we insert spaces to divide this string of letters into words, we could read it two ways—"he is nowhere," or else "he is now here." Such possibilities in Hebrew are endless.

The passage that worldwide Jewry was reading during the week that Rabin was assassinated included Genesis 15:17-18 where God made **a covenant with Abraham promising to give the land of Canaan to his descendants forever. In this very passage**, if the Hebrew is divided differently from the way it appears in the modern Hebrew Bible, the following message appears: "Fire, fire, evil for Rabin." The word "fire" here is used in Hebrew today in the same way it is used in English on the firing range when soldiers are commanded: "Ready, aim, *fire*." Yitzhak Rabin was assassinated when Amir fired two bullets.

The second detail surrounding the assassination of Rabin is related to his assassin, Yigal Amir. Many Israelis wondered if there was a hidden message in the assassin's name. If the first letter of his first name is removed as well as the last letter of his last name, what is left is the Hebrew expression "he will save my people." By snuffing out the life of the man who he believed had allowed Arafat to stand up to him and win, Amir actually thought he was saving God's people from the PLO.

I am convinced that the way in which Arafat stood up to Prime Minister Rabin and the personal cost to Rabin of that confrontation is nothing compared to what Arafat plans to do in the near future. At most, he has only begun to fulfill this prophetic message, and woe to the next Prime Minister against whom Arafat stands up, and woe to Israel!

Will This Also Be Fulfilled By What Will Happen to Shimon Peres?

There is another possible meaning to what Daniel is telling us here. There is absolutely no question that instead of heading for a time of peace, Israel is headed for "the time of Jacob's troubles." There will be no peace for Israel until the nation turns to the Prince of Peace. Shimon Peres became Israel's Prime Minister after Rabin's assassination. Peres is recognized as the real architect of the peace process, and is convinced that "Utopia is coming," as he declared after the May 1994 signing ceremony with Arafat in Cairo.[347] By making huge peace deals, Peres was also seeking to build himself a political kingdom that would not be shaken during his lifetime. He was also seeking a place in history as the man who brought peace to the Middle East.[348]

Could it be significant that his name actually appears in Daniel in both the English and Hebrew Bibles? In Daniel's interpretation of the handwriting on the wall, he declares, "PERES: Your kingdom has been divided, and given to the Medes and Persians" (Dan. 5:28). How awesomely prophetic! In Aramaic, "Peres" means "to divide." It is ironic that by dividing the land of Israel among its enemies Mr. Peres was seeking to assure his place in history as the peacemaker of the Middle East. His kingdom of glory will one day come to an end. Far from being seen as the architect of peace, Mr. Peres will soon be seen as a man who compromised Israel's security and ignored Israel's God and His covenant with them. If we compare Daniel 5:28 with a number of other Scriptures, it seems amazingly prophetic of what will yet happen in the very end to the plans and "kingdom" of Mr. Peres. Sadly enough, it also reveals what will happen to Israel, the people that he has endangered by giving away God's land. The Medes and Persians will destroy his reputation and place in history as the peacemaker. In May 1996, enough Israelis already doubted the outcome of his peace plan to give an election victory to Peres' political opponent, Benjamin Netanyahu.

The Medes and Persians are present day Iraq and Iran, two other extremely virulent enemies of Israel. Several Scriptures inform us that the "Assyrian" will also enter the holy land in the last days. (See Micah 5:3-8 and Isaiah 10:24-27; 14:24-26.) The Assyrian Empire refers to the land of the Medes and Persians. It seems likely, from both the Scripture and current Middle East events, that the Lord finally will permit Iraq to invade Israel and bring horrendous devastation (probably with Russian, and possibly Iranian, involvement as well). Arafat was one of Saddam Hussein's only supporters in the Gulf War. He is *still* one of Hussein's allies—at least in spirit! He will prepare the way for "Assyria" to enter Israel as he succeeds in weakening the nation militarily.

* 42. After Israel Comes to An Agreement With Him He Acts Deceitfully

"After coming to an agreement with him, he will act deceitfully"
(Dan. 11:23a NIV).

The fulfillment of this prophetic word is truly awe-inspiring. Israel did, in fact, come to an internationally-lauded, historic agreement with Yasser Arafat. In that agreement, both sides pledged to take certain measures designed to bring peace between Israel's worst enemy and the Jewish state. The West was ecstatic with the new atmosphere of cooperation from both sides and the mutual declaration of a willingness to make peace. There were several principal commitments that Israel made. One was to withdraw gradually their soldiers from the West Bank, including 450 cities, towns, and villages, and place the administration of these areas under Arafat's Palestinian Authority (PA). Another was to release from Israeli prisons the approximately 11,000 terrorists who were jailed for acts of terrorism against Israel. As a prerequisite for their release, Israel was authorized to demand a signed statement from each prisoner in which they would promise not to engage in any further acts of terrorism.

In return, Arafat pledged that the Charter of the PLO would be changed so that it would no longer call for the destruction of Israel.[349] He promised that terrorist attacks would be halted,[350] and that he would take serious steps to prevent terrorism against Israel from the new autonomous areas, including disarming the terrorists.[351] Arafat promised to make speeches to the Palestinian Arabs encouraging them to reject terror.[352] He promised to extradite terrorists to Israel.[353] He promised to cooperate with Israeli law-enforcement agencies and investigators.[354] Besides these major promises, he made many other minor commitments that would normally be expected from any genuine and sincere "peace partner." How have things progressed during the years since both sides signed this agreement?

At this writing, Israel has almost completed its withdrawal from the territories promised to Arafat. Hebron is the last major city remaining, and was to be placed under the PA very soon when Israel's Labor party lost the election to the Likud in May 1996. What will happen now is unclear, but the Likud is being pressured from within and without to continue with the plan of giving Hebron to the PLO. Israel has already fulfilled its promise to release thousands of terrorists from Israeli jails. The only thing that is preventing the release of those who remain imprisoned is that they are mostly Hamas terrorists, and the Hamas leadership has ordered them not to sign any statement where they promise to desist from terrorism.[355] Arafat is now calling on Israel to release them whether they sign or not.[356] Isn't it amazing that the man who supposedly cannot control Hamas terrorists is requesting that they be released? Is he crazy or cunning?

Arafat just cannot understand why Israel should be so hard-nosed and insist on such extreme measures as demanding a signed statement in return for a gesture so insignificant as granting the release of proven murderers! He must also marvel that Israel could be so naive as to expect their enemies to keep their word and desist from further acts of terrorism. If Arafat wanted to show just how naive the Israeli leadership is, and prove that requiring his terrorists to sign a statement is a waste of time, he could always point to specific examples where those released have reneged on their promise and gone back to terrorism. For example, one of the released prisoners became a suicide bomber in Netanya, Israel, on January 22, 1995. He killed 19 Israelis and wounded 60 in one of the worst terrorist attacks in Israel's history.[357] So what's the big deal anyway? Israel should just release them all knowing full well that they will start killing more Israelis the first chance they get!

How is Mr. Arafat doing with fulfilling his promises? After waiting two years, Arafat finally convened a meeting of the Palestine National Council (PNC) in April 1996. This was supposed to produce a vote on changing the Charter. As we have mentioned, it only produced a vote on forming a commission to *consider* a new Charter! How do we know this? Only because someone videotaped the meeting and the whole proceedings were later exposed. Not to worry. This sham made the world happier than ever with Mr. Arafat, and he has definitely bought some more time through his deceit. The question is, Will the PLO actually retract its old declarations? It seems less likely with the passing of each additional year since the peace agreement was signed.

Arafat promised that terrorist attacks would be halted, when in fact they have doubled, as we have seen. He promised to take serious steps to prevent terrorism against Israel from the new autonomous areas, when in fact, his own security chief, Jibril Rajoub, was in constant contact with the explosives expert, Yihye Ayyash, planning more bus bombs.[358] Arafat promised to disarm the terrorists in the autonomous areas, but now has declared that he will not even attempt to do so, because it might create civil unrest for him, and thereby destroy the peace process with Israel.[359] Arafat promised to make speeches to the Palestinian Arabs to reject terror, but instead has repeatedly made speeches encouraging terror.[360] He promised to extradite terrorists to Israel, but couldn't even find Israel's most wanted terrorist, Ayyash, when everyone knew exactly where he lived openly in Gaza.[361] He promised to cooperate with Israeli law-enforcement agencies and investigators, but now says they are violating the peace accord when they even enter the autonomous areas.[362]

All these peace accord violations have been listed in an official report by the US Attorney General.[363] The same report also cites many other open violations. For the sake of space, I include here only a *partial* list of the violations found in that report. The violations involve: illegal arrest of Israeli citizens; illegal detention of Israeli security forces at PLO roadblocks; illegal movement of Palestinian policemen in blue areas (those under Israeli control); failure to relay a complete list of PLO policemen; use of PLO police weapons during terrorist attack in Jerusalem; PLO police driving stolen Israeli vehicles; illegal movement of PLO police wearing camouflage uniforms; failure to summon witnesses to testify in court; failure to stop released prisoners from leaving

Gaza and Jericho; failure to prevent infiltrations into Israel from Egypt; PLO police weapons found in the hands of civilians; harassment and persecution of "collaborators;" PLO policemen running through IDF roadblocks; issuing documents under the heading "Palestinian National Authority" instead of "Palestinian Authority;" taking over Wakf affairs in Jerusalem, Judea, and Samaria; use of forged documents for entering Israel; illegal construction of a port in Gaza; issuance of stamps contrary to agreement; failure to pay water fees; and the illegal issuance of international driving licenses.

The US Senate has been informed that "Yasser Arafat and the PLO have consistently violated virtually every major and minor requirement in the accords."[364] Of course, to some people, like Penny Wark, a London journalist, Israel is simply asking the PLO to give up too much. She wrote, "[Arafat's] main demand is that Israel pull the troops out of the Gaza Strip and the sleepy West Bank town of Jericho... In exchange, the Palestine Liberation Organisation would recognize Israel, abandon acts of terrorism, and, most importantly, delete passages from its charter which Israel sees as opposing the Jewish state." Wark then assures us, "This is a lot for the PLO to give up."[365] Commenting on Wark's article, another journalist mocked, "Indeed, depriving the lovely [PLO] organization of its right to destroy another nation must be traumatic in the extreme. But Arafat's readiness to make sacrifices for peace is obviously unlimited."[366]

What does Arafat say about all this? He is getting sick and tired of Israel's silly little requests. He recently made known his exasperation with Israel's unreasonable attitude, declaring, "Every time the Israelis come to me they bring up the matter of security, security, security, as if we have signed an agreement about security."[367] The only way Arafat could act more deceitfully toward the agreement that Israel made with him would be to say, "Agreement? What agreement? I don't recall ever having signed an agreement with Israel!"

* 43. He Shall Become Strong With a Small Number of People

"...for he shall come up and become strong with a small number of people" (Dan. 11:23b).

Few of Daniel's descriptions of the little horn fit Yasser Arafat any better than this. Because of *Syria's* terrorist attacks on Israel, done in the name of Arafat's Fatah Hawks, Arafat soon became known as the commander of a mighty guerrilla army.[368] That was early 1965, and his mighty army numbered "no more than a few dozen."[369] In spite of Syrian help in recruiting new members, and an increasing number of endorsements by Arab and non-Arab nations alike, two or three years later his "mighty army" still only numbered five or six hundred.[370]

When he had control of Lebanon between 1970 and 1976, it was much easier for him to "recruit" new terrorists from the refugee camps in the southern part of that nation. After all, when the options during the "carnival of death" were to shoot or be shot, new recruits weren't hard to find! Also, with dictatorial power over the nation for seven years, he was free to use more persuasive methods to convince potential recruits to join his mafia. In spite of all this, when Israel drove the PLO out of Lebanon in 1982, allowing Arafat's great army to flee on ships belonging to PLO sympathizers, the PLO still numbered only 14, 938.[371]

The peace accord that Arafat signed with Israel authorized him to build up a Palestinian "police force" of 9,000.[372] The PLO never tried to hide the fact that their plan was to reunite the gangsters who were scattered after they had raped Lebanon, adding to that group many other terrorists. One PLO official stated, "Under the new interim period arrangements, the Palestine Liberation Army forces will be transformed into security police, with an aim of bringing in thousands of PLO guerrillas outside the camp in stages."[373] That statement was made in 199. By 1995, they had already succeeded in gathering 20,000 "policemen" to form Arafat's new army.[374] Although this is in blatant violation of the peace accord, it is still a "small number of people," especially when compared with Saddam Hussein's army in the Gulf War of approximately one million. Summarizing his history, we can definitely declare that Arafat has "become strong with a small number of people!"

* 44. He Enters the Best Parts of Israel Through Pe

"He shall enter peaceably, even into the richest places of the province" (Dan. 11:24a).

Once again, the Hebrew word here rendered "peaceably" re the atmosphere that prevails as a result of making peace. The "the richest places" is from just one Hebrew word which refers t the "most fertile" or the "most desirable" places.[375] Through pretentious peace dealings, he has already managed to enter most desirable land in Israel. It is the most desirable in at le ways: 1) militarily, 2) naturally, and 3) spiritually.

Consider the **military** importance of the land that Israel has given to Arafat. The West Bank includes the central and only mountain range in the holy land. It runs right up through the heart of the nation. Militarily, this is some of Israel's most desirable land because it is always a military advantage to control the mountains. They have been given to Arafat. According to "The Pentagon Plan for Israel's Security Needs," two thirds of the land that Israel is giving to Arafat is militarily vital for its own security. (See Map 6 in Appendix A.) Isn't it interesting that Israel is seeking to receive promises of "security" from its enemies by placing in their hands territories that, from a military point of view, are essential for the nation's security? The Pentagon also considered Israel's control over the mountains of the Golan Heights to be critical for the nation's security, but the Labor government seemed more than willing to give up even this area to Syria before the Labor government lost the elections. Regardless of what finally happens to the Golan, Israel's enemies have already received much of the land that the Pentagon considered to be vital to Israel's security. It looks like Israel has been set up for a time of great sorrows!

Naturally speaking, the land Arafat has been given is some of Israel's most desirable also. It includes the land on which Jacob's sons were pasturing the family sheep when Joseph was sent to seek for them. It contains some of the more fertile areas of the nation. The psalmist must have seen this day when the enemies would take Jacob's pasture land as they seek to destroy the nation. He wrote, "Do not keep silent, O God! Do not hold Your peace, and do not be still, O God! For behold, Your enemies make a tumult; and those who hate You have lifted up their head. They have taken crafty counsel against Your people... They have said, 'Come, and let us cut them off from being a nation, that the name of Israel may be remembered no more'... Who said, '**Let us take for ourselves the pastures of God for a possession**' " (Psa. 83:1-4,12).

Few people realize just how small the State of Israel really is. (See Map 2 in Appendix A to get a perspective of its size.) Also, some are unaware that a large portion of Israel's land is either desert or semi-arid land. Israel is actually giving to Arafat about one half of the arable land. Besides this, there is something else that is very desirable about the land the PLO is receiving. Arable land in itself is worthless if there is insufficient water. The land that Arafat has been given permits him to exercise control, either directly or indirectly, over 80 percent of Israel's water supply.[376] All three major aquifers (underground sources of water) in the holy land begin in the hills and mountains that Arafat controls. Imagine what will happen if he decides to disturb or cut off Israel's water! The experts say this is a very plausible scenario.

Joyce Starr, one of the leading experts in the field of water resource management, writes, "Overpumping in the West Bank could eventually lower the water table below sea level, causing salt water to flow from the sea into Israel's coastlands. This could lead to permanent destruction of aquifers and farmlands."[377] Of course, the PLO can be trusted to administer Israel's water resources in a responsible manner and not overpump. After all, they drilled only 500 wells in Gaza alone during the two years after taking control of that small strip of land, even though in doing so they threaten the water table of the entire area![378] Having already seen how faithful the PLO is to follow water resource management guidelines in Gaza, the Israeli citizens certainly have no cause for concern. They should have *plenty* of water—at least for another year or two! And besides, after that, there will always be an unlimited supply of saltwater!

In an article in *The Jerusalem Post*, the chairman of the Movement for the Preservation of Israel's Water, Itamar Marcus, wrote: "Whoever controls the pumps in Judea and Samaria determines the amount of water left to flow across the Green Line [the PLO/Israeli boundary]... What life in this country would be like... is beyond imagination. It would affect not just our life style, but our very psyche as a nation. Ecologically, residents of the coastal plain would be at the mercy of residents of the highlands of Judea and Samaria."[379]

A much more sinister scenario also exists. The *Post* writes, "The [Israeli] Ministry of Agriculture is more concerned about the possibility that Israel's water will be polluted. 'While it is possible to monitor excessive water use, pollution is considerably harder to detect.' "[380] Prof. Yair Parag of the Hebrew University believes that, even without malice, the Palestinians can deprive Israel of drinking water. "Some of the area is hydro-geologically very sensitive, with vertical 'slots.' Any sewage spillage will cause immediate, permanent contamination of the mountain aquifer." Geologist Prof. Arnon Sofer of Haifa University, a foremost water expert, has warned that without proper waste management, the addition of a million inhabitants to Judea and Samaria—a development which should be all-too-rapid once families of residents displaced in 1967 are allowed to immigrate—"will finish off the Israeli coast with sewage, dysentery, and typhus."[381] In February 1996, Arafat revealed his plan to import over four million Arabs into this very area within five years.[382] He made it clear that *any* Arab can be legitimately imported, since Israel imports Jews of any nationality.[383]

Spiritually speaking, the land that Arafat has been given, without question, is the most desirable land in the heart and mind of any believing Jew today. We have mentioned the extreme spiritual importance that Hebron, Bethlehem, Shechem, and Jericho have. If Arafat succeeds in getting the Old City of Jerusalem, to an Orthodox Jew, he will be getting the best of the best and the very heart of Judaism. Spiritually speaking, Arafat seems to be taking from God's people something even more desirable than the best land. Arafat's success in taking their land seems to fly in the face of the Lord's promises to Israel through Amos and other prophets. The Lord speaks through Amos, "And I will bring again the captivity of my people of Israel, and they shall build the waste cities, and inhabit them; and they shall plant vineyards, and drink the wine thereof; they shall also make gardens, and eat the fruit of them. And I will plant them upon their land, and **they shall no more be pulled up out of their land** which I have given them, saith the Lord thy God" (Amos 9:14-15). Every time Arafat takes more land, it is a frontal attack on Israel's faith in God's promises. Many fail to understand that the Lord will ultimately intervene to fulfill His Word even though many may be rooted up yet one more time!

* 45. Unlike Other Leaders, He Disperses the Plunder Among His Followers

"...he shall do what his fathers have not done,
nor his forefathers: he shall disperse among them
the plunder, spoil, and riches" (Dan. 11:24b).

"He will distribute plunder, loot and wealth
among his followers" (Dan. 11:24b NIV).

Arafat's "fathers" and "forefathers" are Arabs. Historically, those Arabs who have had the financial means to do so, have had the reputation of living in extreme opulence. In spite of Arafat's own personal wealth, estimated in the billions, and in spite of the billions of dollars that pass through his hands, he is known to live a very frugal life.[384]

Arafat has been accused of stashing away billions of dollars into his own personal bank accounts, and of taking money that was given for either terrorism or as aid to the Palestinians. However, even though the money that donor nations give to the PLO may not always reach its intended purpose, much of it does get dispersed among others—

especially among the PLO officials. While Arafat's personal housing in Gaza and Jericho is said to be very modest, and he never uses money for personal pleasure or entertainment, he has allowed his PLO officials to enjoy the riches and spoil of the PLO. They live like princes. Their extravagant life-styles were detailed in the Jerusalem English-language weekly Al Fajr, an Arabic publication.[385]

* 46. He Will Devise Plans Against the Strongholds

"...he shall devise his plans against the strongholds,
but only for a time" (Dan. 11:24b).

A biblical stronghold is for defense or protection. The concept of a stronghold generally implies there is a population center or land that is being protected. Furthermore, a stronghold without people ceases to be a real stronghold. The Hebrew word here can actually mean "a fortified city" or a city that is "defended."[386] Of course, all of Israel's cities are defended by the Israel Defense Forces, even though those cities do not have walls around them in the way traditional strongholds had. This same Hebrew word is used to refer to cities in Jeremiah 4:5.

In terms of Israel's ancient conquest of Canaan under Joshua, Arafat has already succeeded in taking one of the best-known strongholds in the nation's history—Jericho. It was the first city that Israel conquered as they began to take the land from the Canaanites. It is also the first city or stronghold that Arafat has taken as he begins, to his way of thinking, the final offensive to take the entire holy land from Israel. As we already mentioned, many understand the significance of this PLO "conquest" (through peace, of course) that permitted them to take control of Gaza and Jericho in the first stage of the peace process. That first stage was actually dubbed "Gaza-Jericho First." Arafat has taken a number of other important cities also.

In the holy land, the stronghold of all strongholds is the city of Jerusalem, the Jebusite stronghold that David took 3,000 years ago. Is it not tragic and ironic that during 1996 Israel has been involved in celebrating the 3,000[th] anniversary since David conquered Jerusalem, and, during the same year, they began negotiations concerning the surrender of Jerusalem to their enemies? Does anyone really believe that Arafat would be content and allow Israel to live in peace if he were finally given the Old City of Jerusalem for a Palestinian capital? By his own oft-repeated declarations, he will not stop the holy war until Palestine has been "liberated" from every last Jew. What we will discover in the

very near future is that Mr. Arafat is devising plans against *all* the
strongholds or cities of Israel. Once he is firmly entrenched in the West
Bank, all the major population centers of Israel will not only be within
his sights, they will be within the range of his missiles. He will continue to devise plans against Israel's strongholds, but the glorious part
of this revelation from Daniel is that he will be permitted to do so "only
for a time!"

47. He Turns Against the King of Egypt and Conquers Egypt

*"He shall stir up his power and his courage against
the king of the South with a great army" (Dan. 11:25a).*

At first thought, the concept of Yasser Arafat becoming a threat to the
king of Egypt seems ludicrous—until the facts are considered. How could
Arafat ever manage finally to possess a "great army"? If we attempt to
measure the greatness of a Palestinian army relative to the armed forces
of the US, Arafat will never have what could be termed a great army.
However, if we are measuring the size of a possible Palestinian army
relative to the average size of Middle East armies, he could possibly
raise a sizable force. Presently, there are two to four million people
who call themselves "Palestinians" living in various countries of the
Arab world. One of the demands that Arafat is now making is that Israel permit all "Palestinians" to come and live under his Palestinian
Authority. If Israel permits such a flood of immigrants, or if Arafat
succeeds in declaring Palestinian independence, the situation in the
holy land could change rapidly and certainly will if he imports the millions of Arabs he has promised to import. Arafat could soon have a
much stronger armed forces than he presently commands, especially
since thousands of these "Palestinians" are seasoned terrorists!

We also need to keep in mind that the intra-Arab conflicts are perennial. If one or more Arab nations were somehow to become incensed
with the Egyptians, Arafat might well find himself with many Islamic volunteers from those countries if they knew that he purposed to attack Egypt.
For example, with such "level-headed" Arab leaders like Colonel
Muammar Gaddafi of Libya, amazing things could happen—like fictitious
changes in a person's nationality from Libyan to Palestinian. For example, in a moment of anger, it would not be surprising at all if someday
Mr. Gaddafi were to make the fictitious "discovery" that half of his troops
are actually former "Palestinians" who suddenly feel a call to return to Pal-

estine to help Brother Yasser fight against their common enemy—Egypt! Is this merely wild speculation? Not at all. Gaddafi has already sent a number of "Palestinian" units from his armed forces to help Arafat form his new army. Those units include air force, infantry and naval personnel.[387] The precedent has already been set for this type of cooperation between Libya and Arafat! The relationship between Libya and the little horn will definitely be a very close one in the last days. In fact, we will see that Libya is one of the "three horns" that the little horn will pluck up by the roots. Libya will be following the little horn's orders in yet greater ways as the little horn's strength increases!

Why would Arafat ever turn against his good friends, the Egyptians? Arafat is simply *using* them just as he has always used anyone and everyone possible to further his selfish goals. Besides this, Arafat has several "axes to grind" with the Egyptians. Remember that he once belonged to the "holy Ikhwan." This organization was composed of the Moslem Brotherhood of Egypt, a moderate Islamic fundamentalist group that continues to appear frequently in the Middle East news. One of their primary goals has always been the establishment of an Islamic state in Egypt. They believe that secular governments have no place in Moslem countries and that "Moslem religious law should be the constitution of Egypt."[388] Much of Arafat's early life and thinking were formed by this movement. His father was an Ikhwanite leader, as was Arafat himself throughout his early years.[389] His "holy Ikhwan" was declared illegal by the Egyptian government years ago. In Arafat's mind, this could well be a "score to settle." Remember that one of the first murders he committed was that of Rork Hamid because Yasser thought that he had betrayed the "holy Ikhwan!" He has always been very committed to the vision of the Moslem Brotherhood and still has a relationship with them.[390] He would certainly be their hero if he were to fulfill their vision—a vision that Arafat and his family have dedicated their lives to for decades.

Another ax that Arafat has to grind with the Egyptians is that President Gamal Abdel Nasser ordered his intelligence service to kill Arafat when Arafat was living in Kuwait.[391] This was brought on because Arafat constantly ridiculed Nasser's leadership in a newspaper he once published called *Our Palestine*.[392] Nasser founded the PLO in 1964 for two purposes—to drive the Jews out of Palestine, and to avoid the rise of any more firebrands like Yasser Arafat.[393] However, Nasser's PLO was almost totally unsuccessful on both counts, and Arafat actually ended up taking control of the PLO in February 1969.[394] That was surely sweet success for Mr. Arafat. Would it not be even sweeter success for him if he could one day take control of Nasser's entire nation, also? And even more so since he spent three months in Egypt in one of Nasser's prisons![395] Gaining control over Egypt would be seen by Arafat and his supporters as a clear vindication of his critical attitude toward that nation and its government.

Arafat's hatred for Egypt runs far deeper than is immediately apparent. In fact, that hatred actually became a foundation stone of his life's work. After Nasser dismally lost the 1956 war to Israel, Yasser and his cohorts had an all night meeting where he "ranted for hours about the shame of the Egyptians and about how that shame also stained the soul of every Palestinian."[396] He decided that, since the Egyptian government had been such an abject failure in liquidating the Jews in the holy land, he would organize a group of Palestinian fedayeen who would take it upon themselves to do the job.[397] That night the seeds of hate were sown for the formation of Arafat's Al Fatah terrorist organization.[398] From the outset, their message has been that the "Arab brothers are traitors,"[399] and that Palestine must be liberated by Palestinians without the direct help or interference of others.[400]

If love "keeps no record of wrongs" (I Cor. 13:5 NIV), then it follows that hate must always be at pains to settle old scores. Egypt, beware! The foundation of Arafat's whole organization is based on hate, *not* on a love for the Palestinians. It is true that Yasser Arafat hates the Jews, but there is another principal target for his hatred—Egypt! That hatred seethes in his soul, and he will never lay it down. Woe to Egypt if the day ever comes when he believes he has the military might sufficient to right the wrongs that he perceives have been done to him. His hatred for the Egyptian government grew by quantum leaps with Anwar' Sadat's decision to make peace with Israel. Afterwards, Arafat considered Egypt to be "the most despicable of all Arab states."[401] He seethed, saying: "Sadat sold Palestine for a handful of Sinai sand."[402]

What about Arafat's wonderful "friend," Hosni Mubarak, the current President of Egypt? Time will tell how Arafat will deal with him, but Daniel 11:25-26 shows that Egypt's leader will be assassinated. On June 26, 1995, there was, in fact, an assassination attempt on Mubarak's life that was almost successful.[403] It occurred while he was visiting Ethiopia. What happened when a pale faced Mubarak deplaned in Cairo after the attempt is very interesting in light of Arafat's past and present links to the Moslem Brotherhood in Egypt (his "holy Ikhwan"). The government-controlled news networks had been ordered to black out the news of this event.[404] The Egyptian public did not even know what had happened to Mubarak. Yet, the leadership of the Moslem Brotherhood met him when he landed at the Cairo airport to congratulate him on his amazing escape.[405] It was interesting that they were the first to know about it. The obvious question is, How did they even know about it at all? The plot thickens!

Just five days after the assassination attempt against Mubarak, Arafat, who is known for his total inability to keep secrets, explained that there were in fact two other leaders who were to be assassinated along with Mubarak, and he was one of them![406] Someone should be asking, How did he know this? And also, Did he know it before it happened? If he did, why did he not warn his "friend"? Arafat was also scheduled to be at the place where Mubarak was almost killed. Was it by mere coincidence, or purposeful, that Arafat arrived late for his meeting with Mubarak and that the attempt was made on the Egyptian president's life before Arafat got there? Daniel has already revealed what is in the heart of Arafat and the plans he has for Egypt and its leader. It is doubtful that Mubarak will have the wisdom to see through his "friend" Arafat and his schemes. God has a way of blinding people who are under judgment, as in the case of Samson, who never did open his eyes to what Delilah had planned for him until it was too late!

The revelation that Daniel gives concerning the little horn coming against Egypt, gives us a further indication that the little horn of Daniel is not the worldwide antichrist that comes in the last days. The antichrist is given power over all the nations (Rev. 13:5-7). If the antichrist controls nations like the US, Russia, and all of Europe, why would he choose to initiate a war with an insignificant nation like Egypt as Daniel 11:25 explains he will do. Later, Daniel 11:43 reveals why the little horn does this—to gain control over Egypt's finances. Egypt is one of the poorest of the Islamic nations. If a worldwide antichrist were in need of finances, he certainly would not pick on Egypt! However, we have seen why Arafat would choose to fight against Egypt, and compared with the Palestinians, Egypt is actually quite rich.

* 48. He and the King of Egypt Are Both Bent on Evil

"Both these kings' hearts shall be bent on evil" (Dan. 11:27a).

Before we start to feel pity for President Hosni Mubarak of Egypt, there are a few facts about him that we should understand. A very wise man once wrote, "The curse causeless shall not come" (Prov. 26:2b KJV). If the scourge of Yasser Arafat is permitted to touch Mr. Mubarak, it will be a curse that he has certainly earned. We know that Arafat's heart is bent on evil toward Israel, but what about Mubarak's?

Hosni Mubarak has ruled Egypt since 1981. Egypt is a military dictatorship that has periodic rigged elections only to satisfy the West's desire that every nation be a democracy. As Egyptian journalist Tawheed Magdy explains, "Egypt has been under a dictatorship since the pharaohs."[407] There is almost total censorship of the news media in Egypt.[408] This is a recognized fact of life in the Middle East. In fact, the Egyptian Government even controls what foreign newspapers may be brought into the country. It bans any newspaper that would print anything negative about Mubarak.[409] Understanding that Mr. Mubarak has total control of the media in Egypt, we are permitted to know what is in his heart toward Israel by listening to what is broadcast and printed in Egypt regarding the Jewish state.

More than 17 years ago, Israel signed a peace treaty with Egypt. What Israel got out of it was very similar to what it has gotten from Arafat—almost nothing. Egypt does not abide by the agreement, and Mubarak has declared that the treaty "will fall away the minute another war breaks out between Israel and an Arab country."[410] Although numerous Israeli officials have visited Egypt, Mubarak has never visited Israel during his many years as the Egyptian head of state except for his recent, hurried trip to the funeral of Rabin. He has no plan nor desire to visit his neighboring nation with which he is supposedly at peace.[411] When "an Egyptian police officer machine-gunned seven Israeli tourists, including four children, Mubarak's media declared him 'a national hero.'"[412] Egypt does whatever it can do to hinder Israel from "establishing relations with more countries."[413] That which Mubarak has in his own heart he attempts to instill in the Egyptians. This is demonstrated by the fact that "every night at the close of its broadcast, Egypt Television screens footage of... the opening hours of its treacherous 1973 invasion of Israel on Yom Kippur."[414] Amin el-Huwaidi, former Egyptian minister of war forewarned Israel about what is in the heart of his boss, saying, "The war with Israel is a certainty, and we are ready."[415] The hearts of both Arafat and Mubarak are bent on evil toward Israel; thankfully the heart of God is bent on doing Israel good in its latter end!

* 49. He and the King of Egypt Will Speak Lies At the Same Table

"...[he and the king of Egypt] shall speak lies at the same table" (Dan. 11:27b).

The way Arafat and Mubarak have fulfilled this prophecy is astounding. We must keep in mind that after the signing of the Declaration of Principles on the White House lawn in September 1993, the details of the final peace accord had to be ironed out. Where was that done? In Cairo, Egypt. And who sat often, during a period of months, at the negotiating table where this agreement was being forged? Mr. Arafat and Mr. Mubarak. Together, they spent many long hours hammering out the specific commitments and promises for each side. Mr. Shimon Peres was sent to Cairo to negotiate the deal on behalf of Israel. Poor Mr. Peres! He did not know that he was sitting at a negotiating table that Daniel saw in his vision over 2,500 years ago—a table at which the other two men would be speaking nothing but lies. These two ardent enemies of Israel both knew that Arafat would never fulfill one word of what they were promising to the Jewish people. The facts prove that they "spoke lies at the same table." Arafat has consistently violated every single promise made at that table. In some cases, it must have even required a determined effort on Arafat's part to be sure that everything he promised was purposely violated. He and Mubarak forged lies, not peace, at their negotiating table!

50. His Lies Will Finally Not Prosper Because the End Is Coming

"...but it shall not prosper, for the end will still be at the appointed time" (Dan. 11:27c).

The Lord has every detail under control. Just as Arafat consistently, purposely, and determinedly violates every promise he has made, the Lord consistently, purposely, and determinedly fulfills every jot and tittle of His Word. God's promises to His people will not fail, nor will any of Arafat's efforts to hinder God's purposes succeed. Arafat's efforts will not so much as *delay* the fulfillment of those promises even for one day. Yasser Arafat's end will come at the precise time God has appointed!

51. He Returns From His Encounter With Egypt With Great Riches

"While returning to his land with great riches" (Dan. 11:28a).

In Daniel 11:25-28a we find an interesting series of future events. We are told that the little horn decides to fight against the king of the south (Egypt). The king of the south resists him with a mighty army, something that Egypt definitely has today. Then the king of Egypt is destroyed through a successful assassination attempt from people who are near to him—people that actually eat with him. (See Daniel 11:25c-26.) The result of the armed conflict between the little horn and Egypt will be that "many shall fall down slain" (Dan. 11:26c).

What the angel reveals to Daniel next seems to explain why God allows the king of Egypt to be destroyed—because of the lies that he spoke at the negotiating table with the little horn, and because his heart, like the heart of the little horn, is bent on doing evil to Israel. The next detail gives the hope we discussed in the last point—the end of the little horn is certain. Finally, we are told that the little horn returns to his land (the areas in the holy land over which he governs), with great riches. This seems to hint that he will somehow gain control of the purse strings of Egypt. Later, we will see that Daniel confirms clearly what this passage only hints at—that the little horn will, indeed, gain control over the riches of Egypt.

52. His Heart Will Be Moved Against the Holy Covenant

"...his heart shall be moved against the holy covenant" (Dan. 11:28b).

The little horn's victory over Egypt will cause two things to enter his heart—a far greater pride and a new confidence in his military abilities to do exploits. It seems that at this point he will begin to move against God's land and God's people in a far more determined and open fashion than he had done previously. He will be moved to violate the covenant that God made with Abraham in even greater ways. From humanity's viewpoint, it will seem that the actions of the little horn will spell the end for Israel. However, from heaven's vantage point, the little horn's new zeal to violate God's Word will be correctly interpreted as one giant step toward divine intervention to annihilate him and the rest of Israel's enemies.

* 53. He Shall Do Things Against the Jews and Return to Palestinian Lands

"...he shall do damage and return to his own land" (Dan. 11:28c).

We should keep in mind that Daniel has already shown us that the "land" of the little horn is within the Glorious Land (the holy land) itself. Today, that land is called the "autonomous areas" that are under Arafat's Palestinian Authority. Most people whose eyes were opened to understand what was *really* happening at the signing of the peace accord knew that Arafat would use his newly acquired lands to facilitate the launching of greater terrorist attacks against Israel. After all, we have already seen that he declared this to be his goal on a Jordanian television interview immediately after signing the initial agreement with Israel in Washington. His PLO is already demonstrating just how effectively they can use their new "nation within the nation" for this purpose. Arafat and the PLO are now fulfilling this prophecy in unmistakable ways. Unfortunately, what the PLO has done so far is only a very small beginning to the horrendous plundering of the land and the slaughter of the Jews that is soon to come through the PLO and other Islamic enemies. In the context of what will transpire in Israel in the last days, the Old Testament prophets repeatedly speak of the wholesale plundering that Israel will face in the last days. Through Nahum, God promises that He will "restore the excellence of Jacob like the excellence of Israel, for the emptiers have emptied them out and ruined their vine branches" (Nah. 2:2). From this prophecy, we are permitted to understand part of the reason God promises to restore Israel—they will *need* to be restored after the emptying or plundering that the nation will suffer unjustly.

The plundering of Israel in the last days will be similar to what they experienced under the hand of the Midianites in the Book of Judges where they lost just about everything. (See Judges 6:1-8.) God's answer in these days will be the same as His answer in those days—as soon as Israel cries out to Him for help He will send them deliverance. Gideon was raised up to destroy the Midianites, and God has promised that there will be another battle in the last days like the battle of Gideon. In this battle, the Lord has avowed that He will destroy the yoke that Israel's enemies have placed upon them. During the last days, the yoke will be placed on Israel not only by the PLO but by other nations of Islam also, including "the Assyrian," who will be the last Islamic enemy that will plunder and destroy Israel. (See Micah 5:4-9 and Isaiah 10:5-12.)

Concerning this final enemy, Israel's King has promised His people a victory similar to Gideon's victory over the Midianite plunderers. His Word declares, "And the Lord of hosts will stir up a scourge for him like the slaughter of Midian at the rock of Oreb" (Isa. 10:26). For Israel, deliverance is just a prayer away, but that prayer must be directed to Yeshua (Jesus), their Messiah!

Isaiah reveals Israel's glorious end after they have experienced this grossly unjust plundering in "the time to come," when not even one nation on earth will have the uprightness to demand a restoration of Israel's goods. Isaiah writes, "This is a people robbed and plundered... They are for prey, and no one delivers; for plunder, and **no one says, 'Restore!'** Who among you will give ear to this? Who will listen and hear **for the time to come**? Who gave Jacob for plunder, and Israel to the robbers? Was it not the Lord, He against whom we have sinned?... Therefore He has poured on [Israel] the fury of His anger and the strength of battle; it has set him on fire all around, yet he did not know; and it burned him, yet he did not take it to heart. But now, thus says the Lord, who created you, O Jacob, And He who formed you, O Israel: 'Fear not, for I have redeemed you; I have called you by your name; you are Mine. When you pass through the waters, I will be with you; and through the rivers, they shall not overflow you. When you walk through the fire, you shall not be burned, nor shall the flame scorch you. For I am the Lord your God, the Holy One of Israel, your Savior' " (Isa. 42:22-43:3a). What a glorious end is promised to those who will experience divine discipline through plundering, robbery, burning, and the floods of wickedness!

We have already discussed how the PLO officials actually order the specific make and color of car they want. Their bandits then cross the Green Line, steal the vehicle from some hapless Israeli, and take it back across that imaginary Green Line. Israel has decided not to send its armed forces across the Green Line to capture murderers, much less to recover stolen goods. Arafat is discovering just how wonderfully easy it will be to "do damage [to the Jews] and return to his own land."

The clarity with which Daniel saw these endtime events is absolutely awe-inspiring. He must have been amazed by what he witnessed here—that the little horn could go out from his own land, do damage against the Jews, and then return to his own land with impunity. Something that amazes me, personally, regarding the prophetic word is that the great men of God actually looked ahead and saw these things happening, yet we cannot even see them when they are taking place in front of our eyes!

Some Christians have concluded that it is impossible to understand what will happen in the future through the study of biblical prophecy. Since they have witnessed so many examples of biblical prophecies being misunderstood, misinterpreted, and misapplied, they have come to the mistaken conclusion that it is impossible for a prophecy to be understood until after it has already been fulfilled. However, our God never changes, and throughout history He has revealed His secrets concerning the future to His servants through the written prophetic word. In fact, even Daniel, a man who had great prophetic revelations himself, relied on the prophecies of Jeremiah to determine future events in Daniel 9:2. Instead of assuming that God has changed or that He no longer plans for prophecy to give us insight into the future, let's place the blame squarely where it belongs—our problem is spiritual blindness. Personally, there is one thing that I understand more clearly about myself as the years go by, and that is just how blind I really am. It requires a great miracle for any of us to see and understand any truth in God's Word. With regard to understanding the fulfillment of prophecy, without a miracle, it is just as impossible to see how it *has* been fulfilled as it is to see how it *will* be fulfilled.

If, to any degree, Yasser Arafat is fulfilling Daniel's prophecies about the little horn, the Church today gives a clear example of spiritual blindness—it almost universally ignores the fulfillment of Daniel's prophecies that have already occurred. God's people living during the First Coming of Christ were plagued with spiritual blindness also. Most of them never did see that prophecies were being fulfilled before their eyes by Jesus of Nazareth. Long after the Lord had already returned to heaven, they continued waiting for the Messiah's coming and for the *beginning* of the fulfillment of the Messianic prophecies. Lord, open our eyes that we may see and not blindly ignore the fulfillment of Your prophetic word during the events of Your Second Coming!

54. His Further Intervention In Egypt
Will Bring Foreign Attack Against Him

"At the appointed time he shall return and go toward the south;
but it shall not be like the former or the latter. For ships
from Cyprus shall come against him" (Dan. 11:29-30a).

Apparently, the little horn will see a need to mobilize against Egypt again. The probable reason is quite obvious. The Egyptians will not likely sit by and allow an outsider to continue exercising control over the nation. No king would return to fight against a nation that he had already conquered unless he had lost some or all control over it. On this occasion, the little horn will be hindered by foreign intervention—ships from Cyprus. Cyprus is in the Mediterranean, and that is the direction from where these ships come. This scene could very well involve a United Nations effort to limit Egypt's humiliation. Interestingly enough, the present Secretary General of the UN is Boutros Boutros-Ghali, an Egyptian. Like Arafat, he is also a great "lover" of the State of Israel. He let the world know his feelings toward Israel when he declared, "The Jews must give up their status as a nation and Israel as a state, and assimilate as a community in the Arab world."[416] With a vision like that, it is no wonder that he was chosen as the Secretary General by the Arab-controlled UN! He is surely delighted with Arafat's success. However, he may not be content to see Arafat conquer his beloved Egypt. Such an event might move him to petition the UN to do something to save the Egyptians, especially if he continues as its Secretary General.

55. He Shall Be Grieved and Do
Even Greater Damage to the Jews

"...he shall be grieved, and return in rage against
the holy covenant, and do damage" (Dan. 11:30b).

When the little horn's plans for Egypt are frustrated, it will anger him, and cause him to direct his attacks against Israel in still greater ways.

* 56. He Succeeds In Getting
Unbelieving Jews on His Side

*"...he shall return and show regard for those
who forsake the holy covenant" (Dan. 11:30c).*

Who are those who "forsake the holy covenant"? We can only determine this if we understand what the "holy covenant" is. The angel
told Daniel that he was showing him what would happen to his people,
Israel, in the last days. In the context of Israel, we understand that the
"holy covenant" has to be the covenant that the Lord made with Abraham and the "holy people." The covenant is found in Genesis 17:7-8
where the Lord promises that He will be Abraham's God and the God
of his children, and that Canaan has been given to Abraham and his
descendants forever. Any Jew today who does not accept the God of
Abraham as his God, or who disregards, in any way, Israel's claim to
the holy land, has forsaken this holy covenant in his heart.

There is only one primary reason Yasser Arafat has been succeeding in his plans to form a Palestinian nation within the nation of Israel
and on the holy land itself—Jews who have forsaken the covenant have
been on his side! He showed great regard for Mr. Rabin and Mr. Peres,
who helped him enormously. One of the reasons they helped him was
their own lack of faith in the God of Abraham and in His covenant that
gives Israel a divine right to the land of Canaan. Arafat has shown
great regard for Rabin's widow, Leah Rabin. She has appointed herself as the torchbearer for the peace process that Rabin began.[417]
Arafat visited her home after the assassination of her husband and declared that her children were his children. Even though he is Israel's
fiercest enemy and hates Jews with a passion, he has shown regard for
those who forsake the covenant.

The Prophet Isaiah has a message that seems to apply to Israel today as much or more than at any other time in their history. He warns,
"Therefore hear the word of the Lord, you scornful men, who rule this
people who are in Jerusalem, because you have said, 'We have made a
covenant with death, and with Sheol we are in agreement. When the
overflowing scourge passes through, it will not come to us, for we have
made lies our refuge, and under falsehood we have hidden ourselves.'
Therefore thus says the Lord God... 'The hail will sweep away the refuge of lies, and the waters will overflow the hiding place. Your covenant with death will be annulled, and your agreement with Sheol will
not stand; when the overflowing scourge passes through, then you will

be trampled down by it. As often as it goes out it will take you; for morning by morning it will pass over, and by day and by night; it will be a terror just to understand the report' " (Isa. 28:14-19). The terrorism that will yet come to Israel is so horrendous that just the news of it will, in itself, be a terror to the nation and the world!

It is obvious that Israel's two top national leaders would not have been able to forsake the covenant and give away God's land without a ground swell of support from the Israelis themselves. Israel today is filled with secular Jews who openly state that the land means nothing and that Israel no longer has any right to the land God gave to Abraham.[418] Shulamit Aloni has been a cabinet member in the Israeli government and a well-known member of the Knesset (Israeli Parliament) for years. On Israeli radio, she declared that it is not logical to think that the God of one little people of three million, five hundred thousand is stronger than the god of 200 million Arabs. She speaks for many who have forsaken the holy covenant in their hearts. Remember, there were 100,000 Israelis in the "Peace Now" rally, many holding placards calling for peace, when Yitzhak Rabin was gunned down. The desire to make peace at any cost was not only in his heart but is in the hearts of many Jews. Mr. Arafat will continue to show great regard for the Jews who forsake the covenant, and he will continue to enjoy their support, even as he directs his gunmen in the destruction of the nation.

57. His Army Will Desecrate the Temple Mount

"His armed forces will rise up to desecrate the temple fortress"
(Dan. 11:31a NIV).

This is definitely future, but also, its meaning is definitely very clear. Although some English versions translate this passage to say that the little horn's army will profane "the temple *and* fortress" (emphasis mine), the Hebrew simply says "the temple fortress." As Christians, it is *extremely* important that we take careful note of what is said here. The little horn's army does *not* desecrate the temple or the altar. It desecrates the "temple fortress," which refers to the "place of protection" for the temple.[419] In other words, his army desecrates what is known today as "the Temple Mount." It is the huge walled-in area that protects the place where the temple once stood. For a practicing Jew, it is the most holy place in all of Israel.

If a temple were to exist, a man so hateful and so abominable as the little horn would definitely defile that temple once his armed forces had control of the temple fortress or Temple Mount. Imagine this impossible scenario: 1) for whatever reason, the Mosque of Omar (presently built very near or precisely on the only God-ordained site for the temple) is destroyed, 2) instead of permitting Islam to rebuild their third most holy site on earth, the Jews, whose very existence daily proves that Islam is false, build a Jewish temple, 3) the little horn, who arose out of Islam, manages to take back the Temple Mount, and 4) instead of using his army to desecrate the temple and tear it down, he just desecrates the Temple Mount—all the army does is walk around outside the Jewish temple without doing any damage to the temple itself. Do you see any incongruence between this scenario and the violent, wicked nature of the little horn that Daniel has been revealing in more than 56 previous prophetic descriptions?

Once again, we see that instead of speaking about a temple in the last days, Daniel speaks consistently about the Temple Mount only. The only way a Jewish temple could be built would be for the Mosque of Omar to be destroyed. Many Christians believe that the Jews will rebuild their temple approximately seven years before the physical return of Christ. However, the Mosque of Omar really poses a problem for this belief, because it would have to be removed first. Some Christians have "resolved" this dilemma in a very convenient way. They are now saying that the Jews might agree to build a temple somewhere alongside the mosque. That would definitely provide a very easy solution, *if* it were even remotely possible! To support this speculation, it has even been suggested that the Jews themselves now recognize that the mosque is not really built on the authentic site of the previous temple. This theory reaches the conclusion that the Jews would have no objection, therefore, to building a temple near the Moslem mosque on the proper site. I humbly submit that these ideas would be termed ludicrous by any Orthodox Jew either inside or outside Israel. For Orthodox Jews, these options are not even worth considering. I am aware of an organization in Israel called "The Temple Mount Faithful" that is pressing for a rebuilt Jewish temple, but they are a very small group who will not be the ones to decide. It is very probable that the greatest enthusiasm for a rebuilt temple is found among the evangelical Christians themselves. They "need" a temple to be rebuilt even more than the Jews do because, if one is *not* rebuilt, their doctrine concerning the last days will be proven incorrect! Unfortunately, there are some insurmountable problems inherent in all the talk about a rebuilt temple.

Why No Jewish Temple Will Be
Rebuilt Before the Lord Comes

First, the Jews simply cannot have a temple without a sanctified outer court, and a "sanctified" court precludes the existence of two satanic mosques inside! Second, there is a far more basic and formidable problem with the idea that the Jews would be as quick to build their temple as Gentile Christians are to build a new church building. The problem is that there is no recognized priestly body within Judaism today, and what purpose would a temple serve without having priests who could minister there in accordance with the Mosaic law? There are many rabbis, but rabbis do not even have to be Levites, much less be descendants of Aaron, the only priestly family in the tribe of Levi. There are many Jews who bear the name "Cohen," which actually means "priest" in Hebrew. However, there is not one who has an authentic genealogical record covering the last 2,000 years of Jewish history to prove that he comes from the family of Aaron, the priestly family. Few Jews are even sure of what *tribe* or mixture of tribes they come from, much less to what *family* they belong! After centuries of intermarriage, not only among different tribes, but also with Gentiles, no one claims to be qualified to be a priest. This tremendous dilemma faced Israel in Old Testament times after just 70 years of Babylonian exile. After returning from Babylon, all those who belonged to the priesthood who could not produce an authentic genealogy were "excluded from the priesthood as defiled" and could not even eat of the priests' daily rations much less officiate in the temple (Ezra 2:62-63; Neh. 7:64-65).

The Orthodox Jews believe that the only solution to this dilemma is much the same as it was in the days of Ezra and Nehemiah. In those days, Nehemiah concluded that God would have to supernaturally reveal the qualifications to serve as priests of all those who did not have a genealogy. This was to be done through the "Urim and Thummim" (Neh. 7:65), a method God used to give Israel guidance. The Jews believe that the same thing must be done at the coming of the Messiah. They believe that He is the only one who can tell them which Jews have pure enough blood to be considered true descendants of Aaron. Although most Orthodox Jews continue to reject their Messiah, they still attempt to adhere to every detail of the Old Testament. No Jew would ever appoint himself to be a priest, because the Orthodox Jews believe that if anyone were to be so presumptuous as to do so without the proper genealogy that he would die upon entering the Holy of Holies. As I mentioned, most of the speculation about a temple being rebuilt and "temple fever" is found within the "Gentile church." Not only would the Orthodox Jews oppose such a move, but so would the secular government of Israel, to say nothing of the Islamic world! Islamic law forbids any non-Moslem even to pray on the Temple Mount, as we have already discussed. Moslems are not generally known for being very flexible with the requirements of their religion!

Since Daniel's message concerns natural Israel in the very end, it is vital that we carefully consider what Daniel is revealing here. Understanding Daniel's revelation will help us understand other Scriptures that are sometimes used to "prove" that there will be a physical temple in Jerusalem in the last days. Traditionally, the Book of Daniel itself is one of the primary scriptural sources used to "prove" that a temple will exist in the end, but, in fact, Daniel consistently shows us just the opposite! We will return to this issue a little later on, and we will examine some of the "proof texts" that are used to teach that a Jewish temple will be rebuilt before Christ returns.

58. His Army Shall Take Away the "Continual"

"...they shall take away the daily sacrifices" (Dan. 11:31b).

This detail brings even greater clarity to what will actually happen in the end. We have already seen that in the Hebrew text the "daily sacrifice" is actually the "continual." In point 19 we looked at the reasons this Hebrew word almost certainly refers to the continual prayer and praise of the Jews today. This passage adds further evidence to that study. Once again, the wording here is very interesting and very important. It is the "army" that takes away the "continual." If Daniel is speaking only about a daily animal sacrifice that a group of priests are offering each day in a physical temple, this is a rather unusual way to refer to how it will be stopped. The little horn would not need an army to haul away a continual animal sacrifice once his army controls the Temple Mount. The continual sacrifice of the Mosaic law consists of a little lamb that is one year old—hardly big enough to become a burden for a whole army! (See Exodus 29:38.)

If the "continual" is referring to animal sacrifices, once the little horn's army is in control of the Temple Mount, a simple order from the commander would be sufficient to stop any further sacrifices. The army would not have to "take it away." In addition, the few priests who would be ordained to offer that sacrifice would not even be able to *enter* the temple area to offer it if an army were in control. Just the presence of a ceremonially unclean Gentile army would preclude that possibility; the army certainly would not have to "take away" anything! Furthermore, no Orthodox priest would be *willing* to enter the temple area to offer such a sacrifice if the court of the temple were defiled by Gentiles. The immediate Jewish, biblical reaction to a Gentile defilement of their temple is seen in Acts 21:30. There they thought the temple had been defiled by just four Gentiles, and they immediately ordered the doors shut. What would they do if a whole army were trampling it underfoot? Would they try to force their way in, resisting an army of Moslems, to offer a Mosaic sacrifice in spite of the whole area being ceremonially unclean? For those who have doubts about the answers to these questions, I would recommend asking an Orthodox rabbi!

If the "continual" is, in fact, referring to a multitude of Jews who pray every morning and every evening at the Western Wall or upon the Temple Mount itself, then only an army could take this "continual" away. Arafat and his Moslem leaders, acting as his puppets, have already declared that Jews will not be permitted to pray at the Al-Aksa Mosque or at the wall surrounding the mosque. Continual Jewish prayers *will* become an issue, and *that* continual offering will be taken away by the force of an army when the little horn controls the Temple Mount! Few in the Western world fully realize just how precious the believing Jews consider the Temple Mount to be. An interview with the Israeli army officer who commanded the forces that took control of the Temple Mount in 1967 should help us understand the Jewish heart regarding this matter: "... said the tough commando leader who took the Wall: 'None of us alive has ever seen or done anything so great as [our commander] has done today,' And there by the Wall, he broke down and wept."[420]

59. His Army Shall Place on the Temple Mount the Abomination That Causes Desolation

"Then they will set up the abomination that causes desolation"
(Dan. 11:31c NIV).

Daniel makes it very clear here and elsewhere in his book that an abomination of some sort will be established in Jerusalem. This abomination is established or set up by the army of the little horn and not only by the little horn himself. This abomination will cause desolation to God's people and their land. It will also cause "astonishment," another meaning that the translators have frequently given to the Hebrew word translated as "desolation" here.[421] A very popular concept in the Church today is that the antichrist will offer a swine on a literal altar in a literal temple that will be rebuilt on the Temple Mount in Jerusalem. Let's carefully consider what Daniel and other Scriptures tell us.

In What Way Will the Antichrist "Sit In the Temple"?

Some may point to a popular "proof text" that supposedly shows there will be a physical temple in the last days. That text is II Thessalonians 2:4 where Paul explains that the antichrist "opposes and exalts himself above all that is called God or that is worshipped, so that he sits as God in the temple of God, showing himself that he is God." Is it possible that the "temple of God" to which Paul refers here is the same "temple of God" that he taught the Gentile Believers about throughout the New Testament? We should ask ourselves, Did Paul expect his Gentile readers to forget everything he had taught them about the temple of God being the Body of Christ as they read this passage? Were they supposed to make a huge mental leap over to Jerusalem and begin to think about a temple made of stones and wood? Paul had taught them that, ever since the cross, the Church is the temple of God. (See Ephesians 2:20-22 and I Corinthians 3:16-17.) Far from expecting them to think about a different temple, he exhorts them to remember what he had taught them (II Thess. 2:15). We should recall here that John also explains that the antichrist comes out of the Church, not out of a temple in Jerusalem (1 Jn. 2:18-19).

How could the antichrist sit in the Church saying that he is God in the same way that God does? First, how does God "sit in the Church"? He does not sit in a physical building in a physical way. God sits in the Church in the spiritual realm, and is enthroned by His people through true, Spirit-inspired worship. (See Psalm 22:3 and 29:10.) Note that in Paul's reference to the antichrist above, he confirms that this is how he too will sit in the Church as he "exalts himself... above all that is *worshipped...* **so that** he sits as God in the temple." Worship has much to do with how the antichrist succeeds in sitting as God in the temple. Few would be deceived if a man were to sit in a physical temple in Jerusalem saying that he is God. When did God last do that? However, there are definitely times when people have declared that God was in the church when, in fact, what they experienced was a manifestation of Satan who "transforms himself into an angel of light" (II Cor. 11:14). When we fail to walk uprightly before the Lord, is it possible that our sacrifice of worship might be unacceptable to God just as Cain's was unacceptable? Jude 11-12 explains that there are people in the Church who definitely follow Cain's path and example! When that happens, we may not know whom we are worshipping as Jesus warns in John 4:22.

The Antichrist Comes Out of the True Church

The Apostle John explains that there are many antichrists in the world and that they all went out from the Church.[422] (See I John 2:18.) From the beginning of history, the men who have been used as biblical symbols of the antichrist all came from among the people of God and walked with the people of God. Some examples are Cain, a product of Adam himself and part of the family; Dan, the "serpent" of Genesis 49:17, who does not appear among the tribes in Revelation 7; Abimelech, the wicked judge; Absalom, the very son of David; and Judas, one of the twelve who walked with Jesus and the other apostles and was one of the 12 apostles who rejoiced at the power of God manifested through their ministries. Most people still remember a modern-day example— Jim Jones. He originally came out of the evangelical church, but, in the end, he proved to be a servant of Satan and not of God.

The Dangers of Expecting a Physical Temple to Be Rebuilt

Christians are exposed to two very real dangers if they are incorrect in believing that a literal temple will be rebuilt in Jerusalem as an indication that the end is near. First, if no temple will be rebuilt before the Lord returns, the events of the last days could possibly occur with some Christians not even being aware of it. This would be nothing new. Most of God's people were totally unaware that the events of Christ's First Coming were being fulfilled before their very eyes 2,000 years ago. The second danger is much more serious and very subtle. God's people could be deceived into collaborating with Satan and participating in his system if they do not even recognize what his system involves or that it is already present and functioning. I know that many Christians are certain that they will be raptured before the antichrist is revealed. I deal with this subject in *The Final Victory: The Year 2000*.[423] Again, what if they are mistaken? If Satan's deception was strong enough to blind one third of the angels that lived in God's literal presence, only God's mercy can keep any of us from being deceived. Let's daily present ourselves before the Lord in humility and ask Him to give us greater light and also to give us a heart that is willing to make adjustments in what we believe every time He shows us our need to do so.

We are, by nature, so carnal and earthly that we tend to expect very carnal and earthly events—obvious to the natural eyes and ears—to alert us to Christ's coming. There must be a reason that near the beginning of the message of Revelation, the Church is forewarned seven times, "He who has an ear, let him hear what the Spirit says to the churches" (Rev. 2:7,11,17,29; 3:6,13,22). Without spiritual ears and eyes that are opened by God, we will neither hear nor see what is happening around us in the last days!

The Popular Doctrine About a Rebuilt Temple Is Contradictory to What Most Believe In Other Areas

Most of the Church today is familiar with the teaching of the Bible concerning God's disciplinary measures toward natural Israel, and that His discipline is designed to bring His people back to Himself in the last days. The Church also knows that most Jews continue to rebel against their Messiah to this day. The Church knows that Jesus Christ fulfilled the Old Testament animal sacrifices on the cross, and ordained that his spiritual temple, the Church, now offer Him *spiritual* sacrifices from His *spiritual* temple. (See Hebrews 8:1-2 and 13:10-16.) In light of these beliefs, a Christian of today would strongly reject any attempt to approach God through a return to animal sacrifices. In fact, most Christians would classify such an attempt as "abominable."

In spite of these convictions, the popular doctrine in the Church today teaches that the Jews, with the help or authorization of the antichrist, will rebuild their temple and begin to offer animal sacrifices again on a physical altar. Whether that will happen or not is not the principal issue here. What this popular teaching asks us to do next is totally contradictory to Scripture and to sound doctrinal belief. We are then asked to believe that the Holy Spirit would repeatedly call this temple "God's temple" in the Bible. This teaching assumes that the temple called "God's temple" in II Thessalonians 2:4 is an edifice that Jews will build with antichrist approval. Even though these Jews continue to rebel against their Messiah, it is further assumed that this temple is the same temple referred to in Revelation 11:1,19—"the temple of God." According to this teaching, that which will be an "abomination that causes desolation" is the offering of a pig on the Jews' recently built altar. The unspoken impression that this teaching gives is that somehow, when the Jews return to animal sacrifices, what they build and what they offer will be acceptable enough to the Lord for the Spirit to call their new edifice "God's temple!" Wouldn't the very first lamb offered there be just as much of an abomination as a pig, especially since the Bible declares, "The sacrifice of the wicked is an abomination to the Lord"? (Prov. 15:8) Even during Israel's wilderness journey, God did not accept their sacrifices when they were walking in rebellion. (See Acts 7:42,43.) Isaiah leaves no room for doubt about how God would see any and all offerings that the Jews could possibly offer as long as they continue to go their own way. To God's people who have "chosen their own ways" (Isa. 66:3b), Isaiah writes, "He that killeth an ox is as if he slew a man; he that sacrificeth a lamb, as if he cut off a dog's neck; he that offereth an oblation, as if he offered **swine's blood**; he that burneth incense, as if he blessed an idol" (Isa. 66:3a). Are we supposed to believe, then, that presumably a temple will be rebuilt where abominations are offered daily, and where God considers the worship found there to be idolatrous, and, in spite of all this, the Spirit will still call it "God's temple"? Are we actually to assume that somehow the antichrist could defile this wonderful place by offering a swine on its altar? By definition, something must be holy before anyone can defile it. Could God possibly consider such a place "holy"? This whole interpretation of endtime events is very contradictory to what most of us believe in other doctrinal areas and about other Scriptures!

Christ's Teaching on the Abomination of Desolation

A classic example of our tendency to expect the obvious is demonstrated by the popular teaching regarding the abomination that causes desolation in the last days. In Christ's teaching concerning this subject and the last days, He alerts us to the fact that this event will definitely not be obvious to the casual observer, not even among His people. He warns, "Therefore when you [disciples] see the 'abomination of desolation,' spoken of by Daniel the prophet, standing in the holy place **(whoever reads, let him understand)**, then let those who are in Judea flee to the mountains" (Matt. 24:15-16). Why would this Scripture exhort us concerning the importance of understanding His words in this passage? There is clearly some reason we need a special understanding to perceive what Jesus is talking about. No one would need special understanding if the fulfillment of this were totally obvious to our natural eyes.

If the day ever came when a human being were to offer a literal pig on a physical altar in a physical temple in Jerusalem, most of God's people would perceive it to be an abomination—we would not need very much divine understanding! What if Jesus is not talking about a physical temple or a literal, abominable offering of swine's flesh? *Then*, we would need understanding! Hidden within the words the Lord speaks here, we find a key. This abomination will stand in the "holy place." If He is speaking in the context of a literal temple, then He made a mistake here. Animal sacrifices cannot be offered in the "holy place" of the temple because the brazen altar is in the outer court. What if the abomination is not a *physical* pig, but is a *spiritual* pig that defiles the "holy place"? Both in the Bible, and in the mind of the Jews, Mount Zion or Jerusalem is the holiest part of the holy land, and, within Jerusalem, the Temple Mount is the holiest part of Jerusalem. Could the army of the little horn that takes away the "continual" also be used by the little horn to establish a spiritual abomination that will end up causing desolation in Israel?

Daniel Gives An Indication of What the Abomination of Desolation Will Be

For the sake of clarity on this subject, we will allow ourselves a sneak preview of one of the last details that Daniel gives concerning the little horn. He writes, "He will pitch his royal tents between the seas at the beautiful holy mountain" (Dan. 11:45 NIV). Throughout the Old Testament the "holy mountain" refers to Jerusalem. In fact, this is how Daniel himself refers to Jerusalem. He prays, "Let Your anger and Your fury be turned away from Your city Jerusalem, Your holy mountain" (Dan. 9:16). The "royal tents" of the little horn refer to his seat of government or the seat of his authority. Daniel foresaw that the little horn would "pitch his royal tents... at the beautiful holy mountain." In other words, Jerusalem will, sadly enough, become the capital of the little horn's government in the last days. It is possible that Israel will agree to some sort of international involvement in the administration of Jerusalem, but Yasser Arafat will definitely be a part of any future arrangement to govern the Old City—if not through negotiations, then ultimately through armed intervention.

To make Jerusalem his capital has been precisely the avowed goal of Yasser Arafat from the beginning. He and the PLO continue to declare that there will be war until they possess Jerusalem as the capital of their new Palestinian state. Arafat's army will undoubtedly succeed in establishing him in Jerusalem through terrorism and continued killing. Will Yasser Arafat's control over Jerusalem be an abomination? Do you know what Jerusalem means to God's people? Have you seen the oft-published photograph of the Israeli soldiers weeping when they approached the Western Wall of the Temple Mount for the first time after taking the city back from the Gentiles in 1967? They had waited many long years to walk again within that city! For centuries Jews throughout the world ended their yearly Passover celebration with the expectant shout of joy, "Next year in Jerusalem!" After the war of 1967, many of them would no longer have to say that again.

Does Jerusalem mean anything to you? Is it no longer important that the Lord will literally reign some day soon from His holy mountain, Jerusalem? Does it matter that "at that time Jerusalem shall be called The Throne of the Lord, and all the nations shall be gathered to it, to the name of the Lord, to Jerusalem"? (Jer. 3:17a) In the New Testament age, we are exhorted to speak and sing the Psalms (Eph. 5:19). Therefore, we should obey them. The psalmists reveal God's attitude toward Jerusalem. We are exhorted, "Pray for the peace of Jerusalem: may they prosper who love you" (Psa. 122:6). Also, "If I forget you, O Jerusalem, let my right hand forget its skill! If I do not remember you, let my tongue cling to the roof of my mouth—if I do not exalt Jerusalem above my chief joy" (Psa. 137:5-6).

Before we totally spiritualize these Scriptures and apply them to a Gentile church, we must not forget that God spoke to Isaiah that the natural city of Jerusalem had become a spiritual harlot, and that He therefore called her "Sodom." But He has promised that this **very same city** will have her glory restored as in the beginning! (See Isaiah 1:8-10, 25-27.) Sodom is the name given to natural Jerusalem in both Isaiah and Revelation. According to Revelation 11:8, Sodom is the name of the city where our Lord was crucified. There, His blood was poured out for His people. He will never forget that city for which He wept (Lk. 19:41), for which He cried, "Jerusalem! Jerusalem!" (Lk. 13:34), and for which He died! There can be no doubt about which Jerusalem the Lord is speaking in Isaiah—the natural city of Jerusalem that Isaiah knew so well. That natural city will be restored and will continue to be a revelation of the *spiritual* city of Jerusalem, the Bride of Christ.

Can we now understand why the abominable, satanic vessel of wrath called "the little horn" would want Jerusalem? Only because God calls it *His* city and lays claim to it. What humility on God's part to lay claim to a city so small and so seemingly insignificant as Jerusalem! The Lord will place *His* royal tents there soon! Satan has always wanted to establish his royal tents or his dwelling place in the place where God has chosen to establish His. (See Isaiah 14:13.) As the coming of Christ draws near, Satan will control Jerusalem once again through the Gentiles, manifesting himself through the wicked. What a blessing to have the Lord's assurance that this newly-established Gentile rule will last only 42 months, after which He will return to establish *His* rule over the city and over the world! (See Revelation 11:2 and Daniel 7:25.)

Is it not an abomination for Israel once again to surrender God's holy hill to the Gentiles after the blood of the nation's youth has been shed to win it back in battle? Is it an abomination for Israel not only to give it to the Gentiles, but to give it to one of the most vile, perverse, and abominable Gentile organizations this world has ever known—the PLO? Is it an abomination to exalt an international criminal, Yasser Arafat, and place him over the city of God by choice? Is there a reason Deputy Defense Minister Mordechai Gur, the colonel whose troops actually took the Old City in 1967, committed suicide on July 16, 1995?[424] The excuse given is that he had cancer and did not want to be a burden to his family.[425] Could the news of Israel's willingness to negotiate over the future of Jerusalem have been a factor in his suicide? After all, he had been a national hero for almost 30 years for taking the holy city, a city that now seemed to be worthless to Israel's government. Was he to interpret this to mean that he had been a hero for a worthless cause?

There was no one in Israel that loved Jerusalem and appreciated its significance to the Jewish faith any more than Colonel Gur did in 1967. For him, conquering Jerusalem was the "ultimate mission."[426] Jordan controlled the Old City, but during the 1967 war it looked like Jordan might not get involved in the conflict. In July 1995, *The Jerusalem Post* published an article about Colonel Gur. The article explains that once the 1967 war broke out, the colonel "hoped that Jordan would offer Israel an opportunity to recoup history's 2,000-year-old debt."[427] The Israeli high command had indicated that they were not interested in capturing Jerusalem. Colonel Gur considered taking the city on his own, using the excuse that he was in hot pursuit of enemy soldiers. He asked himself what "history would say about him as the commander who failed to seize this historic opportunity."[428]

On June 7, 1967, Col. Gur's men accomplished the task they had been given—to take the Mount of Olives on the east side of the Old City. From the mount, he stood viewing the Old City. The *Post* article tells us, "As he surveyed the scene, gripped with emotion, his intelligence officer responded to a call on the radio. It was Central Command relaying an order from Chief of General Staff Yitzhak Rabin. The intelligence officer repeated it aloud to Gur: 'You are to enter the Old City immediately and capture it.' Gur had been waiting for that order for the past 24 hours. More to the point, he felt, the Jewish nation had been waiting for it for 19 centuries."[429]

Col. Gur started down the Mount of Olives immediately, but then felt he should turn around and ascend the mount again. He explained to his staff, "I want to give the command for the conquest of the Old City from an appropriate place."[430] Col. Gur most likely did not know just how prophetic his actions were. Very soon, from that very mount, the Lord Jesus Christ, the captain of the armies of heaven, will give the command to conquer the Old City one last time for all eternity! He will descend upon that very mount and fight for Jerusalem. (See Zechariah 14:1-5.) The soldiers who will be with him will be the saints of all ages. Will you be there? Col. Gur may not have fully understood the prophetic import of that moment, but he *did* understand that something deep within the Jewish soul longed to live forever in that city. It is inconceivable that Israel's negotiations to give that city back to her enemies was not at least one of the factors that influenced Col. Gur to despair of life itself.

If delivering Jerusalem into the hands of Yasser Arafat is in fact an abomination, a logical question would be, Will it be an abomination that causes desolation in Israel? In Matthew 24, Jesus explains that the establishment of the abomination of desolation will trigger the beginning of Israel's worst trials ever. (See Matthew 24:1,16,21.) Likewise, Daniel explains that the establishment of the little horn's government in the holy mountain will be the thing that triggers Israel's worst trials ever. As soon as Daniel reveals that the little horn will establish his royal tents in Jerusalem (Dan. 11:45), he declares, "**At that time** Michael shall stand up, the great prince who stands watch over the sons of your people; and **there shall be a time of trouble, such as never was since there was a nation, even to that time.** And at that time **your people shall be delivered**, every one who is found written in the book" (Dan. 12:1). Daniel's revelation here certainly adds weight to the idea that the abomination that will cause desolation is, in fact, the establishment of the little horn's government in Jerusalem.

What a glorious hope!—at *that* time in history, when the little horn enters Jerusalem, Israel will be saved; but what a terrible valley of the shadow of death lies between where we are today and that glorious salvation. It will be a horrendous valley in which Israel will pass through the greatest tribulation it has ever known! Are you praying for the peace of Jerusalem—for the remnant that will survive and be saved? Does your heart weep that the Jews could be so blind that they would allow an abomination like Yasser Arafat and the PLO to take control of God's city and cause unimaginable desolation?

* 60. He Will Corrupt the Jews Who Forsake the Covenant

"Those who do wickedly against the covenant he shall corrupt with flattery" (Dan. 11:32a).

Yasser Arafat has had incredible success in corrupting many Jews already. Many of them now ignore the PLO's continued violence and herald Arafat as a man who is only doing what is best for his people. When Arafat calls for war to be waged until all of Palestine is liberated from the Jews, and when he shouts before huge gatherings of Palestinians, "With blood and spirit we shall redeem thee, O Palestine," many Jews actually make excuses for him. They assure the Israeli populace that Arafat has to make these calls to violence in order to pacify the "extremists in his camp."[431]

The late Prime Minister Rabin went so far as to say, "Arafat wants the peace deal and is committed to the Declaration of Principles. We both are."[432] How could he have actually brought himself to have believed this? Arafat surely corrupted his spiritual sensibilities. Rabin became so protective of Arafat, Israel's worst enemy, that "on more than one occasion Rabin has been known to blame the victims and lash out at all but himself in those moments of acute discomfort produced by the increasingly frequent terrorist attacks."[433] Rabin considered Arafat's massacres as "the inevitable sacrifices for peace."[434] Before he was assassinated, it was said of Rabin that "he doesn't talk about eradicating the terrorist evil, but explains the murderers' motives and modus operandi, why they can't be stopped, and why we should stop demanding that he try more effectively to stop them."[435]

It was well-known in Israel that Mr. Rabin did not believe in the God of Israel or believe that the Jews are under the blessings of a divine covenant. Although most of Israel has not yet acknowledged its Messiah, it is interesting to observe how a Jew's faith in the God of Abraham and the Lord's covenant becomes a spiritual protective barrier around certain areas of his life. For example, I am not aware of a single covenant-believing Jew who sees Arafat and his mobsters in a favorable light—they have not been deceived or corrupted in this area. In fact, it is these people who have raised their voices against giving the holy land to the enemies of the Jews. They were even called "religious fanatics" by the Labor government that lost the May 1996 elections. They find themselves being mocked and ridiculed in much the same way that the "religious right" experiences in the US.

Those who have no interest in the Bible or in what God has promised the nation have actually become corrupted by Arafat's influence over them. They have lied repeatedly to the nation about their intentions and regarding what they have already given away or have already *promised* to give away in their peace negotiations with Israel's enemies—not only with Arafat but with Syria also. For example, on May 10, 1994, Arafat announced that the Israeli government had given him a letter allowing him to continue his political activity in East Jerusalem through the Orient House where PLO offices are located.[436] Both Rabin and Peres flatly denied that such a letter existed.[437] Later, in June 1994, they admitted that it did.[438] It turns out that not only does the letter exist, but it also promises Arafat control over all the Islamic and Christian holy sites.[439] Of course, this includes the Temple Mount, the principal Islamic holy site in Jerusalem. Instead of recognizing the seriousness of what the government had done and apologizing for it, a reporter wrote that Peres' response to the Israeli outcry over the letter was to ask "in his characteristic, sanctimonious simplicity: 'Can't people write articles any more?' "[440] Imagine how corrupt and blind this is—promising control over Jerusalem to the PLO and calling it nothing more than "an article!"

Early in 1996, Mr. Peres, who became Prime Minister after the assassination of Rabin, assured Israel that the government was not willing even to negotiate regarding the possibility of Jerusalem becoming a Palestinian capital.[441] The Israeli Labor government's long list of political flip-flops made it difficult for the nation to believe such declarations. That was surely one reason Labor lost the May 1996 elections to Likud, Israel's conservative party. One of the better known flip-flops was Yitzhak Rabin's change of attitude on the Golan Heights. On June 10, 1992, in Rabin's campaign speech to the settlers on the Golan Heights, he vowed, "Withdrawal from the Golan Heights is unthinkable, even in times of peace. Anyone considering withdrawal from the Golan Heights would be abandoning Israel's security... And you, the residents—those of you who made the Golan Heights what it is—have all my respect."[442] Just over two years later, on September 12, 1994, during his peace negotiations with Syria, Mr. Rabin declared, "The Golan is last on my list of priorities." When the possibility of giving the Golan to Syria raised a tremendous furor among the residents of the Golan, Rabin went so far as to call the settlers "crybabies"[443] who are second-class citizens.[444] These were the same people to whom Rabin had previously declared his respect! The little horn's power to corrupt those who forsake the covenant is surely a satanic spiritual influence that could very well have been affecting the Israeli Labor government's leadership in their negotiations with their other enemies also. The same sort of duplicity seemed to be repeating itself in the recent peace negotiations with Syria!

Christians, Beware! The Little Horn Is Also Corrupting the Church

Upon finishing the manuscript for this book, I asked an Israeli Believer, who is an expert on Israel's recent history, to read it and check to see that I have all the facts right. There were at least four reasons for choosing this particular person. First, he loves and knows the Lord. Second, we had met only recently, so I knew that he would be an unbiased reader. Third, he is another person whose mother tongue is Hebrew, and could, therefore, double check the Scriptures from Daniel. And fourth, he was born and raised in Israel and has firsthand knowledge of what has been going on in the holy land, especially since he personally fought in Israel's last two wars.

When my wife and I dropped off the manuscript at his home, he was not there. His distraught wife met us to receive it. She did not know us personally, and had no idea whatsoever that I was leaving a manuscript, much less its theme. She was distraught because she had just come from a widely publicized series of meetings where thousands of Christians had gathered in Jerusalem from different parts of the world. The speaker was one of the best-known TV preachers in the US. He told the enormous crowd of Christians that a few hours before he had been with Yasser Arafat and had experienced a very wonderful time of prayer with him. Most of the people went away very excited about Arafat's glorious desire to please God. This minister was not the first well-known Christian preacher who has been well-received by Arafat. Nor was he the first to be permitted to lay hands on Arafat and pray for him. Is Arafat sincerely turning away from Mohammed and becoming a Christian who will deeply love Israel so much that he will give God's land back to God's people, or does he have other motives in mind?

Arafat has succeeded in winning the moral support of basically every nation on earth. Most of the news media disseminate his version of the news. But there is a thorn in his side. There is one very influential group of people on earth who have not yet become Arafat fans. It is a group that is gaining influence in the US. Since the US, as a whole, is a country that, at any moment, could become a "wrench in the works" for Mr. Arafat, he urgently needs to win the support of this powerful group also to preclude any possible change in US policy toward the PLO. Over the last few years, enormous sectors of this powerful group of people have become extremely loyal to the State of Israel and are delighted to see God's people being restored. From reports we have been receiving, Mr. Arafat has learned how to win the hearts of this one last group on earth—the Christians!

Arafat now knows that amazing things can happen to his cause if he will simply be willing to give some time to well-known Christian leaders who are either gullible or ignorant of the facts. He has learned that these leaders are looking for great spiritual, soul-winning exploits that they will be able to testify about when they return to the US. He has discovered, by recent events, that if he allows certain influential leaders to spend time praying with him and to lay their hands on him, he can get favorable publicity that will turn millions of hearts toward him in the US and throughout the world. It must bring deep satisfaction to his "righteous" soul when Christian leaders, who have experienced firsthand the "transformed" Arafat, write a book to let Christians know what a wonderful lover of God this man has become. Investing a few minutes to allow these people to pray over him is possibly the most inexpensive and most effectual propaganda this man has ever received. He must stand in awe, as well as laugh, at the glowing reports that are given to multitudes of Christians in the US and elsewhere about the transformed Arafat who loves Jesus, the first Palestinian Christian.

Who knows what else takes place as these well-meaning Christians lay hands on Arafat. This would certainly seem to be a violation of the Apostle Paul's warning, "Do not lay hands on anyone hastily, nor share in other people's sins" (I Tim. 5:22). As a minister, I would consider that laying hands on Arafat to receive the baptism in the Holy Spirit would most likely be a little hasty. My fear would be that I might receive a reverse impartation that Paul seems to indicate is possible in his warning. If that were to occur, I would become a partaker of Arafat's multiplied sins and unclean spirits!

There is a tragic ignorance in the hearts of these Christian leaders. How can it be that the Church today is willing to be the tool that puts the finishing touches on Arafat's transformation before the eyes of the world? The secular world has transformed him from a murderous villain into an international statesman, and now the religious world is being used to transform him from a lifelong hater of God and murderer of His people into a wonderful Christian. If Israel now loses its Christian support, it will truly be all alone in this world; alone in a sea of anti-Semitism and hatred.

* 61. He Will Do All According to His Own Will

"Then the king shall do according to his own will" (Dan. 11:36a).

Arafat is known to be a man who does all according to his own will and is accountable to no one. Financially, he runs a multi-billion dollar operation, but no one is certain of how big it is or of how much money is involved. According to Britain's National Criminal Intelligence Services, the assets of the PLO were around $10 billion in 1993, with an annual income of one and a half to two billion dollars—"mainly from illegal activities."[445] If there is any accounting kept, only Arafat knows about it.[446] Not even the other PLO leaders know how the money is handled, where it is, or how much there is. In 1992, when his cohorts thought he had died in a plane crash, one of their major concerns was if "the secretive Arafat had entrusted anyone with details of the PLO's billions."[447] One of the first questions the PLO officials asked each other was, "Where's the notebook?" referring to the "accounting records of the organization's investments and bank accounts."[448] They realized then that only Arafat knew!

Politically and judicially, Arafat runs the PLO show totally on his own, not only within the organization itself, but also within the new autonomous areas. We have already seen how he handled the so-called Palestinian elections. We have seen that his "democracy" means complete submission to his will or face torture and death. Those who do not submit are placed in the hands of a PLO "tribunal." This means torture and possible death. It is also suspected that he will do what he wants on the issue of Palestinian statehood. He is expected to announce unilaterally the independence of the Palestinians.

Arafat does everything according to his own will on the international level also. It is known that Arafat's PLO is involved in international drug trafficking, theft, and murder.[449]   His organization has many more interests than merely the Palestinian people. Their "love" of the Palestinians is used as a front to cover for what they really are— an international mafia of the worst sort. Proof that Arafat and the PLO's real concern is not for the Palestinians is demonstrated by how little of their vast wealth they have invested in helping them. Now, the US taxpayers are sending Arafat $500 million in aid in spite of his many illegal activities.[450] The US and other countries profess to be fighting a "war on drugs." They pressure Colombia, Mexico, and many other Latin American countries to put a stop to the sale of drugs. Has anyone ever heard of Yasser Arafat being pressured to stop dealing drugs? The US could use their aid package to do so, but it seems that no one would dare do that to a man who does everything according to his own will!

* 62. He Shall Exalt and Magnify Himself Above Every God

"…he shall exalt and magnify himself above every god" (Dan. 11:36b).

"He will show no regard for the gods of his fathers… nor will he regard any god, but will exalt himself above them all" (Dan. 11:37a NIV).

Remember that there are no capitals in Hebrew. Therefore, this reference to "god" or "gods" can very well include the god of Islam! Arafat has already begun to fulfill this by arbitrarily changing Islamic laws. According to this prophecy, the little horn's exalted pride will ultimately lead to total disregard for the god of Islam also, as he has already done for the true and living God. Even greater changes are on the way to the Islamic religion under Arafat's dominion once he decides that he is the god above all gods!

63. He Shall Prosper Until God's Wrath Has Finished Its Work on Israel

"…[he] shall prosper till the wrath has been accomplished;
for what has been determined shall be done" (Dan. 11:36c).

Every great house has both vessels of honor and vessels of wrath, as Paul explains in II Timothy 2:20. In most of our houses, we have containers that are used specifically to carry out the garbage. Even though we are sometimes loath even to touch those containers, they are still ours, and they are under our control. The same happens in God's house. *Every* human being belongs to Him, and He will use every person that comes into this world. If we choose Him, He will use us as a vessel of honor. Maybe we will be like a piece of fine china in His house whose primary purpose is to delight His heart. If we choose to serve sin, then we will still be used, but as a vessel of wrath and judgment. Arafat is a vessel ordained to carry away the garbage that is still in the house of God—in the hearts of God's people.

When God has finished breaking the hardness of heart found in His people, and He has finished purifying their hearts, Arafat will be discarded. It is both awesome and ironic to realize that Arafat hates the Jews with every ounce of his strength, but that he does not yet perceive that he is being used to bless them. In the end, he will turn out to be one of the greatest blessings that God ever gave to the Jewish race. Balaam discovered that it is impossible to curse those whom God has blessed. (See Numbers 23-24.) Just when Arafat thinks he is finally succeeding in wiping out the Jewish race, he will discover that he has been used by the Sovereign One to bless the people whom he fervently hated. God is using him to bring Israel back to Himself and to the fountain of eternal blessing! In the Book of Esther, Haman also thought that he could annihilate God's people, but God sovereignly intervened to bring about a very different outcome—Israel ended up destroying their enemies. If Mr. Arafat would just spend a little time learning some lessons from history, he would discover how the Israeli-PLO story will end also!

* 64. He Is a Homosexual

"…[he shall not regard] the desire of women" (Dan. 11:37b).

The little horn does not regard the desire of women. In other words, he is not moved by women. The Hebrew word for "women" here is most often translated as "wife" in the King James Version.[451] He is not sexually moved by women for the simple reason that, being a confirmed homosexual, Arafat desires men. He recently married for the first time, in his early sixties. This marriage was almost certainly designed to deflect attention from his homosexuality.

There is absolutely no question about Arafat's homosexuality. When he first became a friend of Romanian President Nicolae Ceausescu, Gen. Munteanu was given the task of gathering all the available intelligence information about him from the countries where Arafat had lived.[452] He obtained the intelligence reports of Egypt, Jordan, and Syria, and also included in his report firsthand information gathered through concealed microphones that the Romanians placed in Arafat's guest rooms during his visits to Bucharest, Romania.[453] On one such visit, Munteanu told Lt. Gen. Pacepa, "After the meeting with the Comrade [Ceausescu], he went directly to the guest house and had dinner. At this very moment the 'Fedayee' is in his bedroom making love to his bodyguard. The one I knew was his latest lover."[454] The intelligence reports also contained his first confirmed homosexual relationship as a teenager with his teacher. The report showed that his teacher was the first of a long string of illicit relationships over the years.

65. He Will Invent His Own New Religion

*"...he shall exalt himself above... all gods. But in their place
he shall honor a god of fortresses; and a god which his
fathers did not know he shall honor with gold and silver,
with precious stones and pleasant things" (Dan. 11:38).*

This informs us that at the end of Arafat's long journey as a vessel of wrath, he will initiate a new form of religious worship. It is not hard to imagine how a person who has been taught since his childhood that he is superior would be deceived by the pride of his heart. His great accomplishments will seem to confirm to his own mind his superiority and the greatness of his spiritual call. It requires only a very small leap of the imagination to visualize how Arafat could one day get a revelation that he is not only superior to all other human beings around him, but that he is also superior to Mohammed. Some such "spiritual experience" will surely become the foundation for the pride that will motivate him to "exalt himself above" all gods.

66. He Will Defile the Cities of Israel in the Name of His God

*"Thus he shall act against the strongest fortresses with a foreign god,
which he shall acknowledge, and advance its glory" (Dan. 11:39a).*

As we observed, the word "fortresses" also means "fortified cities" in the Hebrew. Here, the angel is saying that "thus," or in this way (in the way referred to in point 65), he will come against the largest cities of Israel in the name of a foreign god—the "god of fortresses," which can also be translated as the "god of force."[455] He will come against them as he worships the god of force. Just as many great conquerors in history attributed their military success to the power of their gods, so the little horn will do. He will not only "acknowledge" his false god of force, but he will "advance its glory." This is a veiled way of saying that he will win many battles as he attacks Israel's cities.

67. He Will Cause His People
to Have Dominion Over Many

"...and he shall cause them to rule over many" (Dan. 11:39b).

Unfortunately, many in Israel will find themselves under the dominion of Arafat's gangsters—obviously through terrorism and force.

* 68. He Shall Divide the Holy Land for Gain

"...[he shall] and divide the land for gain" (Dan. 11:39b).

Arafat is not interested in the welfare of the Palestinian people. He is interested in both financial and military power—the god that he worships—as will soon be evident to all. He is already fulfilling this prophetic word, even as he becomes established in his new autonomous areas. Presently, it is not possible to get a marketing license under Arafat's Palestine Authority without giving him ten percent of the profits.[456]

69. He Will Be Attacked By Both the King
of the South and the King of the North

"At the time of the end the king of the South shall attack him;
and the king of the North shall come against him like a whirlwind,
with chariots, horsemen, and with many ships" (Dan. 11:40a).

There will come a day when the neighboring Arab states will be concerned about Arafat's intentions, power, influence, and most likely his new religion. The king of the south is Egypt, who will arise against him again, and the king of the north is Syria. Ancient Assyria (modern Iraq) could also be involved. Arafat's relationship with Assad of Syria is not good, as we have mentioned. It will not be good with Egypt either after he attacks that nation! Ironically, God will begin to judge

Arafat through his own Arab brothers that he has called "traitors" for years. In a number of Scriptures, we are told that Assyria will ultimately come into the land of Israel. (See Micah 5:5-8 and Isaiah 10:5-27.) Could it be that Saddam Hussein will be used as the final goad to force Israel to seek the Lord? One thing is certain. The little horn will not be the only instrument God uses to accomplish His purposes with Israel in the last days.

70. Many Countries Will Be Overthrown Because of Him In the End

"...he shall enter the countries, overwhelm them, and pass through... and many countries shall be overthrown" (Dan. 11:40b and 41b).

There will soon be a great military upheaval in the Middle East. The Arabs' propensity for making war among themselves will most likely be a great help for Israel in the end just as it has been for many years. Their warring, however, will be devastating for the Middle East in general. Although the little horn will "overwhelm" other countries, the angel also explains that "many countries shall be *overthrown*." The wording here does not necessarily mean that the little horn himself will *overthrow* "many countries." This could refer to the widespread military involvement of a number of countries and the great destruction that will come to them. What Saddam Hussein did to Kuwait was only the beginning of "the mother of all wars." Neither Saddam nor any of the other major players in the Middle East have laid down the sword yet.

* 71. He Shall Enter the Glorious Land

"He shall also enter the Glorious Land" (Dan. 11:41a).

Although Arafat has already started to enter the holy land, this probably refers to an ever increasing involvement throughout the *entire* holy land or in every part of Israel. We should keep in mind that "the power of the holy people will be completely shattered" (Dan. 12:7). The Jews will be scattered again.

* 72. The Nation of Jordan Will Escape From Him

*"...but these shall escape from his hand: Edom, Moab,
and the prominent people of Ammon" (Dan. 11:41b).*

Edom, Moab, and Ammon are the three peoples that make up the modern nation of Jordan. Jordan did, in fact, escape out of the hand of Arafat. King Hussein successfully drove him out of the land in 1970. After Jordan escaped him, Arafat and the PLO went to Lebanon and raped that country. (See again point 29.) Obviously, he would have done the same to Jordan if King Hussein had not won the battle against him and the PLO. God is sovereign and he allowed the children of Lot and the children of Esau to escape Arafat's butchers. This may very well have another fulfillment in the end when the little horn overwhelms other countries. God has decided that Jordan will not fall into the little horn's hand.

73. Three Horns Will Be Plucked Up By Him

*"He shall stretch out his hand against the countries, and the land
of Egypt shall not escape. He shall have power over the treasures
of gold and silver, and over all the precious things of Egypt; also the
Libyans and Ethiopians shall follow at his heels" (Dan. 11:42-43).*

We have already seen that Egypt is going to suffer great loss at the hand of the little horn. It is important to note that Daniel is *not* saying that the little horn becomes the national leader of three other nations. Referring back to Daniel's fourth point about the little horn, we note that the Aramaic word Gabriel used indicates that the little horn will "humble" the leaders of these nations. This may or may not signify their death. In the case of Egypt, the little horn will gain control over that nation's finances, and we know that its leader will be assassinated. Two other nations mentioned here will also be under his control— Libya and Ethiopia. The Hebrew word that is translated as "Ethiopia" in most English versions of the Bible is more accurately "Cush."[457] Although the land of Cush may well include modern-day Ethiopia, the principal area of Cush is the present nation of Sudan.[458] The angel tells Daniel that Sudan and Libya will "follow at his heels," meaning to follow his march.[459] We all understand what it means for a dog to "heel." Not only is the dog following in the steps of his master, but he is a well-trained and obedient dog. The New International Version translates this as follows: "with the Libyans and Nubians [Cushites] in submission." Another possible colloquial translation is, "with the Libyans and Sudanese marching to his tune." That is, they will receive orders from the little horn as they lose authority over their own people.

There are at least two very interesting details found in this passage. First, it appears to be a revelation of the three specific "horns," or kings, the little horn "plucks up by the roots" (Dan. 7:8). Second, Arafat already has strong and treacherous links with all three of these countries. As we have seen, he not only negotiated the final Israeli-PLO peace agreement in Egypt with Mubarak as the mediator, but he also has several scores to settle with Egypt.

With regard to Libya, I wrote about Libya's "Palestinian" army units that were sent to strengthen Arafat in point 47 above. Gaddafi and Arafat are brothers in terrorism. They understand each other, and many of Gaddafi's terrorists were trained by Arafat. More than this, Arafat exercises a considerable measure of influence and control in Libyan internal affairs as he clearly demonstrated shortly after the 1993 signing of the Declaration of Principles in Washington. He "sent al-Tib [the commander of his personal security forces] to Libya with a letter to Col. Mu'ammar Gaddafi listing the Palestinian army units that [would] be leaving Libya for the Palestinian zones within the [following] two weeks. These units—in Tripoli, Al-Sarah and Al-Kafra—included air force, infantry and naval personnel. These units are said to be the heart of Arafat's new personal guard."[460] If he can give orders to Gaddafi's troops, and simply *inform* him of major changes through one of his subordinates, is not Col. Gaddafi already receiving orders from Arafat? Has not Arafat already "plucked him up by the roots"?

The problem with "friendships" between terrorists is that neither party can be too sure of his own future since both are self-serving murderers! What an example of divine justice. Col. Gaddafi is almost as wicked as Arafat, and the end to his authority will not come through one of his enemies like the US, but rather, through one of his friends—Yasser Arafat!

What about Sudan? Does Arafat have influence there? Not only does he have it, but it dates back many years. In March 1973, the PLO's "Black September" raided the Saudi Arabian Embassy in Sudan and murdered the US Ambassador to Sudan, Cleo A. Noel, Jr., along with the deputy chief of mission, George Curtis Moore. At the very time his men were attacking the Embassy, Arafat was not only in Khartoum, the capital of Sudan, but he was at the government's command center.[461] What about Arafat's connections with Sudan today? On June 25, 1995, the Sudanese government "invited the PLO and... Hamas to Khartoum to try to finalize a cooperation agreement."[462]   Arafat continues to maintain close relations with Sudan where there are more than 20 terrorist camps being used to prepare more waves of Islamic terrorists to win the world and destroy Israel.[463]

It should be noted that Sudan is not only controlled by an Islamic government, but a recent *Jerusalem Post* article dubbed it "the new Iran," and said that it is "replacing Iran as the major inspirational and operational center of Islamic terrorism."[464] The *Post* article goes on to say, "According to Middle Eastern and Western intelligence sources, Sudan directly supports three major Egyptian terrorist movements: Vanguards of Conquest (which warned that it would put the 'nails in Mubarak's coffin' in the next attack); Al-Jihad (responsible for the assassination of President Anwar Sadat in 1981); and Gam'a al-Islamiya, responsible for hundreds of attacks since 1992. It has just claimed responsibility for the latest attempt on Mubarak."

Of the three horns he will pluck up, Arafat's only real battle will be with Egypt, and Daniel has already told us that the little horn will have victory there also. Are we speculating? The only point that could be called speculation is the assumption that Yasser Arafat is the little horn. According to Daniel, the little horn will, in fact, do these things. By now, many readers are probably as convinced as I am that Arafat is that little horn, and that he will definitely end up fulfilling the remaining details.

Even though I did not place an asterisk on this present point as an indication that it has been either partially or totally fulfilled by Arafat, it does actually give us a further confirmation that Arafat is the little horn—especially in light of his hatred toward Egypt and his close ties to Libya and Sudan. .We know that the little horn plucks up three of the ten horns by the roots. Daniel then mentions three nations that will come under the power of the little horn—Egypt, Libya, and Sudan. It is probably no coincidence that current events are continually revealing that Arafat's relations with these three countries are leading to disaster—for them!

74. Countries From the East and North Will Come Against Him

"But news from the east and the north shall trouble him" (Dan. 11:44a).

Toward the east of Arafat's land lies Iran. The "north" could refer to several possible nations—Syria, Iraq, Turkey, or Russia—some or all of which may even be allied against the little horn at this time. Once the little horn plucks up three other countries, the nations of the earth are finally going to understand that this man's goals are not in their own best interest. "News from the east and the north" comes in the context of the little horn's recently acquired influence over Egypt, Libya, and Ethiopia. Once the little horn has direct influence over these three nations, the world is going to become concerned that he could threaten the stability of the entire Middle East. This will bring speedy intervention. The intervention will not be motivated by a concern for lives, but by a concern for petroleum. Tragically, modern history confirms that petroleum has been the bottom line in all international negotiations, intervention, and wheeling and dealing in the Middle East. This corrupt motive caused Britain to side with the Arabs, only to end up losing its empire. This motive will continue to move the hearts of world leaders until they have *all* lost their kingdoms in the battle of Armageddon!

75. He Shall End By Causing His Worst Destruction and Bloodshed

"...therefore he shall go out with great fury
to destroy and annihilate many" (Dan. 11:44b).

We can only begin to imagine the devastation that Yasser Arafat could conceivably bring to the Middle East and the entire earth. If, during the last few years, he has managed to kill tens of thousands with just a handful of terrorists under his command, what havoc will he wreak when he has tens of thousands of terrorists, and untold billions of dollars to finance their acts of terrorism? This is how it will all end. At this time, the Western news media, including its journalists and news correspondents, will discover the true nature of the monster they have been feeding. When this cesspool that they have helped create begins to affect them and their loved ones directly, we can be sure that the news releases will take on a different tone!

76. He Will Establish His Capital In Jerusalem

"He will pitch his royal tents between the seas
at the beautiful holy mountain" (Dan. 11:45a NIV).

We have already discussed at length the significance of this detail in point 59 above. I am convinced that **this event is, in fact, the abomination that will cause desolation** to God's people. Many expect that the abomination will be a physical pig being offered on a physical altar. That was actually done in Old Testament times by Antiochus Epiphanes around 170 BC. During the Old Testament period, God was dealing with the chosen people primarily on a natural, physical level. Once the Messiah came, He began to deal with His people on a spiritual level as well—at least in a deeper way than He had done previously—as He granted His followers the new birth, etc. Since the first fulfillment of an abomination was natural (Antiochus Epiphanes offered a pig on the altar), we might expect the second one to be spiritual. Paul reveals a principle that governs mankind both individually and collectively. He explains, "However, the spiritual is not first, but the natural, and afterward the spiritual" (I Cor. 15:46).

To understand why the establishing of the little horn in Jerusalem and possibly on the Temple Mount itself is the abomination that causes desolation, we must keep in mind the significance of animal sacrifices in the Old Testament. Primarily, they pointed forward in time to the cross of Christ where the Lamb of God would be offered for the sins of the world. Secondarily, they gave another clear message. When the faithful Israelite offered a sacrifice, he first laid his hands on the animal's head. (See Leviticus 1:4.) The Bible shows that the laying on of hands is a God-given way to impart what we are and what we have to someone else, just as Paul imparted a spiritual gift to Timothy in this way. (See II Timothy 1:6.) Therefore, when the Old Testament worshipper laid his hands on the animal sacrifice, he was, in a spiritual sense, imparting his own life to an animal that was destined for the altar. The worshipper became identified with the sacrifice and gave testimony that the Lord calls us all—not just the animal—to give our own lives on His altar. In the New Testament, we are called to become identified with Christ in His sufferings and death. He has called us to follow in His steps, take up our cross, and die with Him. (See Matthew 16:24 and I Peter 2:21.) The Lord calls His people to a total commitment and an absolute surrender to His will and way. Paul admonishes us all, "I beseech you therefore, brethren, by the mercies of God, that you **present your bodies a living sacrifice**, holy, acceptable to God, which is your reasonable service" (Rom. 12:1).

Is it possible that, in the end, instead of a *physical* pig being offered to a false god from the Temple Mount, a *spiritual* pig is being offered to a false god from that holy hill? Peter likens the unclean person to a swine (II Pet. 2:22). Is it possible that a vile, unclean person could offer his life as a living sacrifice to Satan and his service from that holy place? Again, we are not speaking about doing so in a physical way but rather in a spiritual sense—in precisely the same sense that God has always asked us, His people, to offer our lives for the service of the God whom we say we love. Becoming a "living sacrifice" refers to making a total commitment of our lives to Him; dedicating all that we are and all that we have to His service.

Tragically, Israel has not done that—*none* of us who belong to Israel have. Can we see the awesome divine judgment that is soon to fall as God permits one of the most wicked men in history to show Israel what real dedication is all about? This little horn is totally dedicated to Satan, a false god, and to all that comes from the pit of hell. Arafat often expresses his longing to pray with his Moslem brothers on the Temple Mount.[465] He is consumed with the same longing that is in Satan's heart to establish *his* kingdom in the place of *God's* kingdom. When the little horn succeeds in doing that, unspeakable death and desolation will come to God's people. The message is clear. If only we would ascend the hill of the Lord, in a spiritual sense, and offer our lives as a living sacrifice to a loving God; if only we would die, so that He could live through us; if only we would seek first His Kingdom and His righteousness, so that *our* kingdoms would be lost in His Kingdom; if only we would dedicate all that we are and all that we have to reaching His goals for humanity; if only the deep longing of God's heart would become the deepest longing of our hearts—then, we would become a channel for unspeakable life and blessing to flow out to a needy world. For the most part, neither Israel nor the Church has become that living sacrifice. For this reason, Satan will be permitted to gloat over a vile person who will offer himself on the altar of wickedness in the very place God's sacrifices were once offered. For years, that abominable human being has been offering himself fully to the work of wickedness and desolation, bringing death instead of life. He will soon be permitted to do so on God's holy mount. Because our God rules, and because He will continue to deal with us in love, this abomination will come to an end when we all wholeheartedly respond to the Lord's call! Lord, give us a heart to understand and to respond to Your loving call to come to the altar of our God!

77. He Will Come to His End

"Yet he will come to his end" (Dan. 11:45b).

In the Book of Daniel, the angel's revelation of the little horn seems to give God's people a message of hopelessness and desperation, offering a future that holds only sorrow for them. But here he shows in just a few short words who rules, who wins, and that there is hope of a better day. This little horn will come to his end. He is only a man and not God. His days are numbered, and when God has finished His work of righteousness on Israel, the hammer He used to accomplish His purposes will be discarded. Our God reigns! But will we reign with Him? All those who carry a genuine burden for God's people and God's plan in the Middle East will be candidates to be included in that Kingdom of righteousness and justice. Will you pray for the peace of Jerusalem and declare to others the truth about what is happening in the holy land? Let us obey the psalmist's exhortations: "Sing praises to the Lord, who dwells in Zion! Declare His deeds among the people" (Psa. 9:11), and "Declare His glory among the nations, His wonders among all peoples" (Psa. 96:3).

78. He Will Receive No Help at the End

"...no one will help him" (Dan. 11:45c).

The psalmist cries, "My tears have been my food day and night, while they continually say to me, "Where is your God?" Every Christian has experienced times when they have heard the taunts of the enemy. When things seem to be going wrong all around us, and darkness and despair seem to be on every hand, the enemy comes and asks, "If God loves you, why isn't He helping you now? Why would He allow you to face this impossible situation all alone? Where is your God?"

A new day is coming! The Word of God has promised that God's children will not always be mocked. It is written, "But he shall appear to your joy, and they shall be ashamed" (Isa. 66:5c). The Lord is going to appear suddenly and fight for His people and for His city. God will give grace to His "holy people" and they will find a place of deep, sincere repentance. Everything will be turned around. The shame that God's people once endured will then fall on the heads of all those who mocked them. Satan will one day mock Yasser Arafat also, as he finally does to all who serve him. On that day, Yasser Arafat will discover that "no one will help him." Then *he* will be the one who hears, "Where is your god? Why doesn't he help you? Where are all the countries of

Islam that helped you? Where is the unrighteous news media? Where is the UN? Where are all the world's celebrities that thought you were a wonderful international statesman? Where are all your vile followers who heaped praise on you? Where is all your money? Where...?"

Let us pray, "Oh God, keep us from the way of the wicked, and cause your face to shine upon us to deliver us from the pit and from all its ways. Give us the grace to follow You with all our hearts in these last days, and to flee from every unrighteous, selfish motive, and from every crooked way found within the human heart and the world. Thank you for hearing our cry!" He will hearken to the prayer of His people, and His final response has already been given through Isaiah:

"Woe to you who plunder, though you have not been plundered; and you who deal treacherously, though they have not dealt treacherously with you! When you cease plundering, you will be plundered; when you make an end of dealing treacherously, they will deal treacherously with you. O Lord, be gracious to us; we have waited for You. Be... our salvation also in the time of trouble... when You lift Yourself up, the nations shall be scattered; and Your plunder shall be gathered like the gathering of the caterpillar; as the running to and fro of locusts, He shall run upon them. The Lord is exalted, for He dwells on high; He has filled Zion with justice and righteousness. Wisdom and knowledge will be the stability of your times, and the strength of salvation... The ambassadors of peace shall weep bitterly [those who say, 'Peace and safety?']. The highways lie waste, the traveling man ceases. He [the little horn?] has broken the covenant, he has despised the cities, he regards no man... "Now [at this time] I will rise," says the Lord; "Now I will be exalted, now I will lift Myself up... Hear, you who are afar off, what I have done; and you who are near, acknowledge My might" (Isa. 33:1-13).

What If Yasser Arafat Dies Before Fulfilling the Other 30 Details?

This question can probably best be answered by asking a question. What would happen if the king of Jordan were to die before the end? Obviously he would simply be replaced by another king. At the end of Chapter 4 we observed how the Bible uses the term "king" to refer to a political position as opposed to a specific individual. For example, the biblical references to "the king of Egypt" frequently refer to national leaders of Egypt that actually lived in different historical periods that were separated by hundreds of years. The Bible calls any king of Egypt

"Pharaoh" just as it calls any king of the Philistines "Abimelech." (See Genesis 21:24; 26:8, and Psalm 34:1.) We also observed that the Bible uses the term "king" to refer to the leader of a people. The Bible does not use modern-day terms like "president," "prime minister," or "chancellor." All such men would be referred to as "kings" in the Bible.

One of the basic revelations that I have presented in this book is that the ten horns of the last day beast must be ten Islamic nations that arise near the very end of this age, existing as a kingdom for only one "hour." We considered the concept that the "hour" mentioned in Revelation 17:12 could very well refer to a period of 40 or 50 years. This is, in fact, the approximate length of time that most of the key Islamic nations have existed as independent countries. Could it be that when the Bible refers to ten "kings" in the last days, it is continuing its custom of referring to political positions rather than referring to specific individuals? It is self-evident that few national leaders last for 40 or 50 years. If one "hour" represents this length of time, we can expect that these nations will have a number of different individuals ruling over them during that period of time. A change of leadership does not bring an end to a nation's supreme political position any more than it brings an end to the nation's sovereignty.

I have linked my answer regarding the possible death of Yasser Arafat to the possible death of the king of Jordan for a simple reason. If the king of Jordan is one of the "horns" and he dies and is replaced, the supreme political position over Jordan will continue to exist and there will still be a king there. The same is true with the president of Egypt. The death of an individual leader does not do away with the political position or the throne that rules over his nation. Yasser Arafat has been the primary leader and force behind the PLO. This abominable organization, together with its "king" will shortly become the government of a new, independent, Palestinian state within God's land. In the process of accomplishing this goal, Arafat has fulfilled about 50 details regarding the little horn. However, if he were to die and another leader were to become the political leader of this new "kingdom" or "nation," we can fully expect that the new leader, along with the PLO would fulfill the rest of the prophetic revelations concerning the little horn. If the other ten "horns" or kings refer to a political position, there is no reason to assume that the eleventh "horn" is not referring to the same thing—a political position.

Having said that, I am quick to add here my personal feelings on this matter. In the light of all that Yasser Arafat has done himself, and in light of the seeming shortness of time before Christ's return, I would be very surprised if Arafat were to die before he personally fulfills the rest of Daniel's prophetic details. However, if he does happen to die, I would not discount how he has fulfilled so many prophecies while being the head of the PLO and the "Palestinian people." It is no light matter that this people have succeeded in taking the best part of the holy land as their own. It is no light matter that the "Philistines" have been allowed to form a nation within the nation of Israel, right within the very heart of God's land! This new "nation" and any possible new leader it may have will surely finish what Arafat has begun if he were to die. Also, God will surely bring an end to this new nation very shortly, as he fulfills His covenant to Abraham and gives the land to the descendants of Abraham, Isaac, and Jacob!

One Final Word on Arafat, the PLO, and the "Palestinian People"

What if, after all we have seen in this study, it turns out that the world of Islam's centuries' long battle against the Jewish people and against God's plan for the holy land is of no real importance in the fulfillment of the prophetic word? What if the recently created "Palestinian people" along with their claim to the holy land and their subsequent possession of large parts of God's land is really just an unimportant turn of events in the Middle East? What if the fact that Israel's greatest enemy, the man who has murdered more Jews than anyone else alive, is taking possession of God's land and predicting that he will annihilate the rest of the Jews living in God's land turns out to be just one more inconsequential event in a senseless world? What if after seeming to fulfill almost 50 aspects of the little horn it turns out that Yasser Arafat is nothing more than one more foreshadow of the *real* little horn who has not yet even appeared on the world scene?

If all these "what ifs" turn out to be the way it really is, then I would ask the reader to consider a couple more questions. First, as you were reading this book, did you find *anything* in the 78 points we covered that seemed to fit Arafat to some degree? In your mind, is it possible that he is at least a foreshadow of the little horn? If you answered yes to these last two questions, then I have several more questions for you to consider as we come to the close of our discussion on Yasser Arafat. If this man is at least a foreshadow of the little horn, shouldn't the Church today exercise its discernment in this area so that it will be able to recognize the *real* little horn when he comes? What hope is there that we will be capable of recognizing and rejecting the *real* little horn when he comes if we have never been spiritually alert enough to recognize the men who were his foreshadows when they have appeared on the world scene? Should we not at least be aware of the details that Daniel gives concerning the little horn? How else will we recognize him when he comes? If Yasser Arafat has fulfilled a good number of prophetic details without most of us noticing, is there any chance that the prophetic message surrounding the Lord's Second Coming could be fulfilled without most of His people being aware of it—just as happened to His people during His First Coming? Lord, have mercy on all of us, your people, and please open our eyes to see and our ears to hear so that we will know the hour in which we live and not miss the day of your visitation!

Chapter 8

Invited Into the Family

"You say that your God has afflicted your people with famine because they have walked in disobedience?" asked the prospective bride with a tone of amazement. "Our gods do not deal with us in such a harsh, hard way. Just imagine! You are telling me that the famine was so severe that you actually had to leave your country and come to live in mine just to survive your God's punishment. It must be very difficult for your people to serve that kind of God," she continued. Her future mother-in-law responded, "Oh, my God is not hard and harsh! His very name is Wonderful, Counselor, Mighty God, Everlasting Father, Prince of Peace. You see, He is so loving and kind toward His people that He refuses to let them go their own way... a way that would lead them to eternal loss and suffering. In fact, He loves us so much that He will do just about anything to cause us to seek His presence so that He can spend time with us and enjoy our fellowship. The discipline of *our* God shows that He really loves us and that He is sincerely concerned about us just as any true father is concerned for the welfare of *his* children. That's why one of His names is 'Father.' I'm very sorry to learn that your gods don't care for you as our God does."

Later, sitting together with her future husband, the confused bride-to-be confessed, "My spirit was deeply moved this afternoon while talking with your mother. After you had told me why your family came to my country, I expected to find your mother filled with bitterness toward the God of your people. When I brought up the subject, my spirit wept within me as I heard her speak. Instead of expressing resentment or hatred, the only thing that came from her was an expression of unwavering trust and a deep love toward her God. Oh, how my heart longs to feel what she feels and to have planted within me the pure spirit and childlike confidence I witnessed in her today! I just cannot imagine what it would be like to have a heart like hers. Not only was she forced to leave her family, friends, and home, and come here with her husband and two boys to survive, but now she has experienced a deeper sorrow—the death of her husband. How can she face all this anguish and still have a sweet spirit and a love for her God? What a wonderful God He must be if someone who has passed through such deep valleys of suffering can still love Him as she does! You know, for me to hear how she praises Him when I am aware of how difficult her life has been causes my own heart to begin burning also with a love for the God of Israel! Please tell me more about Him, my love." As her future husband shared with her all that he knew about the history of his people, Israel, over and over she would burst into tears of joy to hear of the glory and power of their God. But there was something else that really overwhelmed her in that great love story. She was awestruck at the thought of such a great God seeking to marry Israel as a man marries a virgin. The fact that *any* God would love and care for His people as the God of Israel had done for them melted her heart every time she thought on it.

The days passed quickly, and soon she was the happy wife of a man she dearly loved. Then, almost as quickly, more sorrow and tragedy came to this unusual family. Not only did her own husband die, but so did the only other son of her beloved mother-in-law. Oh, what days of mourning they were! Once again, her mother-in-law was feeling the heavy hand of her God's dealings in her life, but this time the story of suffering and travail had also become part of the daughter-in-law's own experience. She was now drinking from the same cup of sorrow, and the dregs seemed to be so very bitter. She thought to herself, "Surely this time my unusual Israelite mother-in-law will get angry and filled with resentment, now that she has suffered the loss of all things, including her entire family." She mused that, in her own case, the loss of her beloved husband was more than *she* could bear and that loss had already caused a battle with resentment to rage in her heart, but her mother-in-law had lost everyone and now had been left alone! What must she feel?

The daughter-in-law watched and listened intently to every word and every attitude that emanated from her mother-in-law, expecting to hear, at last, an outburst of bitterness. After many days of mourning had passed, she heard the final verdict, spoken with resolve and from a broken and contrite spirit. Her mother-in-law's words came softly as she explained through tears, "My beloved daughter-in-law, you have seen what my God has done to me and what He has allowed me to pass through. You have been with me in my darkest hour of suffering. You have even become personally identified with the sufferings and death that have been at work in my home. You have seen that walking with the God of Israel is a very serious matter. He is deeply concerned about our eternal welfare, even if reaching that eternal goal ends up costing us everything in life. For us, our God and our religion are not simply spiritual additives in our lives. We do not look at our God as a genie who gives us everything that *we* want. As we wholly follow Him, He soon becomes the all-consuming passion of our hearts. He wants to bring all of us to the place where we finally cry out, 'Though He slay me, yet will I trust Him!' Today, I have come to that place in Him, my daughter. You see, instead of being bitter against Him, I love Him more than ever before. I know that He has not given me what I deserve, because I deserve far worse—I deserve to end up in hell. Because of this burning love for Him that I feel in my heart today, I am going to return to my land, to my people, and to whatever He chooses for me there even though it may mean still further suffering. I want to bid you farewell, and weep with you one last time. I am sorry that you ever met us, and that you ever became part of this suffering, dying family. Please leave me now, and go back to your people, to your easy life, and to your god who doesn't afflict his people like our God does. I have nothing to offer you but more suffering and death for His sake!"

At that moment, it was as though a mighty gushing stream flooded from her soul, as the daughter-in-law cried out, "Oh, my mother, you don't know what has been happening within the innermost recesses of my heart during the little time I have known you! It is true that you have experienced great sorrow, but that sorrow has only served to show me that you have seen something in your God that is so wonderful, so glorious, so very special, that *nothing* is able to keep you from running after Him. *Nothing* is able to separate you from His love. Regardless of how much affliction He allows to come to your life, you seem to love Him more every day. Please don't ever again ask me to return to my people or to my god, because wherever you go, I will go with you. You see, I have decided that I want to be like you no matter what the cost may be. Wherever you lodge, there I will lodge, even if our only lodging is in the street, living as beggars. Your people shall be my people. There are no people on earth so blessed as the suffering servants of the Lord who will one day know the fullness of His glory shining through their lives. Your God shall be my God even if the only thing He ever offers me is more affliction and bitterness of soul. I have seen the beauty of His character revealed in your life, and I could never be happy again without drawing near the source of that beauty so that I, too, might be changed into His likeness. Where you die, there will I die, and there will I be buried. Nothing but death will ever be able to separate me from the love of God that I have seen in you.

When she saw that her daughter-in-law was choosing to suffer affliction with the people of God and give up the pleasures of the only life she knew, she invited her to go along and to make her new home in the land of Israel. Once they had arrived in Israel, the daughter-in-law was amazed at how everything was so unlike her past life. She did not understand any of the customs or the laws of God's people, and she felt so alone and so very different from the people she had said would be her own. One day, she said, "Mother, I can see how different I am from these people. In fact, everything about me causes me to stand out among them as an oddity. I know that they will never be able to accept me completely as one of them, and I feel that I will never experience the fullness of the blessing that rests upon them as God's chosen people. But I want to thank you for bringing me here. It is so wonderful to have at least a little part of the blessing, even though I must toil in the fields of Israel as one of the poorest of the poor—just a gleaner in the rich harvest fields of this glorious nation. I know that I am a Gentile and that I will never be called to reap the fruitful fields that God has given to His own people to reap, but I am content to be a servant of servants forever among God's wonderful people!"

Her mother-in-law explained, "Your attitude of humility is very pleasing to the Lord, my daughter, but I know of a mighty Kinsman-Redeemer here in Israel that can change your lot in life among God's people. He is the *owner* of the harvest fields in which you so diligently glean day after day. I want you to place yourself at his feet in total submission to his will and listen for his voice to tell you what you should do."

This submissive, humble handmaiden followed the instructions of the one who was gently leading her in her new walk and new life with God's people. To her infinite delight, after she had placed herself at the feet of her Kinsman-Redeemer, she heard his voice so lovingly say to her, "I will take you to myself, and you shall be my wife and the queen of my home. We both shall become one flesh and one person. All that I am and all that I own I give to you. My very life, with all the blessings of Abraham that I have inherited and now enjoy, will be forever yours also. You will also become the co-owner of my harvest fields. You will no longer be merely gleaning in my fields."

Oh, what joy filled the heart of this Gentile convert. All she could cry out, over and over, was, "Oh God of Abraham, Isaac, and Jacob, I stand amazed at the greatness of Your plan of redemption, a plan that could make two peoples to become one people in You; a plan that could take a Gentile who is without God and without hope in this world, and make her into a full-fledged citizen of Israel according to Your Word" (Eph. 2:19).

Most of us know this beautiful Bible story of Ruth and Boaz. Most likely Ruth continued to have doubts about the degree to which she would actually become one with the Lord's glorious, chosen people. She especially wondered to what extent they would really accept her as one of them. All her doubts were dispelled when she heard the prophetic word that God's people spoke to Boaz regarding his union with her. The people prophesied, "The Lord make the woman who is coming to your house like Rachel and Leah, the two who built the house of Israel; and may you prosper in Ephrathah and be famous in Bethlehem. May your house be like the house of Perez, whom Tamar bore to Judah, because of the offspring which the Lord will give you from this young woman" (Ruth 4:11-12). How could it be? Could this Gentile woman become one with God's people to such a degree that she would actually be like the two principal mothers of Israel, Rachel and Leah? Could she somehow be permitted in the fullest sense to partake of the blessing of Abraham that came on the tribe of Judah? Yes! God did not plan for her merely to taste a little of Abraham's blessing. God's plan was that she actually become one of the very sources of that blessing. The greatest earthly king Israel ever had, the king who will reign over the nation forever, was her great-grandson—King David. And the greatest King in all the universe, the King that will reign over all the earth, the One who is the source and fulfillment of all that God promised to Abraham, also came through her—the Messiah Himself! Ruth was definitely not considered a second-class citizen in Israel either by God *or* His people! Is there any greater blessing found in father Abraham's family than to become one of his children through whom the Messiah comes? Ruth was so totally integrated into God's chosen people, the descendants of Abraham, that she was actually the most blessed and most important woman in Israel during her generation. She was the woman of that generation through whom the Messianic line of Christ came as well as being the great grandmother of David, Israel's greatest king!

God's plan has *always* included the Gentiles. From the beginning, His invitation to become a member of His family was open to any hungry Gentile who wanted, like Ruth, to find a refuge "under His wings" (Ruth 2:12). Not only Gentiles like Ruth the Moabite and Rahab the harlot became part of the nation, but many others did also throughout Old Testament history. Even though Israel has often been a suffering and afflicted people for thousands of years, there have always been some Gentiles who have willingly joined themselves to God's people down through the ages. According to Christ and Daniel, the last days will be the worst time Israel has ever known. In spite of what Israel faces, are you willing to become one with them in your heart and attitude? Will you carry a burden for the remnant that will be saved? Maybe some would respond that there is no need to pray since God has already promised that He would save the remnant. That was not Daniel's response when he learned that God had promised to restore Israel from Babylonian captivity after 70 years. (See Daniel 9.) God moves in response to prayer, and when He decides to do something, He raises up intercessors with whom He can share His burden and also share the reward that comes when their prayers are answered.

Unfortunately, like the Prophet Jonah, most of God's people did not understand that His plan included Gentiles during Old Testament times also. Jonah looked at the people of Nineveh as enemies of God and enemies of Israel. He sincerely believed that the best thing that could have happened would have been their total destruction. God had to bring a tremendous storm that almost destroyed an entire ship and its crew to get Jonah's attention. As with all the questions that people asked and that are recorded in the Bible, those asked by the sailors were surely questions that *God* wanted Jonah to answer in his own heart. God used the sailors to ask Jonah, "Of what people are you?" (Jonah 1:8) The issue was if *Jonah's* people were the same as *God's* people. Of all the questions the sailors asked him, the question concerning who his people were was the *first* question Jonah answered. Maybe he realized it was a root issue that God was dealing with in his life. God wanted Jonah to understand that He also had some people among the Gentiles in Nineveh, who like Jonah, were chosen to be saved.

As Christians, we sometimes make much the same mistake today, only in the opposite sense. Many in the Church have accused the Jews of being "Christ killers." It has been taught that the "Gentile Church" took the place of Israel in God's plan. Do we know who God's people are? They include *all* Jews and *all* Gentiles who believe that Yeshua is the Kinsman-Redeemer of all the spiritually poor and needy throughout the earth. In the early Church, for the first eight or ten years after the cross, the leaders simply could not understand that the Gentiles had also been included in the Lord's plan. It took a tremendous spiritual experience in Peter's life to show him that he should not call any man "unclean" if God had pronounced him clean. According to Acts 11:19, the all-Jewish Church had not yet carried the gospel to any Gentile. It is very ironic that today, after 2,000 years of Church history, many leaders in the "Gentile Church" simply do not understand that the Jews have also been included in God's plan for these last days. Gentiles and Jews form the same family of God.

Through the cross of Christ, the way into the family of God has become much easier than it used to be. Instead of going through a complex religious conversion as Gentiles had to do in Old Testament times and still must do if they desire to become Orthodox Jews, every Gentile can now actually be *born* into the family. When an adopted person discovers how he became part of his family, he sometimes has a struggle with feeling less a part of that family than if he had been born into it. Some students of the Bible have misunderstood Paul's use of the word "adoption" in the New Testament. A careful look at the Greek usage shows that Paul is not speaking about becoming part of the family of God through adoption, but rather about placing a mature son into his position in the family.[1] The Greek word "adoption" used here is "huiothesia" and comes from two Greek words—"huios" and "thesis"— which mean "mature sons"[2] and "placing"[3] respectively. Paul demonstrates how he uses "adoption" by explaining, "We also who have the firstfruits of the Spirit, even we ourselves groan within ourselves, **eagerly waiting for the adoption**" (Rom. 8:23). Paul has just explained that if we have the Spirit, then we have a witness that we are children (teknon) of God (Rom. 8:16), but the "adoption" is something that is future—something for which we eagerly wait. Therefore, the New Testament does not say that we are God's adopted children. The reason we are part of the family of God today is that we have experienced the glorious new birth. In that second birth, the very life of *the* Jew, the Lord Jesus Christ, takes up residence within us. Even when He lives in *us,* He is never seen by God as His Son by adoption! In fact, we become part of the family of God that is called "Israel" because "Israel" is one of the Lord's more than seven-hundred names found in the Bible.

According to Isaiah 49:1-6, Israel is not only the name of His people, but it is the name of our Kinsman-Redeemer. According to Matthew 2:15, when the parents of baby Jesus brought Him back from Egypt the prophecy of Hosea 11:1 was fulfilled. There, Hosea reveals that "Israel" is the name of the Son of God who was called out of Egypt. Isaiah tells us that we are "called by His name" (Isa. 43:1,7). Paul assures us that from that name "the whole family in heaven and earth is named" (Eph. 3:15). The name that God has given to His family is "Israel," and we become part of that family when the very life of its most important member and the One who is its very Creator, lives within us. We became members of Adam's family at our first birth, when the life of the first Adam was given to us. Likewise, we became members of the family of God, Israel, at our second birth, when the life of the second Adam, Christ, was given to us (I Cor. 15:45-49).

Far from being adopted children, the Bible declares that we were "**born** of God" (I Jn. 3:9). This Greek word "born" literally means that we were "fathered by" God or "begotten" of God.[4] Jesus was called "the Son of God" because He, too, was "born" or "fathered by" God (Lk. 1:35). We are also told that He was "the firstborn among many brethren" (Rom. 8:29), and that "both he that sanctifieth [Christ] and they who are sanctified [us] are all of one [from God the Father]: for which cause he is not ashamed to call them brethren" (Heb. 2:11). The same thing that caused the Lord Jesus to be called the Father's "firstborn son"—Christ living in a body of flesh—is what causes us to be called His sons by birth—Christ living in *our* bodies of flesh as a result of us being born again. He calls us "earthen vessels" in which we have this heavenly "treasure" (II Cor. 4:7). Is it not presumptuous to call the Lord Himself, who lives in us, an "adopted son"? What a privilege to be a member of the family of God by birth!

Unfortunately, many Christians are rejecting both God's family and its name today through their attitude of heart and lack of understanding. It is essential that the Gentiles understand that, as true Christians, God has made them one with the nation of Israel. As already mentioned, God has never rejected the people that came out of Egypt. He has never changed His plan for them, and He has never broken His eternal covenant with them. Israel in the Middle East will soon go through the travail of their soul in a way they have never experienced before. Are you, like Moses was, willing to suffer with God's people? Will you stand with Israel in your spirit during their time of severe discipline and cleansing? You can do so, as a beginning, in your heart and attitude towards Israel—maintaining a positive attitude toward Israel in spite of the negative reports of the news media. In your spirit, will you stand with them in their time of severe discipline and cleansing? Will you carry a burden in the Spirit for their sake before the throne of God? Will you pray for the peace of Jerusalem, the city where His throne will be established—the city where He also wants *you* to live with Him? Will you be one who cries out for Israel's salvation as though you were crying for a brother? Or will you, instead, be one who declares that they deserve what they are getting? I fear for many members in the so-called "Gentile Church" today. I fear that, because of an unmerciful attitude, they will also "get what they deserve" from the Just Judge instead of receiving the mercy that our loving God has reserved for all those who recognize their own great need and weakness!

Paul strongly warns the Gentiles, *"For I speak to you Gentiles... if the root is holy, so are the branches. And if some of the branches were broken off, and you, being a wild olive tree, were grafted in among them, and with them became a partaker of the root and fatness of the olive tree, do not boast against the branches. But if you do boast, remember that you do not support the root, but the root supports you. You will say then, 'Branches were broken off that I might be grafted in.' Well said. Because of unbelief they were broken off, and you stand by faith. Do not be haughty, but fear. For if God did not spare the natural branches, He may not spare you either. Therefore consider the goodness and severity of God: on those who fell, severity; but toward you, goodness, if you continue in His goodness. Otherwise you also will be cut off"* (Rom. 11:13a,16-22).

Many Christians feel that the Jews failed God in ways that are almost inexcusable. Some even believe that they would have done better themselves if only they had been alive 2,000 years ago. However, Paul declares, "God has given them...eyes that they should not see and ears that they should not hear to this very day" (Rom. 11:8). If God Himself gives us eyes that cannot see today, we too will do what the Jews did—reject our Messiah! Those who feel that the Jews have failed miserably may be surprised to discover that God still loves them in spite of what they've done! In fact, the severe discipline that will come to Israel through the little horn is proof of God's continued love for the nation. It is *not* proof that He has rejected them!

A critical attitude always sets a person up for a great fall. The Gentile Christians living outside Israel will not face the wrath of the little horn, but without God's grace, they could well face the diabolical power of the spirit behind him—Satan himself and other antichrist forces in the world. God is calling us to weep with those who weep. He is calling us to stand with His natural people through the travail of intercession until the whole remnant comes into His purposes in these last days, along with the Gentile Believers. The Gentiles who love Israel and their God as Ruth did, will also become a channel through which His salvation will come to the entire world. Like Ruth, they will become totally one with Israel so that the life or "fatness of the olive tree" will flow through them to the world in the last days just as it will flow through natural-born Israelites who are in Christ also. Together with Israel, they will inherit the great harvest fields of their heavenly Boaz and will have a part in reaping them. May God grant that we be part of the blessing of Abraham that will come upon all the earth in these last days. As Isaiah 60:1-2 promises, darkness will definitely cover the earth, including every nation upon it, but the light of His glory "will arise over [His people], and His glory will be seen"—resting upon all those who receive His grace to remain grafted into the root along with the natural branches. The Lord invites whosoever will to be part of this suffering, dying family through which He will soon manifest His glorious resurrection life and power!

Appendix A

Maps

1. Israel and the Surrounding Arab World

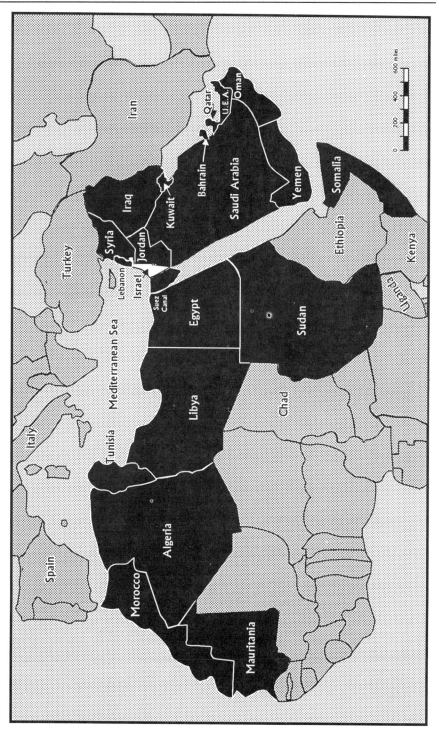

2. Israel's Relative Territorial Size

Israel
10,840 sq. miles

Iraq
280,000 sq. miles

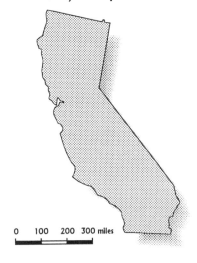

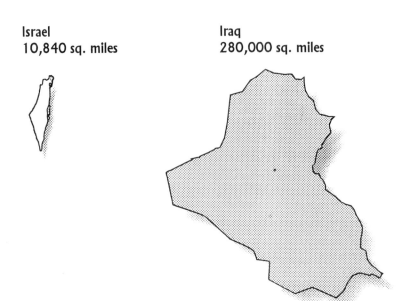

California
160,222 sq. miles

France
213,673 sq. miles

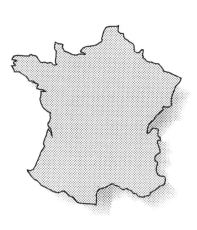

0   100   200 300 miles

3. 1920 Jewish National Home

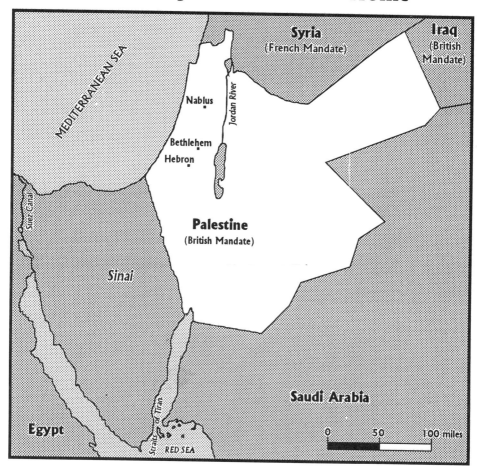

4. 1922 The Jewish National Home

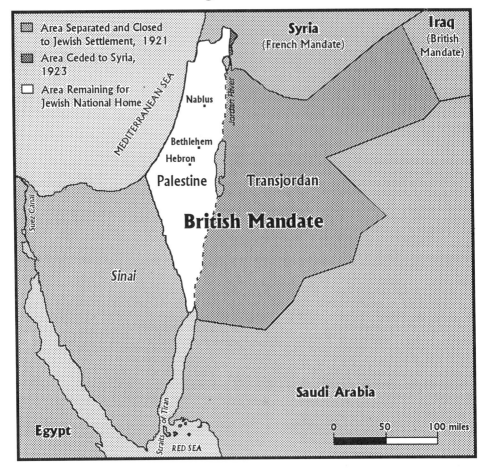

Area Separated and Closed to Jewish Settlement, 1921

Area Ceded to Syria, 1923

Area Remaining for Jewish National Home

MEDITERRANEAN SEA

Syria (French Mandate)

Iraq (British Mandate)

Nablus

Bethlehem

Hebron

Palestine

Transjordan

British Mandate

Suez Canal

Sinai

Saudi Arabia

Egypt

Straits of Tiran

RED SEA

0   50   100 miles

5. 1947 U.N. Partition Plan

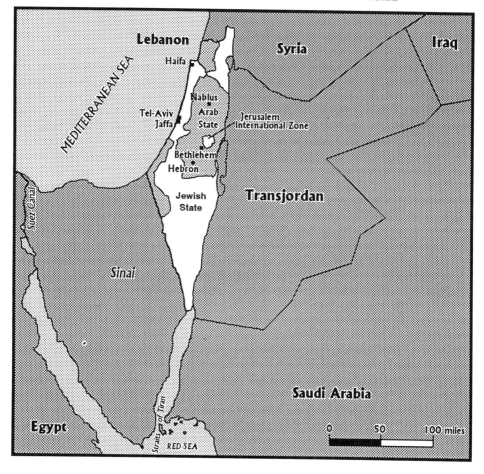

6. Israel with Gaza and West Bank

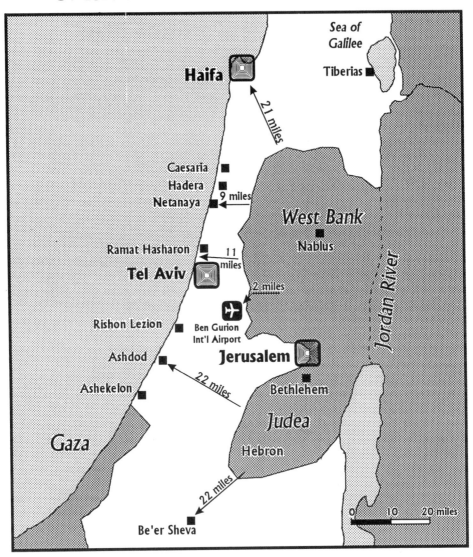

Appendix B

The Relationship Between Daniel 8 and Daniel 11

The Prophet Daniel writes about a supernatural visitation he experienced in the third year of Cyrus (Dan. 10:1a). In this experience, an angel comes to give him understanding of a vision he had received. Daniel explains that he understood the divine message or vision, but also knew that the time of its fulfillment was yet a long way off (Dan. 10:1b). The angel appears to him in Daniel 10:5 and explains, "Now I have come to make you understand what will happen to your people in the **latter days**, for **the vision** refers to many days yet to come." Therefore, from both Daniel and the angel, we understand that his vision is a revelation of the last days.

The angel's declaration here concerning the purpose of his visit is very similar to the purpose for which Gabriel visited Daniel in chapter 8. There he declares, "Understand, son of man, that **the vision** refers to the **time of the end**." By comparing the interpretation of "the vision" that the angel gives in Daniel 11 with the interpretation given in Daniel 8, we discover that the angel is interpreting the same vision in both places—the vision Daniel received in chapter 8. In Daniel 11, he is simply giving greater detail.

I am sure that we would all like to hear the Lord tell us what the angel speaks next to Daniel. He assures him, "O man greatly beloved, fear not! Peace be to you; be strong, yes, be strong!" (Dan. 10:19b) What an honor to be one who is greatly beloved by the Lord! The clarification that the angel now gives helps us to understand the historical and biblical context of what he is about to reveal to Daniel. He explains, "And now I must return to fight with the prince of Persia; and when I have gone forth, indeed the prince of Greece will come" (Dan. 10:20). In other words, the angel is showing Daniel that the Medes and Persians are going to fall, and, after their fall, he will do spiritual warfare against the prince of Greece also. This warfare in the spiritual realm is obviously what brought down both empires and caused Alexander to die at the age of 33. Heaven decides who has power on earth! Daniel revealed this lesson earlier—"The most High ruleth in the kingdom of men, and giveth it to whomsoever he will" (Dan. 4:17b KJV).

The angel then begins his revelation of the future in Daniel 11 by explaining that Darius the Mede had actually prospered because he, the angel, had strengthened him (v. 1). Remember that at the moment of this revelation to Daniel, the united empire of the Medes and Persians was in power with Cyrus and Darius as leaders. (See Daniel 5:28,31; 10:1.) The angel now begins to give greater detail concerning the conflict that was to come between the kingdom of the Medes and Persians and the kingdom of Alexander the Great, the king of Greece. Daniel had already received a vision of this conflict in Daniel 8. The angel reveals that after the Persian king who was ruling at that time (Cyrus of Daniel 10:1), three other Persian kings would arise and that the fourth would be more powerful than his predecessors (Dan. 11:2). This fourth king of Persia would be the king who would make war with Alexander, the king of Greece (v. 2). The angel now repeats the same interpretation that was given for Daniel's vision in Daniel 8, where the king of Greece defeats the Persian king, after which his kingdom is almost immediately divided into four parts (Dan. 11:2-4). This repeat of the interpretation of the vision in Daniel 8 confirms to us that the "vision" to which the angel refers in Daniel 10:14 is the vision of the ram and male goat of Daniel 8. He says he came to Daniel to make him understand that vision (Dan. 10:14). In other words, he now reveals more details than those given in the interpretation provided in Daniel 8.

The angel explains what was to happen with the two parts of Alexander's kingdom that would most directly affect the holy land and the holy people right up to the last days. He speaks of the "king of the south" and the "king of the north" (Dan. 11:5-20). The kingdom of the south, which was centered in Egypt, was first under Ptolemy I, one of Alexander's generals.[1] The kingdom of the north was initially under Seleucus I.[2] These two families and kingdoms came to be known as the "Ptolemies" and the "Seleucids" respectively.[3]

Before we see the rest of the details about the little horn that are re-vealed in Daniel 11, it is important that we understand three keys that will unlock the secrets of this chapter. These keys are the following: a) the events involving the kingdoms of the north and south cover a pe-riod of several generations and, therefore, are not directly related to the last days; b) the latter part of Daniel 11 returns to the subject of the little horn who wars against Israel in the last days; and c) we must conclude, therefore, that the angel here is doing the same thing that the angel of Daniel 8 did—somewhere in this interpretation he takes a huge leap forward in history and arrives at the time of the end or the last days. Of course, we should expect that the angel will do precisely this if Daniel 11 is simply an amplification of the interpretation of the vision in Dan-iel 8. We observed that he made this leap in the interpretation of Daniel 8 between verses 22 and 23 of that chapter. There he jumped from Al-exander, the horn whose kingdom was divided into four kingdoms (v. 22), to "the latter time of their kingdom" (v. 23). Let's look now at the biblical evidence that confirms the validity of these three keys.

A. The History of the Kings of the North and South Covers Several Generations

Consider the facts:

1. The king of the south becomes strong and gains power. This requires some time (v. 5).
2. After "some years" the daughter of the king of the south be-comes involved with the king of the north, but she returns to the south after even more time passes (v. 6).
3. One of the children or grandchildren of this daughter takes the throne of the south and comes against the king of the north and conquers (v. 7).
4. After the king of the south is victorious in battle, he then lives "more years" than the king of the north (v. 8).
5. Afterward, the king of the north comes against the king of the south but must return to the north in defeat (v. 9). We must as-sume that he is a successor to the king of the north that died be-fore the king of the south in verse 8.
6. Afterward, the sons of the previous king of the north take the throne and begin warring with a "multitude of great forces" (v. 10).

7. The king of the south comes against the north and loses the battle (v. 11-12).

8. The king of the south returns to the south and "at the end of some years" he gathers another army to fight against the king of the north (v. 13).

9. After a time, the king of the north, along with others, finally defeats the king of the south (v. 14-16).

10. The king of the north then begins to conquer within the "Glorious Land" or the holy land (v. 15).

11. The king of the north then seeks to make an alliance with the king of the south with the treacherous motive of overthrowing his kingdom, but his plan does not work (v. 17 NIV).

12. After his plan fails, the king of the north begins to conquer the coastlands, which are either a part the holy land or a part of northern Egypt, belonging to the kingdom of the south (v. 18a).

13. A ruler in the south then brings to an end the reproach against the southern kingdom. In other words, he gets the victory over the king of the north and turns back on him (v. 18).

14. It is not clear whether verses 19-20 are now speaking about the ruler from the south, who was the last subject introduced in the dialogue at the end of verse 18, or if this is speaking again about the king of the north. This entire passage concerning these two kingdoms is difficult to translate from the Hebrew. The many differences between the various English translations give us an indication that the meaning of the Hebrew text is not always obvious. Either way, someone dies in verse 19, and is replaced by another ruler who is destroyed in a few days in verse 20.

B. Where the Angel Takes a Leap Forward in History to Arrive At the Last Days

In the interpretation of Daniel's vision that the angel gives in chapter 8, it is very easy to see where he changes from Alexander's day to the last days. In Daniel 8:22, he is speaking about Alexander's kingdom that becomes four kingdoms. He then lets us know that he is jumping ahead in time in the very next verse by saying that afterward a king shall arise "in the latter time of their kingdom"—Daniel 8:23.

We have three indications concerning where this change occurs in the interpretation that is provided in Daniel 11. The first indication is the **wording** of Daniel 11:21 compared with the wording of Daniel 8:23. In both passages, "a king arises" who is extremely wicked. This occurs in Daniel 8 after the leap forward in time.

The second indication that Daniel 11:21 jumps ahead to the last days is that the person introduced in this verse becomes the central theme of the rest of the chapter. And, from this verse on to the end of the chapter, we are given sufficient details about this person to know for certain that he is the same little horn that appears in Daniel chapters 7 and 8. He does precisely the same things.

The third indication comes from the fact that both the little horn of Daniel 8:9 and this "vile person" in Daniel 11:21 definitely come from one of the four kingdoms that arise out of Alexander's kingdom.

C. Proof That the "Vile Person" of Daniel 11 is the Little Horn

There are a number of links that Daniel establishes between the "vile person" who appears in Daniel 11:21 and the little horn of Daniel 7 and 8. Those links are the following:

1. This person takes away the "daily" as does the little horn of Daniel 8. Compare Daniel 8:11 and Daniel 11:31.

2. By means of "peace" this person reaches his goals in both places. Compare Daniel 8:25 and Daniel 11:21,24. The same Hebrew word is used in both places to describe how he gains control over the land and how he destroys many.[4]

3. He speaks against God. Compare Daniel 7:25 and Daniel 11:36.

4. He prospers in his evil way. Compare Daniel 8:24 and Daniel 11:36 where the same Hebrew word is used in both places.[5]

5. As we have already seen, both the little horn and this "vile person" of Daniel 11 have the same origin—one of the parts of the kingdom of Alexander.

6. In both Daniel 8 and Daniel 11, the wicked person who is to arise in the last days arises in the context of the interpretation of the vision in Daniel 8. If the "vile person" of Daniel 11 is not the little horn of Daniel 8, then the interpretations given in the two chapters are parallel except on this point only—something highly unlikely.

Notes

Introduction

1. "Arafat sees Israel's demise," *The Jerusalem Post*, February 23, 1996.
2. "Good Show, by Jove," *Newsweek*, August 1, 1994.
3. Ibid.
4. Ibid.

Chapter 1: The Peace That Brings Sudden Destruction

1. See this same truth in Psalm 8:6 and Psalm 47:2-3 also.
2. Read Revelation 11:2-19 to observe that Christ's coming puts an end to the Gentile rule over Jerusalem.
3. It should be noted that "Palestine" is not a biblical name for the holy land. In the Hebrew, the word "Palestinian" means Philistine. Rome gave the holy land the name "Palestine" to erase its Jewish history. In Joel 3:4 in the King James Version there is a reference to "the coasts of Palestine." However, the other English versions correctly translate this word from the Hebrew as "Philistia," or the land of the Philistines. The Jewish people take offense when anyone uses the word "Palestine" to refer to the holy land, because the connotation is that the holy land belongs to the Philistines or Palestinians.
4. "Negotiations Over Jerusalem," *The Jerusalem Post*, December 8, 1995.
5. Two recent examples are: "Abu Zayyad: Talks on Jerusalem have started," *The Jerusalem Post*, December 7, 1995, and "A no-win situation," *The Jerusalem Post*, December 22, 1995.
6. "Peres Denies Offering Vatican Role in Old City," *The Jerusalem Post*, April 9, 1995.
7. Ibid.
8. United Press International article reporting on the United Nations, written by Rym Brahimi, printed in Guatemalan newspaper as "ONU aprueba resolución sobre Estado de Jerusalén," *Prensa Libre*, December 5, 1995.
9. "Abu Zayyad: Talks on Jerusalem have started," *The Jerusalem Post*, Dec. 7, 1995.
10. " 'Gaza-Jericó primero,' y la maldición de Josué" (" 'Gaza-Jericho first,' and the curse of Joshua"), *Prensa Libre*, from EFE, September 13, 1993.
11. "Borderline concerns," *The Jerusalem Post Magazine*, December 15, 1995.

12.   "Peace on wheels," *The Jerusalem Post*, December 11, 1995.

13.   Ibid.

14.   "Indecent interval," *The Jerusalem Post*, December 6, 1995.

15.   "Mafia-style neighbors," *The Jerusalem Post*, December 7, 1995.

16.   This has happened to seven Israeli buses in just over a year, including two on the same day—February 25, 1996.

17.   *The Jerusalem Post* is a very well-known and well-respected English text daily newspaper, available throughout the world in either a condensed weekly form or the complete daily paper. The *Post* has been publishing the news since 1932.

18.   Benjamin Netanyahu, *A Place Among the Nations*, (New York: Bantam Books, 1993), pp. 421-422. See Articles 15, 19, and 20-23 of the PLO Charter.

19.   "A no-win situation," *The Jerusalem Post*, December 22, 1995.

20.   "Still the Terror-Master," *The Jerusalem Post*, December 28, 1990.

21.   "Syria's Media: Assad Through the Looking Glass," *The Jerusalem Post*, May 18, 1994.

22.   Netanyahu, p. 96.

23.   *Logos Bible Study Software*, (Oak Harbor, WA, Logos Research Systems, 1993), Greek Lexicon, #803.

24.   "Islam's Real Agenda," *Reader's Digest*, January 1996.

25.   Koran, translated by A. Yusuf Ali: 7:169; 13:41; 17:1-8, 104; 24:62; 33:26; 60:1-2,7,9.

26.   "There's Only One Islam," *The Jerusalem Post*, January 26, 1995.

Chapter 2: The Four Beasts of Daniel

1.   Regarding Nebuchadnezzar's dream, Daniel explains to the king, "But there is a God in heaven who reveals secrets, and He has made known to King Nebuchadnezzar what will be in the latter days" (Dan. 2:28a). Daniel's reference to the "latter days" has led some to conclude that Nebuchadnezzar's dream is also a revelation of these last days. This conclusion may be the result of a misunderstanding of what is meant when we refer to the "last days." Many who are unfamiliar with the Bible believe that the Church preaches that the end of planet Earth is at hand. The Bible teaches that the present earth will endure for another 1,000 years. (See Revelation 20:4-6.) When the Bible or the Church refer to the "last days," it is a reference to the days that lead up to the coming of Christ with the accompanying changes. When the New Testament refers to the "end of the world," as in Matthew 24:3, the Greek means the end of an "age or period of time." Just as we are expecting the Lord to come and bring an end to this present age, the men of faith in the Old Testament were looking for the Lord to come and bring an end to their age and to usher in a new age. Therefore, just as we are living in the "last days" that lead up to His coming and a change of the age, the men of faith in John the Baptist's day and before knew that they were living in the "last days" of their age. They knew that those "last days" would lead up to His coming and a change of the age. Not only did the Old Testament age end with the coming of the Lord, but the other major events of that age are being repeated in the New Testament age. The Old Testament period is like a pattern to which the New Testament is conformed. To see that the general events of the entire Old Testament period are being repeated in the New Testament period, and that the Old can actually be superimposed on the New, see Marvin Byers, *The Final Victory: The Year 2000*, Second Edition, (Shippensburg, PA: Treasure House, 1994), Chapters 5-6.

2. J. D. Douglas, editor, *New Bible Dictionary*, (England: Intervarsity Press, 1982), "Alexander the Great," p. 24.

3. Thomas Nelson, *The Open Bible*, (Nashville: Thomas Nelson Publishers, 1983), "Between the Testaments," pp. 1339-1341.

4. *Compton's Interactive Encyclopedia*, (Microsoft: Compton's New Media, 1995), see "Alexander the Great."

5. Nelson, pp. 1339-1341.

6. *Compton's.*

Chapter 3: Why the Little Horn Cannot Be the Antichrist

1. Daniel wrote his book using both Hebrew and Aramaic. Daniel 1:1-2:4b was written in Hebrew. Daniel 2:4b-7:48 was written in Aramaic, and then chapters 8-12 were written in Hebrew.

2. I offer here a possible explanation of the seven heads that are found on the beast—only as food for thought. The seven "heads" could refer to the seven great empires that have ruled over what Daniel calls the "whole earth" in Daniel 8:5 (that is, over the whole known earth—over the biblical or prophetic earth). Those are as follows: 1) Egyptian, 2) Assyrian, 3) Babylonian, 4) Medo-Persian, 5) Grecian, 6) Roman, and 7) Islamic. The angel told John that the seven heads are seven kings (Rev. 17:9-10a), and that "Five have fallen, one is, and the other has not yet come" (Rev. 17:10b). Indeed, five of these empires had fallen by John's day, and one, the Roman Empire, was ruling at that time. Islam had not yet come. The endtime beast or kingdom is a spiritual resurrection of one of the first five. (See Revelation 17:8,11.) Revelation 17-18 hints that it is the spiritual force behind Babylon that will be resurrected, and Jeremiah's endtime message shows that Israel will go into a Babylonian captivity in the last days.

Chapter 4: Daniel Never Heard of a "Gentile Church"

1. Frank Charles Thompson, *Thompson Chain Reference Bible*, Fourth Improved Edition, (Indianapolis: Kirkbride Bible Co.)

2. For more biblical and historical insight into this issue see Byers, Chps. 4 and 15.

3. Michael L. Brown, *Our Hands Are Stained With Blood*, (Shippensburg, PA: Destiny Image, 1992), p. 12.

4. Ibid.

5. Ibid.

6. For biblical confirmation of this see that one of Christ's names is "Israel" by comparing Hosea 11:1 and Matthew 2:15. Also, see that "Israel" is the name of both a nation and also the Redeemer and the light of the world in Isaiah 49:1-6. Isaiah 43:1 and 7 explains this—the nation of "Israel" is called by His name. This is true of any wife.

7. Some might attempt to equate the "mouth speaking great things" of Revelation 13:5 with the little horn of Daniel since the little horn has a mouth that speaks great words. However, the mouth on the beast in Revelation 13:2 is the "mouth of a lion." The lion, along with the bear and leopard, are the three beasts in Daniel 7 that are seen to have been assimilated into the beast with ten horns in Revelation 13. It is the mouth of the lion, not the mouth of the little horn, that is seen to be speaking great things in Revelation.

Chapter 5: Islam and the Deadly Horns

1. "Wrong Ideas About Islam," *The Jerusalem Post*, January 29, 1993.

2. Note that in Habakkuk 3:4 the word "horn" is actually translated as power in the New International Version. See also *Logos*, Greek Lexicon, #2768.

3. The word "mind" used here also means "purpose" in the Greek. See *Logos*, Greek Lexicon, #1106.

4. For those interested in knowing more about who this "harlot" is, refer to Byers, Chapter 17.

5. Ishmael lived in, and populated, the wilderness of Paran, which is in modern-day Saudi Arabia. See Genesis 21:21 and 25:6. The holy sites of Medina and Mecca are in Saudi Arabia.

6. One example is when David asks, "Is not the hand of Joab with thee in all this?" (II Sam. 14:19). See also II Samuel 3:12; Ps. 44:20; 125:3; 140:4.

7. "Behind the PLO Boss's Words," *The Jerusalem Post*, May 27, 1994.

8. "There's Only One Islam," *The Jerusalem Post*, January 26, 1995.

9. "In the month of Ramadan, a test of faith," *USA Today*, February 14, 1996.

10. "There's Only One Islam," *The Jerusalem Post*, January 26, 1995.

11. Students of Greek and Hebrew sometimes speak of the "number value" of a word. In Greek and Hebrew, the letters of the alphabet are also used as numbers. Most people are familiar with this concept through Roman numerals which are letters also. The "number value" of a word is determined by adding the numerical value of each of the letters that form the word. Mohammed in Greek is Maometis, and the numerical value of all the Greek letters that form this name add up to 666. It is also interesting to note that the number value of "Jesus" in Greek is 888. Many interesting "coincidences" can be found in the Scriptures by examining the number value of different words. Although serious students of the Bible should understand that the letters of the original languages were also numbers, I believe that we must be careful not to get sidetracked in secondary issues in our study of God's Word, allowing those issues to become our focus. I am not advocating spending a lot of time in pursuing the number value of biblical words.

12. Ramon Bennett, *Philistine*, (Jerusalem: Arm of Salvation, 1995), pp. 46-48.

13. Joan Peters, *From Time Immemorial*, (USA: JKAP Publications, 1984) p. 73.

14. The Hadith, Sahih Muslim (Siddiqi's translation), p. 1510 (6981).

15. Ibid., p. 268.

16. Russia *does* have a part to play in the last days also; but remember that the population of the former Soviet Union is approximately 50 percent Moslem. This spirit is a deciding factor in the actions and attitudes that are manifested there.

17. "Farrakhan meets Gaddafi on black lobby," *The Jerusalem Post*, January 25, 1996.

18. An Associated Press report from New York entitled, "Jews, Catholics protest Farrakhan, Gaddafi" was printed in *The Jerusalem Post* on February 4, 1996, p. 2.

19. "Farrakhan 'Cavorting with dictators,' US official says," *Los Angeles Times*, February 15, 1996.

20. "Arafat's big mistake," *The Jerusalem Post*, January 10, 1996.

21. "High alert after the death of 'The Engineer,' " *The Jerusalem Post*, January 7, 1996.

22. "Peres the astronaut," *The Jerusalem Post*, January 11, 1996.

23. Ibid.

24. Ibid.

25. "PLO Is Silent on Terror Due to Hamas Links," *The Jerusalem Post*, April 20, 1994.

26. "Arafat: Israel responsible for Yihye Ayyash's liquidation," *The Jerusalem Post*, January 8, 1996.

27. "Boundless Hatred," *The Jerusalem Post*, January 8, 1996.

28. "Security sources: Hamas planning revenge attacks for Yihye Ayyash," *The Jerusalem Post*, January 14, 1996.

29. "Islamic Jihad Member: 50 of us ready for suicide attacks," *The Jerusalem Post*, November 17, 1994.

30. "Ayalon: Hundreds of Palestinians are waiting in line to die as martyrs," *The Jerusalem Post*, March 5, 1996.

31. "The Myth of UN Fairness to Israel," *Dispatch from Jerusalem*, 3rd. Quarter, 1991.

32. Ibid.

33. Ibid.

34. "Middle East Hourglass," *Middle East Intelligence Digest*, March/April, 1995, p. 11.

35. Ibid.

36. This was aired on CNN in the US on May 8, 1996 at 5:07pm EST.

37. Ibid.

38. David Bar-Illan, *Eye on the Media*, (Jerusalem: Jerusalem Post, 1993), pp. 191-192.

39. "Was WTC Bombing An Act of War by Iraq?" *The Jerusalem Post*, January 2, 1995.

40. There have been other world powers who have influenced this region, and, in some cases even exercised a measure of sovereignty over parts of it for very short periods, such as Great Britain, the US, and Russia. However, the region has been completely controlled for extended periods by only seven great empires.

41. Supplement to the *National Geographic*, December 1989, p. 713A, Vol. 176 No. 6 holy land.

42. "Islam's Real Agenda," *Reader's Digest*, January 1996.

43. *Encarta 96 Encyclopedia*, (Microsoft, 1996), see "Martel, Charles."

44. "On the threshold of critical mass Part II," *Middle East Intelligence Digest*, June 1993, p. A3.

45. The Hadith are Moslem holy writings attributed to Mohammed. A Moslem must obey them also.

46. Dr. Anis Shorrosh, *Islam Revealed*, (Nashville: Thomas Nelson, 1988), p. 35, cited in Bennett, *Philistine*, p. 52.

47. Suleiman Al-Khash in *Al-Thaura*, the Ba'ath party newspaper, May 3, 1968, cited in Bennett, *Philistine*, p. 52.

48. Thomas Kiernan, *Yasir Arafat*, (London: Cox & Wyman, 1976), pp. 17, 25.

49. George Grant, *The Blood of the Moon*, (Brentwood, TN: Wolgemuth & Hyatt, 1991), p. 53, cited in Brown, p. 54.

50. *Logos*, Hebrew Lexicon, #398 and #399.

51. Stephan Karetzky & Peter E. Goldman, *The Media's War Against Israel*, (New York: Shapolsky Books, 1986).

52. "A Palestinian Version of the New Testament," *The Jerusalem Post*, January 3, 1992.

53. "Syrian press lauds Clinton-Assad summit," *The Jerusalem Post*, January 18, 1994.

54. "Arafat and the Church, " *The Jerusalem Post*, December 25, 1995.

55. Karetzky & Goldman, pp. 203-204.

56. Ibid. p. 35.

57. Netanyahu, p. 56.

58. Ibid., p. 57.

59. Ibid., pp. 55,64.

60. For the history of the *Achille Lauro* affair in October of 1985, see Neil C. Livingstone and David Halevy, *Inside the PLO,* (New York: William Morrow and Company, 1990), p. 252.

61. In the spring issue of *Foreign Affairs*, cited in Raphael Patai, *The Arab Mind* (New York: Macmillan, 1983), p. 337, cited in Bennett, *Philistine*, p. 27.

62. Ibid.

63. Netanyahu, p. 104.

64. Ibid., p. 105.

65. Kiernan, pp. 139, 144, 178.

66. John Laffin, *The Arab Mind*, (London: Cassell, 1975), p. 143, cited in Bennett, *Philistine*, p. 28.

67. Netanyahu, pp. 100-101.

68. Jillian Becker, *The PLO*, (London: Weidenfeld and Nicolson, 1984), pp. 196-197.

69. Netanyahu, pp. 100-101.

70. *Logos*, Hebrew Lexicon, #7512 and #7511.

71. "Can the US Hide from the Real PLO?" *The Jerusalem Post*, June 17, 1990.

72. Bennett, *Philistine*, p. 29.

73. Andrew Gowers & Tony Walker, *Arafat*, (Great Britain: Cox and Wyman Ltd., 1994), p. 98.

74. These details are taken from: Becker, p. 77, and Gowers & Walker, pp. 120-121.

75. For example, in Exodus 3:19 there is a reference to the "king of Egypt." Later, in I Kings 3:1 the Bible tells us that Solomon made an affinity with the "king of Egypt." Someone unfamiliar with history and the Bible's use of the word "king" to refer to a position, might think that these references are speaking about the same man, when, in reality, they were separated by 500 years.

76. Divide 1,000 (the years in God's "day") by 24 (the hours in a day). The result is exactly 41 and two thirds years, or 41 years, 8 months.

77. Kiernan, p. 131.

78. Ethiopia has been "independent" from ancient times, although its present form of government is recent. Oman received its independence from Portugal in 1650. North Yemen was the first to receive its independence after Oman, becoming independent in November 1918. Iran was the last according to its declared date of independence—April 1, 1979. All the other middle east nations became independent between 1923 (Turkey) and 1971 (U.A.E.).

Chapter 6: The First Indications of the Identity of the Little Horn

1. If you do the calculation, don't forget to add a day for leap-year in 1996. If the actual hours are counted, based on Israeli time, it turns out that there will be 2,300 days plus about 6 hours from the actually signing until the New Year, 2,000. In other words, the precision is quite amazing.

2. For those who are not aware that most prophetic Scriptures have more than one fulfillment, I recommend the reader obtain a book on Biblical Hermeneutics. Most of them explain this well-known principle of Bible interpretation.

3. Byers, pp. 174-176.

4. Included in a number of quotes at the top of the front page where the headline was: "Peace Dawns in Mideast," *Detroit Free Press*, September 10, 1993.

5. Although I cannot document this (only because I have been unable to locate the place I read it), we do know how many invited guests were present—3,000! See "Every detail scripted in signing ceremony," *The Jerusalem Post*, September 14, 1993.

6. C. I. Scofield, *Scofield Reference Edition*, (New York: Oxford University Press, 1945), pp. 914-915 notes on Daniel 9:27.

7. "Arafat: Esto es el inicio del fin," ("Arafat: This is the beginning of the end"), *Siglo Veintiuno*, September 14, 1993, reported from Washington by EFE.

8. Nelson, see footnote on Daniel 2:4, p. 868.

Chapter 7: Is Yasser Arafat the Little Horn of Daniel?

1. Reprinted with permission from the September 15, 1995 issue of *The Jewish Press*, Brooklyn, New York.

2. The Bible presents this concept, beginning with the Creation. Romans 1:20 explains that the invisible, spiritual or heavenly things are understood by the things that are found in the natural realm. Solomon received much of his wisdom by considering what God had made in the Creation. (See I Kings 4:31-34.) Both Jesus and the Apostle Paul constantly compared the natural world with the spiritual world. They spoke of trees, beasts, fowl, creeping things, fishes, sowing, reaping, fishing, baking bread, farming, buying and selling land, shepherding, warfare, armor, racing, sand, fire, rocks, the wind, the waves, and much more.

3. "You can't dance with a murderer," *The Jerusalem Post*, September 3, 1993.

4. Kiernan, p. 24.

5. Ibid.

6. Ibid., p. 65.

7. Danny Rubinstein, *The Mystery of Arafat*, (Vermont: Steerforth Press, 1995), p. 1.

8. Ibid.

9. Ibid., p. 2.

10. Ibid., p. 4.

11. Ibid., p. 7.

12. Ibid., p. 1.

13. Ibid. p. 8.

14. Ibid., cover flap.

15. Ibid., foreword.

16. Ibid., p. 15.

17. "Arafat's Moment of Truth," *The Jerusalem Post*, April 11, 1995.

18. Livingstone and Halevy, p. 65.

19. "Arafat: Peace Process Must Go on Despite Land Dispute," *The Jerusalem Post*, May 2, 1995; "Arafat's View on Peace," *The Jerusalem Post*, March 13, 1994; "Arafat's Moment of Truth," *The Jerusalem Post*, April 1, 1995; "Arafat: Israel responsible for Yihye Ayyash's liquidation," *The Jerusalem Post*, January 8, 1996.

20. "No way back," by Moshe Sharon, in *Middle East Intelligence Digest*, January 1994, p. 8, and also "Arafat's big mistake," *The Jerusalem Post*, January 10, 1996.

21. "No way back," by Moshe Sharon, reprinted in *Middle East Intelligence Digest*, January 1994, p. 8, and "PA plans to unveil its own currency within two years," *The Jerusalem Post*, December 21, 1995.

22. "Arafat's big mistake," *The Jerusalem Post*, January 10, 1996.

23. Kiernan, p. 55.

24. Ibid.

25. Ibid., p. 60.

26. Ibid., p. 108.

27. Ibid., p. 138.

28. Ibid., p. 146

29. Ion Mihai Pacepa, *Red Horizons*, (Washington, DC: Regnery-Gateway, 1990), p. 24.

30. Rubinstein, foreword, p. xii.

31. "Rabin: Arafat's Call for 'Jihad' Puts Peace Process in Question," *The Jerusalem Post*, May 18, 1994.

32. "The stark reality of Jerusalem," *The Jerusalem Post*, June 24, 1994.

33. Kiernan, p. 34.

34. Ibid., p. 35.

35. Rubinstein, p. 4.

36. Kiernan, p. 35, 43.

37. Ibid.

38. Ibid., pp. 35-36.

39. Ibid., p. 30.

40. Ibid., p. 137.

41. Ibid.

42. Ibid., p. 138

43. Ibid., pp. 147-148.

44. "*The American Heritage Dictionary*," Third Edition, (Boston: Houghton Mifflin Company, 1992), see "sanctify."

45. "You can't dance with a murderer," *The Jerusalem Post*, September 3, 1993.

46. "The first step," *Middle East Intelligence Digest*, September 23, 1993.

47. Kiernan, pp. 29, 65-71.

48. Mitchell G. Bard and Joel Himelfarb, *Myths and Facts*, (Washington, DC: Near East Report, 1992), pp. 305-309.

49. Becker, p. 107.

50. Ibid.

51. Livingstone and Halevy, p. 38.

52. Ibid., pp. 31-32.
53. Ibid., p. 32.
54. "You can't dance with a murderer," *The Jerusalem Post*, September 3, 1993.
55. "The earth shakes under our feet," *The Jerusalem Post*, May 5, 1995.
56. Rubinstein, p. 1.
57. Gowers & Walker, p. 500.
58. Ibid., p. 488.
59. Ibid., p. 489.
60. Livingstone and Halevy, p. 108.
61. Gowers & Walker, p. 282.
62. Ibid.
63. Livingstone and Halevy, p. 232.
64. Gowers & Walker, p. 301.
65. Livingstone and Halevy, p. 21.
66. Ibid., p. 22.
67. "They are not expendable," *The Jerusalem Post*, July 5, 1995, and " 'Smely' government reeks of whoredom," *The Jerusalem Post*, February 3, 1995.
68. "They are not expendable," *The Jerusalem Post*, July 5, 1995.
69. In "A nation torn apart," *Middle East Intelligence Digest*, January 1994, p. 1.
70. Rubinstein, p. 32.
71. Peters, p. 139.
72. "Arafat asks Bonn to help pull Iran into peace process," *The Jerusalem Post*, November 26, 1995.
73. "Donors pledge $13.7B in aid to Palestinians," *The Jerusalem Post*, January 10, 1996.
74. "Arafat asks Bonn to help pull Iran into peace process," *The Jerusalem Post*, November 26, 1995.
75. Peters, p. 3
76. Joan Peters, *From Time Immemorial*, (USA: JKAP Publications, 1984).
77. Dutch daily *Trouw*, March 1977, cited in Peters, p. 137.
78. Peters, p. 149.
79. Ibid., pp. 149-150.
80. *Palestine Royal Commission Report*, p. 11, para. 23, cited in Peters, p. 147.
81. Netanyahu, pp. 23-26.
82. Bennett, *Philistine*, pp. 148-149.
83. Peters, p. 411-412.
84. Ibid., p. 230.
85. Ibid., p. 412.
86. Ibid., p. 7.
87. Prittie, "Middle East Refugees," in Michael Curtis et al., eds., *The Palestinians: People, History, Politics*, (New Brunswick, NJ: Transaction Books, 1975), p. 71, Associated Press interview, January 1960, cited in Peters, p. 23.
88. Peters, p. 406.

89. Official information release in January 1988, by the Israeli Embassy in Wellington, New Zealand, cited in Bennett, *Philistine,* p. 118.

90. "Oh little town of Bethlehem," *Middle East Intelligence Digest,* February 1995, p. 6.

91. "Churchmen Against Israel," *The Jerusalem Post,* December 24, 1990.

92. "Bethlehem's Future," *The Jerusalem Post,* March 19, 1995.

93. Bennett, *Philistine,* p. 55.

94. Yasser Arafat's recorded speech in a Johannesburg mosque, May 10, 1994, cited in Bennett, *Philistine,* p. 102.

95. *Logos,* Hebrew Lexicon, #1080.

96. Becker, p. 68.

97. Nadew Safran, *Israel: The Embattled Ally,* (Cambridge: Harvard Press, 1981), pp. 49-50.

98. *The Jerusalem Post,* 1986, cited in Ramon Bennett, *When Day and Night Cease,* (Jerusalem: Arm of Salvation, 1993), p. 181.

99. "Hussein and Arafat in Conflict," *The Jerusalem Post,* October 28, 1994.

100. Kiernan, pp. 7-24, 30, 133-148.

101. "Hussein and Arafat in Conflict," *The Jerusalem Post,* October 28, 1994.

102. Ibid.

103. "Ramadan Moon Boosts PA'S Mufti," *The Jerusalem Post,* February 3, 1995.

104. See James Strong, *Strong's Exhaustive Concordance,* (Grand Rapids, Michigan: Baker Book House, 1977), *Strong's Hebrew Dictionary,* # 3064 and #3063.

105. See *Strong's Greek Dictionary* to note that "Judas" comes from *Strong's Hebrew Dictionary* #3063, which is "Judah."

106. Becker, pp. 149-150 and accompanying photos of Arafat's office in the UNRWA school in Siblin, Lebanon.

107. Grant, p. 53, cited in Bennett, *Philistine,* p. 50.

108. "PLO-Hamas connection," *The Jerusalem Post,* January 17, 1993.

109. Monitored by BBC Caversham, July 28, 1992, cited in "PLO-Hamas connection," *The Jerusalem Post,* January 17, 1993.

110. "Even as they speak peace," *Middle East Intelligence Digest,* November 1994.

111. "The Summit Against Terrorism," The McLaughlin Group, aired on American Airlines Inflight video service on flight #990, March 22, 1996.

112. "Peace at last," *Newsweek,* September 13, 1993, p. 21.

113. Announced on CNN Headline News on March 4, 1996.

114. To see that Daniel and Revelation both use the expression, "time, times and half a time" to refer to a three-and-a-half-year period, compare Revelation 12:6 with 12:14 and Daniel 12:7 with 12:1-12.

115. Most encyclopedias cover these events.

116. The Bible never uses titles like "President," "Prime Minister," or "Chancellor." The biblical term for any head of state is "king."

117. Rubinstein, p. 12-13.

118. Kiernan, p. 24, 30.

119. Ibid., p. 26.

120. Rubinstein, p. 12.

121. Ibid.
122. Ibid., pp. 15-16.
123. Ibid.
124. Kiernan, pp. 52-53.
125. Ibid., p. 29.
126. Ibid., pp. 160-161.
127. See how Lebanon is part of the promised land in Deuteronomy 1:7; 3:25; 11:24 and Joshua 1:4, along with other references.
128. For example, this word is used in reference to the armies of Israel in the King James Version in Numbers 2:9-25; 10:14-28, and in most versions in Psalms 44:9 and 60:10.
129. In Joshua 5:13-15 the Lord appeared to Joshua to inform him that He was taking command of the armies of Israel, whom He called the "army of the Lord" (NIV, NKJV, RSV, NRSV). God considered Israel to be His army or the army of heaven often, because he often fought with it. Compare Psalm 44:9. He is also called "the God of the armies of Israel" (I Sam. 17:45). When Israel is almost annihilated in the last days, He will fight with them again. See Zechariah 14:1-3.
130. I am aware of the fact that this could also be referring to the spiritual help that God gave to Israel in this battle. However, the reason that the righteous will "shine as the stars" (Dan. 12:3) is because of heaven's light and life shining through them. When God came upon the armies of Israel under Deborah, His light and life was shining through Israel's soldiers. That is what made them to be "stars" who fought in the battle also.
131. Kiernan, p. 117.
132. Ibid.
133. Ibid., pp. 199-200.
134. Ibid., pp. 196, 198-200.
135. Ibid., p. 203.
136. Brown, p. 12.
137. Bennett, *When Day and Night Cease*, pp. 243-245.
138. Netanyahu, p. 70.
139. Ibid.
140. Ibid., p. 50.
141. Ibid.
142. Ibid., p. 147.
143. "The heart of the matter," *Middle East Intelligence Digest*, March/April, 1995, p. 4.
144. Official information release in January 1988, by the Israeli Embassy in Wellington, New Zealand, cited in Bennett, *Philistine*, p. 118.
145. Falastin, Jordan, May 30, 1955, cited in Bennett, *Philistine*, p. 120.
146. Becker, p. 73.
147. Ibid.
148. Some would be quick to point out that Arafat is only claiming the West Bank and Gaza for his Palestinian nation. However, he repeatedly verbalizes his plans to use these areas as launching grounds for the "liberation of the rest of Palestine," meaning the whole Jewish state.
149. Rubinstein, p. vii.

150. Ze'ev Schiff, *History of the Israeli Army*, (New York: MacMillan Publishing Co., 1985), p. 22.

151. Ibid.

152. Dan Kurzman, *Genesis 1948*, (New York: World Publishing Co., 1970), p. 244.

153. Ibid.

154. Larry Collins and Dominique Lapierre, *O Jerusalem*, (Israel: Steimatzky, 1993), pp. 434-435; 506-507.

155. Connor Cruise O'Brien, *The Siege*, (New York, Simon and Shuster, 1986), p. 522.

156. Ibid., pp. 522-523.

157. "You can't dance with a murderer," *The Jerusalem Post*, September 3, 1993.

158. Rabin and Arafat received the Nobel Prize along with Shimon Peres on December 11, 1994.

159. "On toeing the line," *The Jerusalem Post*, December 23, 1994.

160. Scofield, Daniel 9:27 footnotes.

161. Refer to *Logos*, #8548 to see that this word is a noun.

162. Some versions translate Psalm 22:3 as "He is enthroned in the praises of Israel." However, the Hebrew word they render as "enthroned" appears almost 1,100 times in the Old Testament. The King James Version translates it as "to dwell" 437 times and as "inhabitant" or "to inhabit" 260 times. It is never translated as anything like "enthroned." Again, the translators were taking their liberties!

163. David's tabernacle was a simple tent that he pitched near his house in which he placed the ark of the covenant. The manifest presence and glory of God dwelled there for about 30 years during the reign of David. See I Chronicles 13:11-14 and 16:1. The offerings that David offered had to be offered on the brazen altar that was still being used at that time in Moses Tabernacle (I Chr. 16:39).

164. Colossians 2:16-17 explains that the Old Testament rituals were shadows or figures of the New Testament life found in the Body of Christ, which is the true Temple or Church. Hebrews 8:1-5 reveals the same truths about God's dwelling. The earthly tabernacle of the Old Testament was a shadow of His true Tabernacle or dwelling place (the Church).

165. "Temple Mount may close to Jews today," *The Jerusalem Post*, August 6, 1995.

166. "Hussein and Arafat in Conflict," *The Jerusalem Post*, October 28, 1994.

167. "Wakf: Temple Mount Is For Moslems Only," *The Jerusalem Post*, April 26, 1995.

168. There are a number of reasons we know Joel is a message for the last days. One is in Acts 2:16-17 where Peter understood that Joel was speaking to the last days. Another is Joel 3:1-2 where the Lord declares that He will judge the nations for parting His land. He specifies that this will occur in the time when He brings Israel back from their captivity among the nations. Then, the rest of Joel 3 is seen to be apocalyptic if it is compared with New Testament passages on the last days.

169. "Wakf Holds the Keys to Eight Temple Mount Gates," *The Jerusalem Post*, November 2, 1994.

170. "You can't dance with a murderer," *The Jerusalem Post*, September 3, 1993.

171. "A Palestinian Version of the New Testament," *The Jerusalem Post*, January 3, 1992, and "Pictures of murder," *The Jerusalem Post*, December 4, 1992.

172. "Pictures of murder," *The Jerusalem Post*, December 4, 1992.

173. "Horror show of the absurd," *The Jerusalem Post*, July 7, 1991.

174. Ibid.

175. "Silenced strip: The Gaza story almost no one tells," *The Jerusalem Post*, December 8, 1995.

176. Becker, p. 154.

177. "Eight churches versus Israel," *The Jerusalem Post*, March 9, 1995.

178. Rubinstein, p. 3.

179. Ibid.

180. Arafat's official text, Geneva, December 13, 1988, cited in Netanyahu, pp. 212-213.

181. *Logos*, Hebrew Lexicon, #6743.

182. Live TV interview with Leah Rabin on December 17, 1995, from Mainz, Germany with Leah Rabin in Israel, Channel ZDF, *Menchen '95* (program), with Güenther Jauch (interviewer).

183. "New world disorder," *The Jerusalem Post*, November 4, 1994.

184. *Logos*, Hebrew Lexicon #6944. Some are not aware that the *Strong's Hebrew and Greek Lexicons* give the precise definition of each word first, and then, at the end of the definition a colon and dash appear. After the dash is a list of the various words that the translators used to translate the particular word into the King James Version. However, it is important to understand that those words are *not* part of the definition itself.

185. Yasser Arafat on Jordan Television, September 13, 1993, as cited in Bennett, *Philistine*, p. 94.

186. "The earth shakes under our feet, " *The Jerusalem Post*, May 5, 1995.

187. "Nablus wakes up to Palestinian rule," *The Jerusalem Post*, December 13, 1995.

188. Ibid.

189. "Pictures of murder," *The Jerusalem Post*, December 4, 1992.

190. "Arafat mocks the Jews," *The Jerusalem Post*, December 21, 1995.

191. Ibid.

192. *Logos*, Hebrew Lexicon, #6440.

193. Ibid. #2420.

194. "Sign of contempt," *The Jerusalem Post*, June 7, 1994.

195. Yasser Arafat's recorded speech in a Johannesburg mosque, May 10, 1994, cited in Bennett, *Philistine*, p. 102.

196. Moshe Sharon, professor of Islamic history at the Hebrew University, writing in *The Jerusalem Post*, "Behind the PLO Boss's Words," May 27, 1994.

197. Ibid.

198. Ibid.

199. Ibid.

200. Ibid.

201. Ibid.

202. Ibid.

203. Arafat quoted in Saudi News Agency, January 2, 1989, cited in Netanyahu, p. 123.

204. Ibid.

205. "A no-win situation, " *The Jerusalem Post*, December 22, 1995.

206. Livingstone and Halevy, p. 165.

207. Ibid.

208. "The menu for the talks: cocktails and coffee," *The Jerusalem Post*, October 15, 1993.

209. Bar-Illan, p. 291.

210. Ibid., p. 91.

211. Ibid.

212. Ibid., p. 283.

213. Ibid., pp. 283-284.

214. Alexander Schloch, "The Demographic Development of Palestine," in *International Journal of Middle East Studies*, vol. 17, 1985, p. 488, cited in Netanyahu, p. 37.

215. A PLO official's statement made on August 31, 1993. Quoted in "On Destroying Israel," Yesha Report, Sept.-Oct. 1993, p. 4, cited in Bennett, *Philistine*, p. 87.

216. "Recruits for Palestinian police force may come from up the river," *The Jerusalem Post*, October 3, 1993.

217. Livingstone and Halevy, p. 82.

218 Ibid.

219. Gowers & Walker, p. 85.

220. Becker, p. 149.

221. Ibid., p. 150.

222. Ibid.

223. Ibid.

224. "Frauds and advocates," *The Jerusalem Post*, January 24, 1996.

225. Ibid.

226. Ibid.

227. "The election myth," *The Jerusalem Post*, January 26, 1996.

228. "Gazans vote again at two polling stations," *The Jerusalem Post*, February 1, 1996.

229. "Observers blast 'police intimidation' in Jerusalem," *The Jerusalem Post*, January 21, 1996.

230. "Arafat's plan for democracy: freedom from the press," *The Jerusalem Post*, December 3, 1993.

231. "Arafat accused of intimidating Palestinian journalists," *The Jerusalem Post*, January 25, 1996.

232. Karetzky & Goldman, p. 182.

233. Ibid., p. 167.

234. "Come, let us reason together," *Middle East Intelligence Digest—Document*, February 1993, p. A1.

235. Karetzky & Goldman, p. 250.

236. Ibid., p. 245.

237. Ibid., p. 172.

238. Ibid., pp. 245-247.

239. Ibid., 191.

240. Ibid., 202.

241. Becker, p. 159.

242. Ibid.

243. "Arafat has editor arrested over slight," *The Jerusalem Post*, December 27, 1995.

244. "Al-Quds editor freed after personal reprimand from Arafat," *The Jerusalem Post*, December 31, 1995.

245. "Arafat accused of intimidating Palestinian journalists," *The Jerusalem Post*, January 25, 1996.
246. Ibid.
247. Becker, p. 117.
248. This explanation came from my Hebrew-speaking friends, but is also understood from the Hebrew words themselves. The King James translates it as "destroy wonderfully," meaning to "destroy in an extraordinary and surpassing way."
249. Karetzky & Goldman, pp. 242-243.
250. Ibid.
251. Ibid., pp. 244-245.
252. Ibid., p. 234.
253. Ibid., p. 230.
254. Ibid.
255. Peter Grace, *The Rape of Lebanon*, (Beirut: Evangelical Press, 1983).
256. Karetzky & Goldman, pp. 242-243.
257. John Markham of the *New York Times*, cited in Karetzky & Goldman, p. 171.
258. Becker, pp. 117-121.
259. Ibid., p. 120.
260. Ibid., p. 124.
261. Ibid.
262. Ibid., pp. 122-123.
263. Ibid.
264. Ibid.
265. Grace, p. 177, cited in Bennett, *Philistine*, p. 78.
266. Ibid.
267. Grace, p. 16, cited in Bennett, *Philistine*, p. 77.
268. Ibid., p. 17.
269. Karetzky & Goldman, p. 236.
270. Becker, p. 271.
271. Bard and Himelfarb, p. 98.
272. Karetzky & Goldman, p. 223.
273. Ibid.
274. Rubinstein, p. 34.
275. "Silenced strip: The Gaza story almost no one tells," *The Jerusalem Post*, December 8, 1995.
276. Ibid.
277. Used with permission and reprinted from *The Jerusalem Post* of January 9, 1996.
278. "Boundless hatred," *The Jerusalem Post*, January 8, 1996.
279. "Arafat's big mistake," *The Jerusalem Post*, January 10, 1996.
280. "Arafat's Nablus speech," *The Jerusalem Post*, December 17, 1995, and "PA gets Kalkilya without incident," *The Jerusalem Post*, December 17, 1995.
281. "High alert after death of 'The Engineer,'" *The Jerusalem Post*, January 7, 1996.
282. Ibid.
283. Ibid.

284. "Arafat: Israel responsible for Yihye Ayyash's liquidation," *The Jerusalem Post*, January 8, 1996.

285. Ibid.

286. "2 Suicide Bombings in Israel Kill 25 and Hurt 77, Highest Such Toll," *The New York Times*, February 26, 1996.

287. "The awakening," *The Jerusalem Post*, March 5, 1996.

288. Ibid.

289. Ibid.

290. "PLO is silent on terror due to Hamas links," *The Jerusalem Post*, April 20, 1994.

291. "Peres the astronaut," *The Jerusalem Post*, January 11, 1996.

292. "Terrorism ups and downs," *The Jerusalem Post*, January 12, 1996.

293. "The awakening," *The Jerusalem Post*, March 5, 1996.

294. *Logos*, Hebrew Lexicon, #4820.

295. John Laffin, *The PLO Connections*, (London: Transworld, 1982), p. 18, cited in Bennett, *Philistine*, p. 71.

296. Kiernan, p. 42.

297. Ibid., p. 210.

298. Ibid., pp. 153-154.

299. "Arafat's plan for democracy: freedom from the press," *The Jerusalem Post*, December 3, 1993.

300. Ibid.

301. "Jurists to Arafat: Postpone vote, stress democracy," *The Jerusalem Post*, December 7, 1995.

302. Yasser Arafat, *El Mundo*, Venezuela, February 11, 1980, cited in Bennett, *Philistine*, p. 100.

303. *Logos*, Greek Lexicon, #803.

304. Ibid., Hebrew Lexicon, #7962.

305. "A true man of his word," *The Jerusalem Post*, September 13, 1994.

306. "The earth shakes under our feet," *The Jerusalem Post*, May 5, 1995.

307. "A no-win situation," *The Jerusalem Post*, December 22, 1995.

308. Ibid.

309. Ibid.

310. Ibid.

311. Ibid.

312. Pacepa, p. 24.

313. Ibid., p. 19.

314. Ibid., p. 36.

315. Ibid., pp. 24-25.

316. Ibid., p. 36.

317. Ibid.

318. "Terrorism pays," *Middle East Intelligence Digest*, November 1993, p. 8.

319. Ibid.

320. "PLO Envoy to UN: Some settlers can stay in 'new Palestinian areas,' " *The Jerusalem Post*, April 6, 1994.

321. Terrorism pays," *Middle East Intelligence Digest*, November 1993, p. 8.

322. Ibid.

323. "Peace lullaby," *The Jerusalem Post*, November 22, 1994.

324. "Rabin's decision time," *The Jerusalem Post*, April 27, 1995.

325. This was Arafat's declaration directly to Leah Rabin. She appreciated it enough to mention it as something very meaningful to her on Günther Jauch's live TV interview with her.

326. Pacepa, p. 25.

327. "Arafat: Israel responsible for Yihye Ayyash's liquidation," *The Jerusalem Post*, January 8, 1996.

328. Kiernan, pp. 136-137.

329. Arafat's speech upon receiving the Nobel Peace Prize in Oslo, Norway.

330. Ibid.

331. "*The American Heritage Dictionary*," see "slippery."

332. Pacepa, p. 25.

333. "Palestinian Charter can't be changed—Shaath," *The Jerusalem Post*, January 12, 1995.

334. "Settlement likely in '*Achille Lauro*' suit," *The Jerusalem Post*, January 17. 1996.

335. This includes only the population of the ten nations which I listed as candidates for being the ten horns in Chapter 4.

336. *A History of Israel, Volume II: From the Aftermath of the Yom Kippur War*, (New York: Oxford University Press, 1987), cited in Bennett, *When Day and Night Cease*, pp. 179-180.

337. Ramon Bennett, *Saga*, (Jerusalem: Arm of Salvation, 1994), p. 77.

338. "Saddam *could* have destroyed Israel," *Middle East Intelligence Digest*, September 1995, p. 8.

339. Moshe Arens, an ex-defense minister of Israel confirmed that Israel does, in fact, have technology that others are not even aware of in "Arens: 'We can deter Iraq,'" *The Jerusalem Post*, September 19, 1990.

340. "Saddam *could* have destroyed Israel," *Middle East Intelligence Digest*, September 1995, p. 60.

341. Netanyahu, pp. 23-26.

342. bid.

343. Ibid.

344. "A curse of death gets the kiss of death," *The Jerusalem Post*, December 8, 1995.

345. Ibid.

346. Ibid.

347. Shimon Peres in Cairo after the signing ceremony and broadcast over Voice of Israel Radio, May 4, 1994, cited in Bennett, *Philistine*, p. 69.

348. "Peres' terrible choices," *Time Magazine*, March 18, 1996.

349. "Lawmakers examine the expiration date and the PLO produce," *The Jerusalem Post*, June 23, 1995.

350. Ibid.

351. "Check up," *The Jerusalem Post*, May 30, 1995.

352. Ibid.

353. Ibid.

354. "Lawmakers examine the expiration date and the PLO produce," *The Jerusalem Post,* June 23, 1995.

355. "Hamas orders its prisoners not to sign non-violence pledges," *The Jerusalem Post,* May 12, 1994.

356. "PA gets Kalkilya without incident," *The Jerusalem Post,* December 17, 1995.

357. "Released Arab prisoner kills 19 in suicide attack," *Middle East Intelligence Digest,* February 1995, p. 2.

358. "Peres the astronaut," *The Jerusalem Post,* January 11, 1996.

359. "The peace watch report," *The Jerusalem Post,* June 22, 1995.

360. "Check up," *The Jerusalem Post,* May 30, 1995.

361. "High alert after the death of 'The Engineer,' " *The Jerusalem Post,* January 7, 1996.

362. "Arafat: Israel responsible for Yihye Ayyash's liquidation," *The Jerusalem Post,* January 8, 1996.

363. "PLO Violation of Israel-PLO Agreements," as enumerated in an official Attorney-General report, compiled by the Yesha Report, March 1995.

364. "Check up," *The Jerusalem Post,* May 30, 1995.

365. "A tabloid's-eye view of the Israeli-PLO accord," *The Jerusalem Post,* September 23, 1993.

366. Ibid.

367. "No security," *The Jerusalem Post,* July 25, 1995.

368. Kiernan, p. 203.

369. Rubinstein, p. 51.

370. Kiernan, p. 216.

371. Samuel M. Katz, *Israel Versus Jibril,* (New York: Paragon House, 1993), p. 88.

372. "The State Department's whitewash," *The Jerusalem Post,* June, 5, 1995.

373. A PLO official's statement made on August 31, 1993. Quoted in "On Destroying Israel," Yesha Report, Sept.-Oct. 1993, p. 4, cited in Bennett, *Philistine,* p. 87.

374. "The State Department's whitewash," *The Jerusalem Post,* June, 5, 1995.

375. This is seen by comparing the definition of the word from *Strong's Hebrew Dictionary,* #4924, and by considering its usage in the Old Testament. It refers to the chosen or desirable part as in Nehemiah 8:10; Psalm 78:31 and Genesis 27:28.

376. "Water dispute: No immediate solution on tap," *The Jerusalem Post,* July 21, 1995.

377. "Impasse over water, " *The Jerusalem Post,* July 19, 1995.

378. "News bytes," *Middle East Intelligence Digest,* September 1995, p. 2.

379. "Impasse over water, " *The Jerusalem Post,* July 19, 1995.

380. Ibid.

381. Ibid.

382. "Arafat sees Israel's demise," *The Jerusalem Post,* February 23, 1996.

383. Ibid.

384. Rubinstein, pp. 85-86.

385. "Cracking open the PLO's piggy bank," *The Jerusalem Post,* June 24, 1994.

386. *Logos,* Hebrew Lexicon, #4013.

387. "Arafat reappoints Force 17 commander," *The Jerusalem Post*, December 1, 1993.

388. "50 seconds and Sadat was gone!," *The Jerusalem Post*, October 4, 1991.

389. Kiernan, p. 130.

390. "Martyr's breeding ground," *The Jerusalem Post*, February 10, 1995.

391. Kiernan, pp. 191-192.

392. Ibid.

393. Ibid., p. 194.

394. Ibid., p. 219.

395. Gowers & Walker, pp. 27-28.

396. Kiernan, pp. 167-168.

397. Ibid.

398. Ibid.

399. Rubinstein, p. 33.

400. Kiernan, pp. 167-168, 198.

401. Rubinstein, p. 33.

402. Ibid.

403. "Egyptians kept in the dark by government after attack," *The Jerusalem Post*, June 27, 1995.

404. Ibid.

405. Ibid.

406. "Arafat says he was also on hit list at African summit," *The Jerusalem Post*, July 2, 1995.

407. "Egyptian democracy, press have come a long way," *The Jerusalem Post*, March 15, 1995.

408. Ibid.

409. Ibid.

410. "Gaza—soft underbelly of the Jewish state," *Middle East Intelligence Digest*, February 1993.

411. Bennett, *Philistine,* p. 234.

412. Ibid.

413. "Warm ties compete with chill factor," *The Jerusalem Post*, November 25, 1994.

414. Bennett, *Philistine,* p. 237.

415. "Whirlwind on the rise?," *Middle East Intelligence Digest*, March/April, 1995.

416. "Blowing in the wind," *The Jerusalem Post*, February 24, 1995.

417. "Leah Rabin: 'I'll carry my husband's torch of peace,' " *The Jerusalem Post*, December 21, 1995.

418. "Whose statute of limitations?," *The Jerusalem Post*, October 7, 1994.

419. *Logos*, Hebrew Dictionary, #4581.

420. "Israel at war," *Time Magazine*, June 16, 1967, cited in Bennett, *When Day and Night Cease*, p. 154.

421. *Logos*, Hebrew Dictionary, #8074.

422. For a more in-depth study of this subject, see Byers, Chapter 17.

423. Ibid.

424. "Mordechai Gur takes own life. Deputy Defense Minister had cancer," *The Jerusalem Post,* July 17, 1995.

425. Ibid.

426. "Gur: The man who opened the gates of Jerusalem," *The Jerusalem Post,* July 21, 1995.

427. Ibid.

428. Ibid.

429. Ibid.

430. Ibid.

431. "Arafat's Nablus speech," *The Jerusalem Post,* December 17, 1995.

432. "Rabin gives Arafat 'clean bill of mental health,' " *The Jerusalem Post,* December 17, 1993.

433. "Clinton showed he cares," *The Jerusalem Post,* April 25, 1995.

434. Ibid.

435. Ibid.

436. "The Arafat bombshell," *The Jerusalem Post,* May 18, 1994.

437. "The Arafat bombshell," *The Jerusalem Post,* May 18, 1994, and "Mr. Peres' Deception," *The Jerusalem Post,* June 10, 1994.

438. "Peres defends gov't over Jerusalem letter," *The Jerusalem Post,* June 8, 1994.

439. "A Jerusalem without Jews," *The Jerusalem Post,* June 14, 1994.

440. Ibid.

441. "Peres: 'Jerusalem not up for negotiations,' " *The Jerusalem Post,* January 28, 1996.

442. Yitzhak Rabin in his campaign speech on June 10, 1992, printed in *Middle East Intelligence Digest,* October 1994, p. 1.

443. "A good start," *The Jerusalem Post,* November 24, 1995.

444. "They are not expendable," *The Jerusalem Post,* July 5, 1995.

445. "Poor, wealthy Yasser," *The Jerusalem Post,* November 22, 1994.

446. "Cracking open the PLO's piggy bank," *The Jerusalem Post,* June 24, 1994.

447. Gowers & Walker, p. 488.

448. Ibid.

449. Livingstone and Halevy, p. 186.

450. "Poor, wealthy Yasser," *The Jerusalem Post,* November 22, 1994.

451. *Logos,* Hebrew Lexicon, #802.

452. Pacepa, p. 36.

453. Ibid.

454. Ibid.

455. *Logos,* Hebrew Lexicon, #4581.

456. "Arafat's corruption creates instability," *Middle East Intelligence Digest,* September 1995, p. 57.

457. *Logos,* Hebrew Lexicon, #3568.

458. *Compton's Interactive Encyclopedia,* see "Sudan."

459. *Logos,* Hebrew Lexicon, #4703 comes from #6805.

460. "Arafat reappoints Force 17 commander," *The Jerusalem Post,* December 1, 1993.

461. "Poor, wealthy Yasser," *The Jerusalem Post,* November 22, 1994.

462. "PLO, Hamas invited to Sudan," *The Jerusalem Post,* June 26, 1995.

463. "Muslim Arabs... the fine line between moderate and fanatic," *Middle East Intelligence Digest,* March/April, 1995, p. 10.

464. "Sudan, the 'new Iran,' " *The Jerusalem Post,* July 5, 1995.

465. "Arafat: Israel responsible for Yihye Ayyash's liquidation," *The Jerusalem Post,* January 8, 1996.

Chapter 8: Invited Into the Family

1. Refer to W.E. Vine, *An Expository Dictionary of New Testament Words,* (New Jersey: Fleming H. Revell Company, 1966), see "adoption," pp. 31-32.

2. Refer to Vine, under "son," p. 47 of the Addenda. He explains that in Matthew 5:9,44, and 45 Jesus exhorted his disciples, "Blessed are the peacemakers for they shall be called sons (huios) of God," and "love your enemies... and pray for those who spitefully use you and persecute you, that you may be sons (huios) of your Father in heaven." Vine's conclusion is, "The disciples were to do these things, not in order that they might become children of God, but that, being children (note 'your Father' throughout), they might... 'become sons' " (huios) who manifest the character of Christ. The Greek word for a child is "teknon."

3. Vine, p. 31.

4. *Logos,* Greek Lexicon, #1080.

Appendix: The Relationship Between Daniel 8 and Daniel 11

1. Nelson, "Between the Testaments," pp. 1339-1341.

2. Ibid.

3. Ibid.

4. *Strong's Hebrew Dictionary,* "#7962.

5. Ibid., #6743.

Bibliography

Bar-Illan, David, *Eye on the Media*, Jerusalem: Jerusalem Post, 1993.

Bard, Mitchell G. & Joel Himelfarb, *Myths and Facts*, Washington: Near East Report, 1992.

Becker, Jillian, *The PLO*, London: Weidenfeld and Nicolson, 1984.

Bennett, Ramon, *Philistine*, Jerusalem: Arm of Salvation, 1995.

Bennett, Ramon, *Saga*, Jerusalem: Arm of Salvation, 1993.

Bennett, Ramon, *When Night and Day Cease*, Jerusalem: Arm of Salvation, 1995.

Brown, Michael L., *Our Hands Are Stained With Blood*, Shippensburg, Pennsylvania: Destiny Image, 1992.

Byers, Marvin, *The Final Victory: The Year 2000*, Shippensburg, Pennsylvania: Treasure House, 1994.

Collins, Larry and Dominique Lapierre, *O Jerusalem*, Israel: Steimatzky, 1993.

Compton's Interactive Encyclopedia, Microsoft: Compton's New Media, 1995.

Curtis, Michael, et. al., ed., *The Palestinians: People, History, Politics*, New Brunswick, NJ: Transaction Books, 1975.

Douglas, J. D., ed., *New Bible Dictionary*, England: Intervarsity Press, 1982.

Encarta 96 Encyclopedia, Microsoft, 1996.

Gowers, Andrew & Tony Walker, *Arafat*, Great Britain: Cox and Wyman Ltd., 1994.

Grace, Peter, *The Rape of Lebanon*, Beirut: Evangelical Press, 1983.

Grant, George, *The Blood of the Moon*, Brentwood: Wolgemuth & Hyatt, 1991.

Karetzky, Stephan & Peter E. Goldman, *The Media's War Against Israel*, New York: Shapolsky Books, 1986.

Katz, Samuel M., *Israel Versus Jibril*, New York: Paragon House, 1993.

Kiernan, Thomas, *Yasir Arafat*, London: Cox & Wyman, 1976.

Kurzman, Dan, *Genesis 1948*, New York: World Publishing Co., 1970.

Laffin, John, *The Arab Mind*, London: Cassell, 1975.

Laffin, John, *The PLO Connections*, London: Transworld, 1982.

Livingstone, Neil C. and David Halevy, *Inside the PLO*, New York: William Morrow and Co., 1990.

Lockman Foundation, The, *New American Standard Bible*, A.M. Holman Company, Philadelphia, Pennsylvania, 1973.

Logos Bible Study Software, Oak Arbor, Washington: Logos Research Systems, 1993.

Morris, William, ed., *The American Heritage Dictionary*, Third Edition, Boston: Houghton Mifflin Company, 1992.

Nelson, Thomas, *The Open Bible*, Nashville: Thomas Nelson Publishers, 1983.

Netanyahu, Benjamin, *A Place Among the Nations*, New York: Bantam Books, 1993.

New International Version, The Holy Bible, Zondervan Bible Publishers, Grand Rapids, Michigan, 1978.

O'Brien, Connor Cruise, *The Siege*, New York: Simon and Shuster, 1986.

Pacepa, Ion Mihai, *Red Horizons*, Washington DC: Regnery-Gateway, 1990.

Patai, Raphael, *The Arab Mind*, New York: Macmillan, 1983.

Peters, Joan, *From Time Immemorial*, USA: JKAP Publications, 1984.

Rubinstein, Danny, *The Mystery of Arafat*, Vermont: Steerforth Press, 1995.

Safran, Nadew, *Israel: The Embattled Ally*, Cambridge: Harvard Press, 1981.

Schiff, Ze'ev, *History of the Israeli Army*, New York: MacMillan Publishing Co., 1985.

Scofield, C. I., *Scofield Reference Edition*, New York: Oxford University Press, 1945.

Shorrosh, Dr. Anis, *Islam Revealed*, Nashville, Tennessee: Thomas Nelson, 1988.

Strong, James, *Strong's Exhaustive Concordance,* Grand Rapids, Michigan: Baker Book House, 1977.

Thompson, Frank Charles, *Thompson Chain Reference Bible,* Fourth Improved Edition, Indianapolis: Kirkbride Bible Co.

Vine, W.E., *An Expository Dictionary of New Testament Words,* Old Tappan, New Jersey: Fleming H. Revell Company, 1966.

_____, The Hadith, Sahih Muslim (Siddiqi's translation).

And the following publications:

The Jerusalem Post (Israeli newspaper)

Detroit Free Press (American newspaper)

Los Angeles Times (American newspaper)

The New York Times (American newspaper)

The Washington Post (American newspaper)

USA Today (American newspaper)

Newsweek (American magazine)

Time Magazine (American magazine)

Prensa Libre (Guatemalan newspaper)

Siglo Veintiuno (Guatemalan newspaper)

El Mundo (Venezuelan newspaper)

Trouw (Dutch daily)

Dispatch from Jerusalem (Israeli periodical)

National Geographic (International Periodical)

Middle East Intelligence Digest (International Periodical)

Reader's Digest (International Periodical, English edition)

For more information write to any of the following addresses:

Hebron Ministries
Section 0374 PO Box 02-5289
Miami, FL   33102-5289

Hebron Ministries
2203 E. 11 Mile Rd.
Royal Oak, MI   48067

Or call:

1-800-LAST-DAY (1-800-527-8329) in the U.S.

or

(502)-333-2615 in Guatemala City, Central America